TO RAISE A
JEWISH CHILD

TO RAISE A JEWISH CHILD

A Guide for Parents

RABBI HAYIM HALEVY DONIN

Author of TO BE A JEW

BasicBooks
A Division of HarperCollinsPublishers

Library of Congress Cataloging-in-Publication Data

Donin, Hayim.
    To raise a Jewish child.

    Includes index.
    1. Jewish religious education of children.
2. Children—Management.   3. Education of children.
I. Title.
BM103.D66   296.7'4   76-7679
ISBN 0-465-08626-8 (cloth)
ISBN 0-465-08635-7 (paper)

91 92 93 94 CC/CW 9 8 7 6 5 4 3 2 1

To my wife

<small>TZIVIA</small>

a woman of grace and charm

a true helpmate

and a wise and loving mother

Contents

Contents

~~~~~~

Part Two

TO RAISE A JEWISH CHILD: TRANSMITTING THE VALUES

Contents

Part Three

SELECTING THE RIGHT SCHOOL

Contents

Contents

Acknowledgments

I WISH to thank many friends, colleagues, and young parents who read the manuscript and whose comments and suggestions were most valuable. My sincerest appreciation is extended to Haya Rafael for typing the manuscript and to Iris Topel for her enthusiasm and devotion in the copyediting of this book. And above all, I am deeply indebted to my publisher, editor, and friend, Erwin Glikes, whose guidance and counsel contributed greatly to the development and refinement of this book.

Introduction

THIS BOOK was written to help parents raise their children to become affirmatively aware of themselves as Jews, to be happy with their Judaism, and to be prepared to find meaning and purpose in their Jewish identities and traditions. It intends to focus on contemporary issues, problems, and goals involved in educating the Jewish child, but not only in those matters usually considered when we use the term "religious education." We are interested, like *every* parent and teacher, in the *whole* child, and every aspect of his or her intellectual, psychological, and spiritual development and growth. This book therefore includes a central chapter about those principles of child-raising that are encouraged by Jewish teaching and that are considered essential for developing healthy personalities. It seeks to bring to the attention of Jewish parents the opportunities and options available to them in the Jewish upbringing of their children. Formal schooling, with which Jewish education is largely identified, is only one part of it. However important the professional educator's role may be, unless parents themselves appreciate the essence of the educational process and have a clear view of their own goals, the Jewish educator will find himself defeated before he has even begun.

Introduction

I have drawn upon the traditional insights of Judaism as well as on my own twenty years of practical experience in Jewish education and family counseling while serving as rabbi of a large, in many ways typical, suburban congregation. Most directly, my experience grew out of my responsibility for the educational programs of both an afternoon Hebrew school and a Hebrew day school over many years and was invaluable to me in the development of this book. Not the least, I have drawn on what I know best of all, the experience shared with my wife in raising our own four children.

When we consider the fact that society seems to set no requirements for parenthood in terms of the training, education, skills, or common sense necessary to qualify for being entrusted with the life and character of the next generation, it is one of the miracles of civilization that so many children turn out as well as they do. But it is also obvious that there are many parents who needlessly fail their children. Of course, there are situations over which the very best parents have little or no control and, in which, despite their best efforts things go wrong. The environment can be overwhelming. But very often, parents themselves create and add to the problems they later bemoan.

The decisions that parents make or, more often, neglect to make for their children during their earliest, formative years greatly determine the character and the quality of life of their children, both in a general and a Jewish way. A child has just *one life*. One cannot always depend on correcting serious errors of judgment and starting all over again. Once such questions as "where have we gone wrong?" must be asked, the problem is harder to solve, if it can be solved at all. In child-raising especially, the proverbial ounce of prevention is worth more than its weight in gold.

Child-raising is not a science; there is no one proven way to "do it right." There are too many variables. But, whatever the approach, all good child-rearing calls for the loving acceptance of each child. Being a parent is really an art, requiring imagination, skill, and sensitivity. But even those who were not born to be "gifted" parents can learn the basic guidelines and acquire sufficient skill to produce creditable results. At the very least, one can minimize avoidable errors and their sometimes tragic results.

Raising children means training them to meet the daily demands of their early years and preparing them for their adult lives. In addition to the normal responsibilities of the average parent, Jewish parents who want their children to retain their Jewish loyalties have another obligation. They must teach their children to live in two worlds and to function in two cultures. Each world makes its demands and each culture leaves its impact. Often they pull in different directions. Jewish parents must see the education of their children in terms of harmoniously bridging the gap between these two worlds and must seek to find a formula for blending them together without sacrificing the essential aspects of either. They need to educate their children to find meaning and satisfaction in their Jewish heritage—while, at the same time, participating fully in the civic and cultural life of the nation. Educators differ on how and what to teach children even where the goal is only to adapt to one culture. How much more complex is it when the aim is to impart two distinct cultures!

Some Jews do not have to solve this problem. The assimilationist Jew who chooses to disassociate himself and his family from all Jewish experiences and involvements is one example. The other is the isolationist Jew who rejects much of western culture and attaches himself to a sheltered community where he finds complete fulfillment. But between them is the vast number of Jews who reject both extremes, yet differ considerably among themselves about how to successfully pursue the dual goal. Some of the paths have obviously failed; others have been moderately successful; still others, remarkably successful. Good intentions do not necessarily imply effective means, for the path to unintentional assimilation is often paved with the best of Jewish intentions.

From their earliest history the Jewish people have been aware that transmitting their heritage depended upon sound educational programs and effective child-raising methods. The Torah tells us that God chose Abraham with whom to make the Covenant because: "I have known him, that he may (knows how to) instruct his children and his household after him, that they may keep the way of the Lord" (Genesis 18:19). Throughout history Jewish scholars have written extensively on the education of children and have consistently devoted themselves to solving its problems in every age. And today, effective child-raising and Jewish education is still the key to Jewish survival.

I have not resorted in this book to such usages as *he/she* simply because it results in awkward and cumbersome style. Inasmuch as the English language does not always provide for suitable neutral words from which all sexual bias is absent, it is difficult to always make it clear that no such bias is intended. The reader should, however, be aware that everything in this book, except where specifically indicated otherwise, refers to the upbringing of both boys and girls.

It is my hope that this book will help young families who have little or no religious background as well as those who have retained a strong religious tradition. Even families which are meticulous in their observance of every aspect of Jewish ritual sometimes neglect the essential spirit which should govern the Jewish parent-child relationship. I trust that each will find in this book some insights that will prove helpful in raising their children to reflect the nobility of the Jewish heritage. Those who seek more practical guidance in all areas of Jewish observance or desire to read about the basic principles of Jewish faith may find my book *To Be A Jew: A Guide to Jewish Observance in Contemporary Life* (Basic Books, Inc., 1972), a useful companion volume.

And, after having done everything right, you will still need a little *mazel*. Add a prayer!

Make it known to your children and to your children's children.　　(Deuteronomy 4:9)

~~~~~~

And He shall turn the heart of the fathers to the children, and the heart of the children to their fathers.　　(Malachi 3:24)

~~~~~~

And all your children shall be taught of the Lord; and great shall be the peace of your children.　　(Isaiah 54:13)

Part One

SETTING
THE GOALS

CHAPTER

1

Defining the Problems in Our Time

Recovering Our Jewishness

JEWISH PARENTS who sincerely wish to transmit to their children an attachment to Judaism and to the Jewish people need to do some serious thinking and planning. Today, raising a child to feel, think, and live the life of a Jew cannot be taken for granted. The environment in which most Jewish children are raised today differs radically from that which nurtured their parents and grandparents even if they were born or grew up in the United States. In the time of our parents and their parents, complete assimilation, intermarriage, and the widespread erosion of Jewish identity seemed a distant threat. The average Jewish parent was concerned with the *Americanization* of the child. Today his concern must be with the child's *Judaization*.

It is no longer enough, if it ever was, to believe that one is giving the children a Jewish education by exposing them to a smattering of

Jewish schooling. Such a Jewish education is bound to fail. The education of a child must be seen as the sum of his experiences at home as well as at school. The influences exerted by friends, the attitudes and values reflected by the community in which they live, and the entertainments and pastimes to which children are exposed, all must be seen as a part of their overall education.

We sometimes hear older people compare the contemporary afternoon Hebrew school to the one they knew many decades ago. They are favorably impressed with the fact that today there are a variety of interesting textbooks and audiovisual materials available, that there is a set curriculum and an administrative order that was lacking in their day, and that professionally trained and licensed teachers are found on many staffs. Granting the professional superiority of the afternoon Hebrew school of today to that of the past, we must sadly observe that this does not mean that children are receiving a better overall Jewish education. However deficient formal Jewish schooling may have been a generation or two ago, children then acquired much more religious and cultural knowledge, more Jewish feelings and values from their parents at home and in their Jewish neighborhoods, than they do in today's average Jewish school. Today the school is too often expected to be the major, if not the *only*, resource for a child's Jewish upbringing.

Jewish identity was so inherent in the lives of the immigrant and first-generation American Jew that little thought was given to the danger of losing that identity. Jewish parents and community leaders thought in terms of helping their child integrate into American society. This meant gaining command of the English language and acquiring a broad secular education. It meant helping their children aspire to one of the professions. For many, it also meant shedding distinct Jewish practices that set the Jew apart from other Americans. An immigrant generation, awestruck by America, enthusiastically endorsed the opportunities of the great American "melting-pot" in which all ethnic groups could look forward to coalescing into homogeneous "Americans." American values and mores were accepted unquestioningly and unconditionally by the majority of Jews. Economic success and rising on the social ladder seemed clearly dependent on the degree to which such *Americanization* was achieved.

Except for a distinct minority of Jews who continued to regard their own Jewish heritage and way of life as more valuable than anything that the western world could offer, most East European Jews who came to America developed a feeling of inferiority about themselves and their heritage. And while most immigrant Jews were literate people, many well educated in a Jewish culture that was rich in learning, intellect, and sophistication, their inability to speak English or to speak it without a distinctive accent contributed daily to their sense of inferiority, to the conviction that as "greenhorns" they would always be treated as outsiders. This feeling was communicated to the first American-born generation, which acted on it. Many judged the worth of their own religious faith on the basis of its compatibility with American principles and values, instead of assessing the worth of American values in terms of their own traditions.

It is likely, when one looks back, that few then thought of ever becoming un-Jewish. It was widely believed that Jewishness would survive without much formal attention—there seemed to be other priorities. For many, the only formal Jewish education considered necessary to maintain their Jewish identity was limited to training for the Bar-Mitzvah and for the saying of Kaddish. The historic Jewish emphasis on religious-moral education and the traditional appreciation for studying the Torah was now directed almost exclusively toward secular studies which could lead to professional status and success. As a result, most of the Jewish educational programs that were established in America were minimal and diluted from the very start. Very few people foresaw the long-term danger of this early neglect or took steps to avoid it if they did recognize the danger. The historical and social forces of the times were overwhelming. Even rabbis and lay leaders who did understand the need for Jewish education felt helpless and made few efforts to provide true religious educational leadership. Except for a handful, to whom we must be everlastingly grateful, Jewish leadership in America resigned itself to the disappearance of Judaism in its traditional forms and surrendered to what it regarded as inevitable; the leaders despaired of stemming the tide.

This Jewish educational neglect led to a distorted understanding of Judaism on the part of a whole generation of American-born Jews and further encouraged a shedding of those religious disciplines and rituals that were most distinctly Jewish. Nevertheless, somehow, the emotional ties of this generation to "things Jewish" remained strong.

The Jewish ethic, morality, and value systems, and many distinct cultural traits had permeated their souls and remained an uneradicable part of their lives. For *their* children, however, it was quite another matter!

The Jew became so integrated into the life of America, so thoroughly had he absorbed the culture of the secular-Christian country, so accepted a citizen had he become in an atmosphere relatively free of anti-Semitism, and so little did he give expression to his own Jewish heritage, that the Jewish problem today is to *undo* the consequences of their own *success* in the great effort to become "real" Americans.

In addition, it cannot be denied that the rapidly changing mores of American society, increasingly conducive to the breakdown of family life, has also affected Jewish life. The general environment of secular society has always been corrosive to the religious content of Judaism. Today it is also corrosive of those social and moral values which have for so long been a source of pride and strength to Jews. Even Jews who nominally identify with synagogues or temples reflect the thought and the life-style of a secular, non-Jewish society, with little trace of Jewish religious content. It is no wonder that their children see little reason to exclude the non-Jew from consideration as a marriage partner. They are usually *not* choosing a person whose upbringing, culture, and way of life is appreciably different than their own. This may explain why recent studies show a great surge in the rate of intermarriage. One is not being an alarmist or exaggerating in any way to observe that this process, if allowed to continue unchecked, will insure that American Jewry will suffer the fate of tens of thousands of Jewish families who settled in America from 1653 through the early 1800s. Their Jewish descendants should today have numbered in the hundreds of thousands. Yet in the Jewish community there is hardly a trace of them. Will we, will our children, also disappear as Jews? It is really up to us.

The great "success" in the *Americanization* of the Jew has now alarmed even those who were originally among its greatest proponents. And even in Reform circles there has been something of a swing back to more traditional values and practices. "Tradition," a word once in considerable disfavor, has now been restored to an honorable place in the lexicon of the Reform rabbinate and in the practices which are now encouraged. The *Judaization* of the Jew is now the task facing *all* of American Jewry.

The Spiritual Crisis in Contemporary Society

In moving away from a distinctive heritage, the contemporary Jew also fell victim to that crisis of the human spirit threatening all of western society. William Barrett writes that "religious life had once been a structure that encompassed man's life, providing him with a system of images and symbols by which he could express his own aspirations towards psychic wholeness. With the loss of the containing framework, man became not only a spiritually homeless being, but a fragmentary psychic creature." [1]

The radical decline of religious faith over the past several centuries was at first welcomed by many as a great triumph of the human spirit over symbols and ceremonies, over restrictive and narrow practices. But in "freeing" himself from religion, man in fact lost his psychic vessel and cast himself spiritually adrift on the face of the earth.

The alienated, and the multitudinous candidates for alienation, not only became strangers to God and to the conventions and traditions which once supplied their basic needs, but worst of all, they became strangers to themselves. "Know thyself" was Socrates' advice to the young at the very beginning of Western-cultural development. The message of the new, social prophets of today seems to be either "lose thyself"—in drugs, alcohol, momentary thrills, and dubious pleasures—or, equally delusional, to "find thyself"—by going as far afield as possible and by resolutely denying and abandoning every known social and cultural value. In the words of Ecclesiastes, contemporary society appears intent in the pursuit of "vanity"—of nothingness itself raised to the highest good.

Aggravating the spiritual crisis in Western society is the very nature of our technological, postindustrial society and the very affluence to which we have become accustomed. There is nothing inherently wrong with technology, or with affluence. On the contrary, both are potentially good for the human spirit, for they promise to spiritually enrich and elevate life. They remove or at least lighten daily burdens. They provide the leisure needed to improve the mind and the body and they challenge the soul to reach greater heights.

Yet, instead of man's using leisure to free himself for nobler pursuits, modern man has instead found himself confronted by what Abraham Joshua Heschel has called the "trivialization of life." Modern man spends more and more of his time in activities that are less and less meaningful, purposeful, and necessary. When life becomes filled with unessentials, after the basic struggle for survival has been won, it is not long before the human spirit becomes a very fragile thing and the joy for living is easily destroyed by minor difficulties. Instead of using affluence to improve oneself and others, it has been used to open up a Pandora's box of hedonistic pursuits which bring immediate pleasures but with them, inevitably, social decadence and personal despair. Instead of sustaining man's capacity to dream and strengthening the will to reach out for new challenges, our affluence has produced a peculiar apathy and a steady erosion in vitality, creativity, and hope for the future.

Modern conditions have introduced a mechanization that has made life more and more impersonal. We are no longer known to most of the central institutions in our society by our faces and names, but instead by identifying numbers. It is not particularly stimulating or emotionally rewarding to engage in conversation with a computer. There are many who eventually see themselves as they think the society sees them, as interchangeable bodies with blank unrecognizable faces. Anonymity is the final blow to human dignity, and may in time utterly corrode one's sense of responsibility. It means one is not accountable. The effect of one's actions on family, friends, or simply innocent bystanders is disregarded.

This is the crisis of the spirit that permeates all of western society. In a desperate effort to extricate ourselves from this crisis, contemporary existentialist philosophy has attempted nothing less than "to exhume the features of Hebraic man (as distinct from Hellenistic man) and bring it to the reflective consciousness of our time." [2] "Exhume" is a troubling but significant word here. It suggests that there has been a burial, "Hebraic man" died. In truth, it is the learned mourners who are in need of resuscitation. Hebraic man, while not numerous, is still alive and well.

And the Jewish people's contribution toward alleviating the contemporary crisis of the human spirit can best be made by remaining living examples of what these philosophers call Hebraic man. The task of the contemporary Jew is to project more vividly the authentic Hebraic man. This requires first the solution of the Jews' own internal spiritual crisis. Jewish influence on the spiritual history of mankind has always been greatest when Jews were true to themselves and to their own heritage.

The Judaization of the Jew, consistent with traditional values, will provide the Jew with the means by which to overcome those problems of the spirit that engulf Western society. It will serve to give our children not only what they need to live *with*, but what to live *for*.

Vagueness of Goals

Even if we assume that an awareness of the problem as presented now exists, as well as a readiness to become "more Jewish," there are still few who have any clear views as to the kind of Jewish personality they are really trying to develop. Jewish education is encouraged by all Jewish groups yet most seem strangely unclear about their specific goals. Most Jewish parents, educators, and leaders still avoid coming to grips with the central question: "How does one remain a Jew in an overwhelmingly non-Jewish environment, and in what practical ways ought that Jewishness be expressed?" While there is unanimous agreement among all concerned Jews that "appreciation of Judaism as a way of life" should be one of the major values conveyed to Jewish students, a terrible vagueness emerges when an attempt is made to *define* what that way of life is or should be.

Professor Eugene Borowitz, a leading educational thinker of the Reform movement, admitted to that vagueness in response to the question: "What is the image of the American Jew that the non-traditionalists are seeking to create?" He states: "In most [educational] programs, it is never quite clear what the ideal is which animates the program. . . . The absence of such a definition is a persistent source of guilt and apprehension among parents and educators. . . . The question of knowledge and will [to live as a Jew] all hinges upon the picture of a Jew no one has yet seen and few are willing to commit themselves to attempt to describe." [3]

This statement was written over a decade ago. The educational problem has not appreciably changed in the intervening years. The vagueness remains. Many Jewish parents and educators simply do not know how to describe the distinct Jewish personality they wish to create. When the goal is not clear, the chances of reaching it are slight. One of the purposes here is to help create a definition of, and an appreciation for, the consciously Jewish personality in contemporary life.

Religious Labels: A Source of Confusion

Contemporary Jews tend to identify themselves in terms of a specific "denomination"—Orthodox, Conservative, Reform, and Reconstructionist. This practice is a major source of confusion. While there are institutions that are decidedly Orthodox, Conservative, Reform, or Reconstructionist in their orientation and policies, and the labels do serve to identify the respective rabbinic groups and their synagogues, I have found these labels largely meaningless when used to identify the people and their beliefs or practices. Therefore, the use of the labels makes the parents' decisions about Jewish education more difficult. Although the labels are intended to place a person's religious orientation in sharper perspective, it succeeds in doing just the opposite. It also puts an end to intelligent discussions and makes it that much harder for parents to evaluate the strengths, weaknesses, and appropriateness of different educational institutions. Labels make it difficult to discuss various issues and questions on their own merits, especially if they affect the "life-style" of a family or the policy of a Jewish community. Too often, the simplest thing to do is to retreat to the protective coloration of one's label as an adequate defense of one's position. It successfully makes thinking, real choice, and responsibility seem unnecessary.

The following examples will demonstrate how meaningless and misleading the current use of labels is to divide Jew from Jew.

1. Consider the ideologically secular Jew who belongs to a truly Orthodox synagogue in order to maintain a family association that goes back a generation or two, or because he wishes his children to make use of the synagogue's social or educational or even recreational facilities. Is he Orthodox, Conservative, or Reform?

2. Consider the Sabbath-observant Jew whose only compromise with strict Orthodoxy is that he attends a Conservative synagogue because it is the only one in town, or the only one within walking distance of his home. Is he Orthodox or Conservative?

3. Consider the Jew who believes in the traditional principles of Jewish faith, but joins a Reform temple because his wife never learned to read Hebrew and she insists on going where the prayers are recited primarily in English. Is he Reform or Conservative, or perhaps even Orthodox?

4. What about the Jew whose theological views and religious practices coincide with those of Reform but, because of his youthful upbringing, cannot tolerate the services at a Reform temple. "The services are too 'unJewish,' too 'churchy,'" so he attends a Conservative synagogue. Is he really a Conservative Jew?

5. What about the fifty percent of American Jewry who are not affiliated with any synagogue? Are they all secularists? If not, to which denomination do they belong?

Since American Jews join synagogues without necessarily sharing the religious views or practices of that "denomination," the validity of using synagogue affiliation as an adequate label of religious orientation is highly dubious.

Furthermore, it might be argued that if a person who does not observe the traditional rules of conduct expected by Orthodoxy, no longer identifies himself as Orthodox, and others no longer regard him as Orthodox, then the person who deviates from the religious requirements of the Conservative movement should not be identified as Conservative. This same would hold true for Reform. On this basis, it is clear that the number of those who can truly be called Orthodox, Conservative, or Reform would be but a small fraction of those who are now so identified.

Most Jews will, of course, balk at this conclusion, logical though it may be, but only because they choose to understand the denominational labels, especially Conservative and Reform, in a way that is totally at odds with how these terms are defined by those who are ideologically committed to these movements. The religious leaders of these movements teach specific theological positions and insist on definite religious commitments. The people, however, use these labels as adjectives to describe a *lack* of religious commitment. Thus, Conservative is used to describe a person who is less observant of the traditions than the Orthodox, and Reform is used to describe the least observant of the traditions. While these popular definitions cannot make conscientious Conservative or Reform leaders happy, it has made it possible for more people to identify with them, thereby contributing to a numerical swelling of their ranks.

I cannot count how many times a person has said to me, "Our family is Conservative." I would then say, "Tell me, what do you mean by Conservative?" "Well, we observe the holidays," they would reply, which upon further inquiry meant attending services on the High Holydays, conducting a Passover seder, and possibly the lighting of Hanukah candles. "And we wouldn't think of going to a Reform temple," was usually the final justification for this claim to Conservatism.

Even when used accurately, the various labels do not tell the whole story. A wide range of different views on many crucial questions are found within the Orthodox camp itself. The existence of four separate Orthodox rabbinic bodies testifies to this division.* There is a world of difference between the Hasidic Jew of Williamsburg, New York, and the religious-observant scientist at Harvard University. Yet the same Orthodox label applies to both. And while the Conservative movement is organizationally united, it contains within its fold those whose views and practices border on Orthodoxy and those whose views and practices border on Reform.

To see the confusion is a necessary prerequisite to begin emerging from it. The advice is to avoid labeling people, if only to reverse the process of institutionalizing the confusion and to stop giving the prestige of a denominational *hechsher* † to what is simply religious laxity and not an ideological commitment. If identification is needed, let a Jew be identified by the level of his religious, moral, and ethical observance. Is he a Sabbath observer? Is he honest in business? Is he truthful? Is he charitable? Does he regularly put on tefillin? Does he

---

* Rabbinical Alliance of America; Rabbinical Council of America; Union of Orthodox Rabbis of the United States and Canada; Union of Grand Rabbis (Hasidic).

† A rabbinic seal of approval to indicate that a food product is kosher.

study Torah? Does he believe in God? Assigning labels creates meaningless divisions; learning to see what is behind them is what is important.

Jewish Respect for Scholarship: An American Myth

If we really want to raise children imbued with a Jewish spirit and rich in Jewish knowledge, then we must first restore the traditional value that Jews have placed on learning and scholarship. For that tradition is eroding. We pride ourselves on something that is no longer true. We point to a long history of respect for scholars and scholarship, and of support for education. It is customary to recall that a system of free public compulsory education was established among the Jews of Eretz Yisrael as far back as 64 C.E. Talmudic sources, too, emphasize the priority that must be given to education: "A city that does not have a school for children is deservant of destruction" [4] and "one does not cancel school for the children even to build the Holy Temple." [5] While education among Jews always meant a knowledge of Torah, today American Jews would like to claim that the tradition is being continued in the Jewish community's well-known support for quality secular education, and by the record number of Jews who attend colleges and universities and go on to graduate and professional schools for advanced degrees.

But we are deceiving ourselves. While it is true that the traditional respect for learning led many Jews to encourage their children to enter the learned professions, it is also true that Jews gradually shifted from their own learning-oriented culture to America's job-oriented culture. Reflecting the pragmatism and materialism of secular American culture, education gradually focused almost exclusively on the occupational goal. The importance of a good education is now stressed because it is the route to higher earning power and not because it possesses intrinsic merits that expand both the mind and the soul. "If he can't make a really good living, what good is it?" is typical of the attitudes of many middle-class American Jews toward truly scholarly professions with limited earning power. Do you recall the intensive campaigns on radio and television during the 1960s that urged American youth to get as much schooling as possible?

Why? Because as a people we love and respect knowledge and wisdom? Hardly. The reason given was that a comparison of the average lifetime earnings of elementary school, high school, and college graduates indicated that the higher up the educational ladder one went, the greater the earnings to be expected. In the same vein, more recent campaigns praise technical careers that require no college background because it is now possible to earn as much in those jobs. If education has come to be widely regarded in America, and by Jews as well, only as the door to a good job, then it should come as no surprise that the study of Torah * and the acquisition of the knowledge needed for a satisfying Jewish life is looked upon as not worth serious effort. It is clearly no way to make money.

Even for those who wish for status within the Jewish community, it is the sad truth that Jewish education is not essential. Philanthropy is today's most valued form of Jewish expression and the quickest road to high honor in the Jewish community. Sensitive Jewish apologists may be critical of such a statement, but no objective observer of the Jewish scene can dispute this fact.

A comment often heard from parents resisting the suggestion that they give their child a more intensive Jewish education or that they encourage them to continue on to secondary or even higher levels of Jewish study is, "but what does he need it for? He's not going to be a rabbi anyway." The underlying but obvious assumption is that Jewish studies are worthwhile *only* insofar as they contribute to a professional goal and provide the tools for a livelihood. A secondary implication, of course, is that such a parent does not want his son to become a rabbi which more than anything else lays to rest our much cited respect for Jewish scholars. It is hard to imagine the same parents deriding advanced courses in mathematics or biology on the claim that they do not really expect their son to become a physicist or a physician. After all, it's always possible!

Surely, American Jews appreciate the need for a professional school designed to train rabbis and they can understand why a person who wants to become a rabbi will attend such a school. Certainly, they would be made very uneasy by a school that claimed no occupational purpose and they would find it difficult to understand why anyone should want to attend it. Yet, that is precisely the nature of those in-

---

* See pp. 33–35 and 43–45 for a fuller definition of what is meant by the study of Torah.

stitutions of higher Jewish learning called *yeshivot*. They are generally referred to as rabbinical seminaries, but they have never been that at all. Even today, very few *yeshivot* actually train students to become professional rabbis. These are schools where students immerse themselves for a period of time in the study of Torah, acquire an intensive knowledge of the Talmud and the Codes, and where their religious commitments are intensified. Some *yeshivot* may make provisions to ordain those who show an inclination toward becoming rabbis or teachers. But the greatest number of students who attend these schools do so without any intention of ever seeking ordination. Of those who do, there are many whose only interest is the knowledge they can acquire in the process of ordination, rather than because they are interested in a rabbinical career. The existence today of a whole cadre of men having rabbinical ordination, or who stopped just short of it, and who pursue careers in law, business, medicine, science, and education attests to this. Yet, most American Jews prefer to believe that *yeshivot* are more or less like graduate or professional schools, "training" those who make a career of their Jewishness.

The desire to acquire a general education and to train for a secular profession need not be a barrier to a good Jewish education, although the anti-intellectual, job-oriented view of education which pervades our society is a definite obstacle. This view limits the pursuit of Jewish study to the shallow, elementary level, suitable enough for children through the elementary grades when "real" education is less demanding, but dispensed with as soon as "real" education is taken more seriously.

The much treasured claim that Jews have a special love of learning in and for itself was once valid. We now need to recover our awareness that intensive Jewish studies enrich and add meaning to life—regardless of one's occupation or profession.

Fear of Success

Let us gather our courage and admit the sad truth that most American Jewish parents simply have mixed feelings about Jewish education. On the one hand, they insist that they want their children to

have a Jewish education and honestly believe they are doing everything in their power to provide it. On the other hand, they do not
want "too much" Jewish education, but just enough to make the
children aware of their Jewish identity and keep them from a mixed
marriage. But, in truth, *they are really afraid that a good Jewish
education might succeed.* They are afraid that it might make their
children "too" Jewish.

This fear is revealed to any observant Jewish educator in most
casual conversations with parents and in the parents' reactions to
the programs and policies of Hebrew schools. While the limited
achievements of contemporary Jewish education in America is widely
bemoaned, many are secretly very satisfied with it. If they weren't,
most parents would have revolted a long time ago and demanded
more, as did in fact a minority group of parents who opted for more
intensive programs offered by day schools. And even among them, the
fear is not wholly gone.

Jewish parents in America have largely chosen to walk an educational tightrope; their objective being to move the children along
without falling into an unwanted success (becoming "too Jewish")
or outright failure (rejection of Jewish loyalties). The Jewish educational establishment is under constant pressure to maintain that
tightrope.

It is a difficult compromise to maintain. It calls for disassociating
Jewish studies from life experiences, while simultaneously expecting
those studies to provide emotional satisfaction, intellectual stimulation, and psychological support. We expect Jewish education to
provide the magic formula whereby the child will learn to think
and feel like a Jew, while continuing to live like a gentile. It is completely unreal.

Jewish parents expect education to be relevant and support those
philosophies that view education as an integral part of life itself. Yet,
in Jewish education, many actually insist on irrelevance. How else
can one categorize the inevitable demand by parents who have themselves drifted far from religious tradition to "teach my child to know
he's a Jew, not to be religious." What parents are essentially asking
is for Jewish education to transmit a "feeling" of peoplehood and an
"appreciation" for Jewish values, while stopping short of inspiring the
youngster to abide by those values, or stopping short of the religious

practices with which that peoplehood has been historically identified. While such parents would like Jewish education to affect their child's emotions, they want it to be irrelevant to their behavior. The difficulty in granting that wish is that everything having to do with being Jewish is ultimately grounded in the Jewish religion. The religion and culture of the Jewish people have been so intertwined from its very inception as to make any attempt to separate them doomed to failure. Any division between peoplehood and religion is wholly artificial. What such people may not realize is that even the so-called "nonreligious" Jewish values that they possess—i.e., a commitment to education; a sensitive sense of justice; a basic humanitarianism; an emphasis on charity; the quality of their family life; universalism— are also the fruits of the spiritually rich Jewish environments in which they were raised and, notwithstanding their rejection of the ritual elements, it is the religious tradition that is the origin and source of their basic views.

It is certainly possible for people raised in a religious or a culturally positive Jewish environment to "feel" their Jewishness long after they themselves no longer reflect it in their daily lives. The Jewish loyalties and the more universal Jewish values of a nonobservant family may perhaps survive on the strength of religious memories and nostalgic associations. But they should not expect to succeed in building Jewish loyalties in their children on the basis of *their* memories and *their* nostalgia. It is foolish to assume that mere nostalgia can be perpetuated, or that schools can be programmed to transmit Jewish nostalgia. If the opportunities to experience Jewishness are no longer provided, the erosion not only of Jewish behavior but of Jewish feeling is also inevitable. If *Jewish* children are to be raised, a family may just have to accommodate itself to a fuller return to religious practices. Parents have to overcome the fear of "losing their children" to successful Jewish education, which among some parents is apparently as real as the fear of "losing a child" to a mixed marriage. The accommodation should be welcomed with the realization that any return to a traditional pattern of behavior also involves emphasis on the obligation to "honor thy father and mother." Religious duty teaches and demands a respectful relationship to parents, even where parents themselves do not abide by the traditions. Far from losing one's children, parents may find their children tied to them ever closer. And if parents will feel themselves pressed into adopting some traditional Jewish disciplines, they might also discover a new source of delight.

If Jewish education is to fulfill its task of raising Jews to whom Judaism and the Jewish people are central and not peripheral to their lives, it will have to be precipitated by a real parental desire for it to succeed and a simultaneous readiness to come to terms with all the implications of an effective Jewish upbringing.

Assessing the Environment: Promising Conditions

Even if the general environment is more hostile than ever before, to the spirit of Jewish life and to raising a generation committed to Jewish living, it is also more conducive to it than ever before. The psychological, sociological, economic, and legal conditions are making it easier.

The psychology of young Jews is far healthier today. Earlier generations reflected a decided inferiority complex about their Jewish status. There was a sense of shame. One's Jewishness was not publicly projected. Indications of this complex are legion. Jews hesitated to open a Yiddish newspaper or book in any public place; they felt awkward about being seen outdoors in a skullcap; they avoided wearing a Star of David or any symbol of their Jewish status; and they felt uneasy in using their Hebraic name, as though it invited others to think of them as odd. One is reminded of the report brought back to Moses by ten of the men he sent out to scout the Holy Land. They reported seeing "giants" and that "we were as grasshoppers in their eyes," a confession of their own lack of self-esteem. This inferiority complex has been given theoretical rationale in Europe by the Jewish leader of the *Haskalah* (Enlightenment), Yehudah Leib Gordon (1830–1892), who had written "Be a Jew in your home and a man when you go out," as if being a Jew and a man were two separate aspects of the human personality and could function independently of each other. Today, one is not apt to look kindly on any prescription that counsels schizophrenia, two separate standards of behavior, one for home and one for outside the home.

The younger Jewish generation feels itself very much part of America, and much more natural and candid about its Jewish identity. It doesn't try to hide it and doesn't hesitate to show it. The identity crisis about which one hears and reads so much is not due to any sense of inferiority, but rather to an overwhelming ignorance about themselves as Jews. Young Jews openly admit their Jewishness. They simply do not understand how that makes them different, for there is very little difference between them and non-Jewish persons in the way they live and the things they believe. This is reason enough for crisis. They regard the Judaism of their parents as being quite shallow; as making few demands; imposing no disciplines; and providing no emotional satisfaction, no intellectual stimulation, and no spiritual inspiration. It is to this ersatz Judaism on which they have been raised that many have become apathetic or openly hostile. However, their revolt is qualitatively different from that of their parents' or grandparents' rejection of the Jewish regimen. Decades ago, the motivation was to pass as an American. Today, it is in response to a genuine spiritual yearning that is open to an infusion of real Jewish experiences.

Today there is also a greater tolerance for ethnic differences in America. While a tolerance for religious differences presumably existed all along, it manifested itself primarily in a person's right to his preferred ritual in his own house of worship. It did not encompass an acceptance of different behavior patterns resulting from those religious convictions. Since Judaism is more than a set of beliefs and a way of worship, the effects of this intolerance were disastrous to Jewish life. Jews were made to feel that the distinct elements of the Jewish way of life, such as the Sabbath and kashrut, would be a barrier to their Americanism. To gain acceptance in America, their Jewishness had to be sacrificed.

This is no longer the case. Differences resulting from religious convictions or ethnic customs are now seen as enriching the cultural life of America, and enhancing the democratic nature of American society. The concept of America as a pluralistic society has supplanted the old homogeneous melting-pot concept. "Ethnic diversity" is the new American theme. It is no longer hard to find Jews who are committed to the Jewish way of life accepted in politics and government, in company management, in universities, and in all professions. It is an indication of the changed atmosphere which no longer insists that "making it" in America has to be done at the expense of one's Jewish heritage.

Economic conditions today are also such that it is rarely, if at all, an impediment to the observance of the Sabbath and the Jewish festivals. The five-day business week, and the greater flexibility enjoyed by most salaried employees in determining their days of leave or leisure, removes most of the external pressures that made it difficult for earlier generations. Even where work on the Sabbaths and festivals is expected, today there is greater understanding on the part of management for the religious needs of employees and a greater readiness to accommodate sincere convictions and practices. In the absence of goodwill, employees wishing to observe their traditions have been granted legal protection on the basis of the Civil Rights Act of 1964 and in court decisions that have since been handed down. The contemporary Jew may choose to ignore the Sabbath, and business pressures may at times be great, but the explanations of earlier generations who "justified" their working on the Sabbath in order to provide bread and butter for their families ring hollow today.

Institutions, programs, and personnel who can help one have a Jewish education are more prevalent today. Until a decade or two ago, such facilities simply did not exist throughout most of America. In most Jewish communities, the Jewish parent could count on little outside help in raising a Jewish child. The local synagogue was of little assistance. While the afternoon Talmud Torah was available, its limitations were great. The Jewish day school, with its Jewish atmosphere and more intensive program of study, was almost non-existent. The handful that existed three or four decades ago were all concentrated in the old Jewish neighborhoods of New York City. Jewish high schools, or schools of higher Jewish learning in all of the United States, could be counted on the fingers of one hand. All this has changed. Every city in America that has a Jewish population of more than 7,500 now boasts of at least one day school. There are now over 500 day schools throughout the country. Jewish high schools are more readily available, as are schools of higher Jewish learning. Jewish studies are now offered at countless American colleges and universities. A new generation of American-born and trained rabbis communicate much more easily with the youth. Opportunities for religious-educational experiences to fill periods of leisure—week-end retreats, Jewish camping, trips to Israel, and synagogue youth organizations—exist to a degree that was hitherto unknown. These changed conditions help make the task of raising a devoted Jewish generation much more promising than ever before.

The hostile conditions of the contemporary environment need not invite abject surrender and cause us to throw up our hands in despair and say it's too much to overcome. The promising conditions are also present and must be exploited. While it requires swimming upstream against the current, it's also a sign of life. Only dead fish drift with the current; live fish swim upstream. And if fish can do it in their natural habitat, so can people in theirs. It would, in fact, be in keeping with the entire history of the Jewish people, who have historically been the first to challenge the idolatries others docilely accepted. Jews have contributed much to the spiritual progress of all humanity by acting to preserve and protect themselves against becoming spiritually engulfed by antagonistic ideologies.

The choices are clear:

> One can choose to surrender to the non-Jewish environment either consciously or by just being indifferent and apathetic to the significance of one's Jewishness.

> One can choose to withdraw culturally into insulated Jewish communities that avoid all but peripheral contact with the surrounding culture and society. That is one way to preserve an authentic Jewish existence.

> Or, one can choose to engage in a spiritual confrontation with the environment. Even the family with very little Jewish background has this option. The "spark of faith" (*dos pintele Yid*) resides in every Jew. It needs only be drawn out to become all aglow.

If the decision is to surrender, you can stop reading. If the choice is for insulation, the ghetto environment will decide for you. If you have chosen the third alternative, read on. It is our hope that this book will make a modest contribution in helping Jewish parents clarify goals, avoid some basic errors, and make sounder decisions relating to the Jewish upbringing of their children.

*The Basic Values of Judaism:
What Kind of People Do We
Want Our Children to Be?*

FAITH ALONE does not suffice. The entire moral-ethical-religious system of Judaism rests on the notion that faith, to be meaningful, must be translated into deed: "Not study is the supreme thing, but the doing." [1] Action is a necessary companion to both study and belief.

Many contemporary Jews are known to boast, "I am a good Jew at heart." What they mean by it is that as long as one means well, and one's heart is in the right place, it does not matter what one does. Judaism insists that it does matter. On the contrary, if one's actions are deficient, it really does not matter how well one's "heart" may function. What good is it if one believes it is wrong to murder, steal, lie, and deceive if one proceeds to commit such crimes? What significance is it of how strongly one believes in the importance of charity or of education if one does not practice those duties? While the examples cited have been drawn from the ethical-moral obligations, the principle applies also to the ritual obligations. One must not only believe as a Jew, but also live as a Jew.

A good Jewish education is one that not only succeeds in transmitting knowledge or inspiring faith, but that transforms it all into the reality of practice. Although creed and deed are both essential, greater importance is attached to correct living. The ancient sages were able to conceive of God saying: "Even if My children were to leave Me, as long as they keep My commandments." [2]

No discussion of the goals of a Jewish upbringing would be complete without some understanding of the essential spiritual, social, and moral values that constitute the living center of the Jewish heritage.

It is true that *some* of Judaism's values are by now regarded as universal. Other religions teach these values too. Humanists who espouse no religious preference also proclaim them. This does not detract from their importance as a Jewish teaching. On the contrary, the very fact that the source of these now universal values lies in Judaic sources is all the more reason for Judaism to be appreciated, not only for that which it has already contributed to humanity but for what it may still contribute to the refinement of the individual.

Judaism itself does not distinguish between its universal values and those that are still distinctively, if not uniquely, Jewish. They are all interrelated and interdependent; each emanates from and leads into the other. In transmitting such particular Jewish values as reverence for God, study of Torah, love for the Jewish people, a basis is also built up for strengthening and transmitting such universal values as love for mankind, justice, compassion, and respect for the dignity of all people.

It is possible that one will say: "I know people who have acquired a good Jewish education and are even considered to be scholars, yet they lack some of the values mentioned." The answer is that either such people did not assimilate everything they learned, or their education was deficient in some areas, or that human weakness, together with environmental temptations, combined to undermine its effectiveness.

After all, no education can offer a one hundred percent guarantee. Basic to Judaism, as it is to other faiths, is the view that man does have free will, namely, the power to choose the way in which he goes. A good Jewish education can influence good decisions or correct behavior; it does not automatically guarantee them.

The Torah understands this. It guides and instructs, it commands concerning the direction a person is to take; and it even warns of the dire consequences of ignoring the guidance: "I have put before you life and death, blessing and curse. Choose life, if you and your offspring would live" (Deuteronomy 30:19). But in the final analysis, it recognizes that it is man himself who makes the choice. Otherwise, man would be nothing more than a robot programmed by the Almighty to live his life in a certain way. The good life would merit no reward. The evil life would deserve no punishment.

Taking into consideration all the limitations of human character and environmental influences, Jewish education worthy of its name at least strives to instill those values that are deeply imbedded in the entire fabric of the Jewish heritage. These values, which we will now attempt to outline in capsule form, are clearly defined in the immense religious literature of the Jewish people. They are the measuring rod by which all else is judged and by which alternative courses of action are selected. They provide the basis of the legal, religious (halakhic) rulings and set the framework within which the Jewish personality develops and from which a way of thinking emerges. These values influence character, determine priorities, and define the way one relates to the world. Judaism strives to create people who reflect these values in their daily lives.

To Love and Revere God

The noblest spiritual virtue stressed in Judaism is undoubtedly the love of God. The Hebrew expression is *ahavat haShem*. In the passage known as the *Shema* ("Hear O Israel"), the central affirmation of God's unity is immediately followed by: "And you shall love the Lord your God with all your heart, with all your soul, and with all your might" (Deuteronomy 6:5). The charge to "love the Lord your God" is repeated over and over again in the Torah, the Prophets, and Sacred Writings, which together make up the Hebrew Bible.

The Talmud,[3] basing itself on the verse from the *Shema* just quoted, teaches the lesson that both the good and the "evil" inclinations of the heart must be directed toward doing the Divine Will. It is not easy to ascertain whether every religious-observant person is truly imbued with the capacity to truly love God—as Job unselfishly loved Him. It is not a level easy to reach. However, it remains an everpresent goal in the Jewish value structure.

A spiritual step below that of love for God is reverence for God. The Hebrew words for this concept are *yirat haShem.* Although it is often translated as *fear of God*, it does not mean fear in the same way as one might fear a wild beast, a hostile ruler, or a dangerous situation. For this kind of fear, the Hebrew word is *pahad.*

While *yirat haShem* does harbor the notion of fearing punishment for wrongdoing, to limit the concept of *yirah* to this definition would be to define it in its most primitive form. Rabbi Abraham Isaac Kook (1865–1935), first Ashkenazic Chief Rabbi of Eretz Yisrael, regarded this form of *yirah* as suitable only for the "spiritually ill or weak." On a more sophisticated spiritual level, *yirah* connotes a sense of awe or reverence for the greatness and overwhelming majesty of God. The closest example might be the feeling one experiences when coming before a powerful ruler or before a great and famous personality. The extra care that one exerts in one's dress, behavior, and manner of speech on such occasions is an expression of awe, not of "fear." The feeling is much more intense when relating to the King of Kings.

A religious upbringing ought to inspire children with a sense of reverence for God that comes from contact with nature. Jewish tradition prescribes a blessing to be recited when coming upon great scenes of natural beauty: "Blessed art Thou Lord our God King of the universe who has made the works of creation." The Psalmist put it more spontaneously: "O Lord, How great are Thy works!" (Psalms 92:6).

A sense of awe toward God should emanate from studying the intricate ways of the human body or of the natural universe. The complicated orderliness should be a source of continuous amazement. Jewish tradition saw fit to prescribe a blessing to be said when meeting a person who has distinguished himself in acquiring such scientific knowledge: "Blessed art Thou Lord our God King of the universe who has given of Thy wisdom to mortals." Before a scholar allows such adoration to go to his head, he should realize that it is not he who is the subject of adoration; it is the Almighty. Reverence and awe toward God imply humility in man. The absence of such reverence is conducive to the sort of "intellectual arrogance" that ill suits those who truly aspire to wisdom.

Awe for God's greatness ought also to emanate from the study of His teachings and Israel's experiences: "For what great nation is there that has a God so near to it as the Lord our God is to us, whenever we call upon Him? And what great nation is there, that has statutes and ordinances so righteous as all this law which I set before you this day?" (Deuteronomy 4:7–8).

Each day's prayer begins with the verse from Psalms: "The beginning of wisdom is reverence for the Lord" (111:10). The Ethics of the Fathers add: "Where there is no wisdom, there is no reverence (of God); where there is no reverence (of God), there is no wisdom." [4]

The interrelationship between true wisdom and reverence for God was stressed by Rabbi Kook: "Reverence for God is the deepest of all wisdom, and serves as the fundamental basis for all science and all Torah, for all matters both sacred and secular. As long as reverence for God is not a basis for science, the latter can only float on the superficial level of concepts that cannot qualify as wisdom." [5]

Our twentieth-century generation, more so than those who preceded us, ought to appreciate the full impact of Kook's words. For this is the generation that has seen the achievements of scientific technology used not only to advance human life but also to systematically and barbarically destroy it; this is the generation that has seen scientific theories not only put to many good purposes, but also to many ignoble uses.

Most people find it so much easier to fear or revere people than to fear or revere God. Rabbi Yohanan ben Zakkai chastised his disciples: "When a person wants to commit an offense, he says [to himself] 'I hope *no man* will see me.' " [6]

The moral significance of reverence is emphasized in the Torah where, at the conclusion of an entire series of laws relating to moral offenses not punishable in a court of law, we find: "You shall revere the Lord," or simply "I am the Lord, your God" (see Leviticus Chap. 19). The awareness of the Divine presence provides effectiveness to conscience as a deterrent to many offenses that are not within the jurisdiction of any court or where there is no fear of being caught and judged in any human court of law.

Religious education strives to instill such reverence for God. It too is not easily achieved. Once attained, however, *"yirat haShem* adds strength and courage to the human soul, it adds purpose and great aspirations to life, and fills it with heightened spirituality." [7]

To Love Our "Neighbor"

Paralleling the love and reverence for God is the Jewish tradition's emphasis upon the verse in the Torah, "Love your neighbor as yourself" (Leviticus 19:18). The Hebrew text uses the word *rai-akha* which means more than neighbor. It implies fellow human beings. Rabbi Akiva called that verse *the* great principle of the Torah.[8] When the great sage Hillel was asked to summarize the essence of the entire Torah, he quoted that same verse, adding the explanation that its practical implementation is in terms of "what is hateful to you, do not do to your fellow men." [9] He was even more direct in the statement attributed to him in the Mishna when he said: "Love all people and draw them close to Torah." [10] In an unbroken chain of tradition, this value continues to be emphasized by the great scholars of the twentieth century. Rabbi Kook writes: "The love of all people must pulsate in one's heart and soul, the love of every human being individually and of all nations collectively, expressed by a desire to assist in their spiritual and material growth. Hatred must be directed only towards the acts of evil and the corrupt deeds in the world." [11] This teaching requires one to see the good inherent in all people even if their beliefs and their ways of life differ from that followed by the Jewish people, and demands that one give others the benefit of the doubt.

While it is necessary to emphasize the love of all people, to overcome the tendency to be suspicious of, or hostile to, the stranger, it is equally important to stress the virtue of loving one's *own* people. Sibling rivalry and conflict among the members of a family are as old as the history of man. And so, Judaism places special emphasis on the importance of love for all Jews, *ahavat Yisrael*. The Torah warns that "you shall not hate your brother in your heart" (Leviticus 19:17). One can be suspicious of those who are so enamored of mankind that they have no room in their hearts to love their fellow Jews. There are also those who tend to relate sympathetically only to such persons within Jewry with whom they can personally identify and to be hostile to those who belong to different cultural or ideological subgroups. The sages caution against this: "A man should not say: Love the sages, and hate the disciples; love the disciples and hate the common people, but love them all." [12] The Talmud ascribes the destruction of the Second Temple in the year 70 C.E. to "causeless hatred." [13] While there was much religious devotion and Torah scholarship, the people, split as they were into many sects, hated one another. This was an intolerable sin.

Ahavat Yisrael is reflected by the sense of responsibility that Jews are taught to feel for one another. The Talmud teaches: "All Jews are responsible one for the other." [14] Where there is *ahavat Yisrael*, there will also be found unity and a working together for the common good. This lesson is also derived from the Midrashic interpretation of the Four Species used on the Sukkot festival.[15] The *etrog* (citron), which possesses the qualities of taste and smell, is compared to those people who possess much Torah learning and are rich in good deeds. The *lulav* (palm), which possesses taste but no smell, is compared to those people who have acquired much Torah knowledge, but are poor in good deeds. The *hadas* (myrtle), which has smell but no taste, is compared to those who have many good deeds to their credit, but are poor in Torah knowledge. The *arava* (willow), which has neither taste nor smell, is compared to those people who possess neither Torah nor good deeds. The parable teaches the lesson that just as one cannot fulfill the duty of rejoicing before the Lord if any of the Four Species is missing, so, too, the Jewish purpose cannot be attained if sections of the Jewish people are omitted. Where there is unity, and all benefit from whatever merits each possesses, one makes up for what the other lacks. The High Holyday prayer book makes the point in a prayer: "May they all form a single bond to do Thy will with a perfect heart." Israel's highest spiritual aims can only be attained through unity. A good Jewish education strives to imbue *ahavat Yisrael* in the heart of a child.

To Respect Human Dignity

The love of "neighbor" is inseparable from the Jewish concept of man, derived from the passage in Genesis (5:1–2): "When God created man, He made him in the image of God; male and female He created them." Rabbi Eliezer, one of the Talmudic masters, was said to regard this passage as *the* great principle of the Torah.

The word "image" or "likeness" does not imply a physical representation, but a spiritual one. We are taught the lesson that the human being possesses qualities that are Divine-like in their essence and that set him aside from the rest of the animal kingdom. The human being is capable of reasoning and feeling compassion, and is capable of a dimension beyond the senses.

While the religious view sees man as an extension of God, as "but little lower than the angels" (Psalms 8:6), the secular view sees man as an extension of the animal, as a creature governed by physical drives and needs. The moral implications of this distinction are great.

In the social dimension, this provides a religious foundation for the view that all human beings are worthy of being treated with dignity for the spark of the Divine is within everyone. Implicit in this view is the parallel lesson that human beings have a responsibility to behave with dignity, to act in a manner that befits the Divine holiness that is an essential part of their selves.

The stress upon acting with due regard and consideration for the feelings of others is found throughout Torah sources. The Mishna teaches: "Who is worthy of honor? He who shows respect for others." [16] The sages of the Talmud added: "The dignity of the human being is a great thing." "Let the honor of your student be as dear to you as your own" is an application of this lesson to the classroom. [17] Be as "careful with the honor of your friend as with the reverence due your [spiritual] teacher" is a guide for all social situations. [18]

This basic value is reflected in the religious prohibition against publicly embarrassing a person which is treated as the moral equivalent of murder. [19] To violate this prohibition is to automatically invite loss of one's share in the world to come. [20] The application of this teaching is found in many different rulings and customs: one may not remind a repentent person of his former life, nor call attention to a convert's former status; one may not call another with a derogatory nickname; one may not demean a mentally retarded person who does not even understand the implication of what is being said or done to him; one must not embarrass a poor man by ostentatious display of one's own wealth; one must not request a contribution from another unless it is known that he is in a position to give; and a teacher must not ask a question that he knows his pupils cannot answer, nor may students throw questions to a teacher on a topic far removed from what is being studied, lest it cause him confusion and embarrassment. The treatment accorded the dead in burying everyone in the same simple white garment is based on the prohibition against demeaning the poor. Even in death, the vessel that housed the "image of God" must be accorded its deserved dignity. Many Jewish laws relating to burial derive from this value. It is applied to every area of human relations. The essence of this value emerges constantly from every page of Torah and Talmud.

To Treat All People Equally

Inherent in the Jewish value system is the view that looks upon all people as equal and that refutes all ideas of racial superiority. The idea is embodied in the answer given to the question as to why God chose to create just one human being and then commanding, be "fruitful and multiply and fill the earth," when He could just as easily have started with many hundreds or thousands of people and quickened the process of filling the earth. It was done, says the Mishna, to enhance the peace of mankind, so that no man should be able to say to another, "my father was greater than yours." [21] If many people were created simultaneously, it would be possible to claim that some were created with superior qualities. But if all mankind is descended from the same one person, such a claim loses all merit. While differences in ability, skill, and talent among individuals are obvious, the claim to being of superior racial stock falls by the wayside. Thus, the laws that are based on the dignity of people and the sacredness of life relate equally to all humanity.

To Regard Life As Sacred

Still another reason given in the same Mishna for the initial creation of one person is to teach the importance of human life. "He who destroys just one life among people, it is though he destroyed an entire world," for not only is that one life destroyed, but so are all those later generations who might have descended from that person.[22] The Nazis in World War II slaughtered not only six million Jews and millions of others as well, but also the many additional millions to whom the victims might have given birth. Likewise, "he who saves a life among people, the Torah credits him with having saved an entire world."

The importance of life is underscored throughout Jewish tradition. Jewish law suspends all prohibitions except for idolatry, murder, incest, and adultery in order to save a life. It forbids taking part in needless activities that might be dangerous to life.

While other nations have created such toasts as "cheers" and "bottoms up" to emphasize the conviviality of the occasion, Jews use the word "l'ḥayim" which means "to life." That they do so is not mere chance. It is the reflection of a value that runs deep in Jewish sources.

To Strive for Holiness

The call upon the Jewish people to become "a kingdom of priests and a holy nation" (Exodus 19:6), able to serve as a spiritual example to all nations, is inherent in Jewish purpose and central to the spiritual values of Judaism. It involves a striving for holiness: "The Lord spoke to Moses saying, Speak to the whole Israelite community and say to them: You shall be holy, for I, the Lord your God, am holy" (Leviticus 19:2). It means to implement the values discussed till now and those still to be discussed. Holiness in Judaism does not mean being removed from life. It does not mean the total suppression of human drives or the denial of physical comforts. As a matter for fact, within the framework of what the Torah regards as permissible, it encourages the enjoyment of the "good things" of life in moderation. Holiness means striving for ethical perfection; it means a disciplined life where one learns to master one's passions instead of being enslaved by them; it means removing oneself from the vulgar and the profane.

The state of holiness is expressed through the disciplined life enjoined by Judaism. Samuel Belkin writes:

> Our Sages looked upon passion, excessive desire and undisciplined indulgence in food and drink as causes of evil. . . . Philosophers, too, emphasized that the control of human desire is one of the great virtues. But to the Greeks, such terms as self-control, temperance and the discipline of the passions were philosophic virtues. . . . The Torah, however, regulates human life; it checks the unrestricted sensual and gluttonous desires through divine disciplines. It encourages man to enjoy life, but at the same time, it limits his passions and desires by statutes. . . . They restrain man's desires and teach him to live like a being created in the image of God instead of like an irrational beast.[23]

The centrality of this value is evidenced by the fact that all of Jewish law can be classified in terms of enhancing (1) the sanctity of the person, (2) the sanctity of time, and (3) the sanctity of place.

Concern for the *sanctity of the person* is reflected by laws dealing with social and business ethics, sexual relationships, eating habits, patterns of dress and speech, family relationships, personal hygiene and health care, the supreme importance of life, and the honor and respect due even to a lifeless human being.

Concern for the *sanctity of time* is emphasized by the laws relating to the Sabbath and the festivals. The *sanctity of place* is reflected in the commandments relating to the ancient Temple in Jerusalem and in laws relating to the synagogue and the study hall.

The sense of purpose inherent in the call to holiness gives this deeply spiritual concept a very significant role in the development of the human personality. Viktor E. Frankl insists that "the striving to find a meaning in one's life is the primary motivational force in man." [24] He finds that this supersedes the pleasure principle on which Freudian psychoanalysis is centered or the power principle stressed by Adlerian psychology. While meaning in life can also be found outside the religious framework, Jewish spiritual values provide an early and firm basis for it, by focusing on the ultimate purposes of present activities, and by diverting attention from preoccupation with oneself toward God and humanity. Samuel Belkin, in fact, see Judaism's call to holiness as "a spiritual design for purposeful living" and as providing "a *raison d'être* to man's continued existence." [25]

To Study Torah

The study of Torah provides the basic content to Jewish education. To study Torah is to study the Five Books of Moses and the rest of the Hebrew Bible; it is to study Mishna and Gemara, together known as Talmud; and all the commentaries to all of these texts. Studying Torah is a basic Jewish value in itself and the way one learns all the other values. That is why the sages equate the importance of studying Torah with the observance of all other duties combined.

To study Torah is to partake of a spiritual experience. It is a form of worship and one is expected to enter into it with the same concentration and devotion as that required for prayer. In fact, studying Torah enjoys a status even higher than that of worship. One is not required to interrupt one's Torah study to engage in prayer unless the obligatory time for the prayer is about to pass. Prayer is a *monologue* where man talks *to* God. Torah study is a *dialogue* where man talks *with* God. His words are discussed, analyzed, and interpreted by man. The purpose of Torah study is to come to know the mind and the will of the Almighty. In the process of doing so, one finds not only intellectual excitement and the joy of discovery, but a sense of spiritual elevation as well.

Torah is studied by both the young and the old. The same page, the same material, is studied by the beginner at the age of eight, ten, or fifteen as by the venerable scholar at the age of sixty, seventy, or eighty. To each one, on his own level of understanding, it has something to offer. To the young, it offers a level of sophisticated study that general subjects geared to his level do not approach. To the older student, Torah is an entire world of thought that puts man in touch with the Divine. There is the everpresent excitement of new insights, of penetrating intellectual debates. In disciplining the mind, in developing mental acuity, in probing philosophical and human problems, and in its integrated interdisciplinary contents, the study of Torah is a unique experience.

To the uninitiated it must be explained that Torah is not limited to the study of ritual questions, to subject matter thought of as belonging exclusively to the category of religion. Its subject matter touches upon every branch of human knowledge. Though not in any systematic form, it is a curriculum that encompasses law and philosophy, history, and legend. It touches upon the elements of psychology and sociology, mathematics and biology, ethics and government. Within the framework of Torah, one studies matters related to business and labor, marriage and divorce, civil damages and criminal law. It is all religious study inasmuch as it is rooted in the Sinaitic revelation and reflects the spiritual views of the Hebraic faith and doctrine. When one of the sages said about Torah: "Turn it and turn it over again for everything is in it," he meant to emphasize its broad scope and the depths to which it was possible to plumb when studying Torah.[26] The tradition makes the same point when it refers to "the sea of the Talmud."

The study of Torah was the basis for the democratization of Jewish life. Unlike the aristocracy created by royalty or by the priesthood, the aristocracy of Torah scholarship was open to people from the humblest of origins. In due course, the "crown of Torah" surpassed the "crowns of royalty and of priesthood" in power, influence, and importance.

Torah study is credited with adding to the strength of one's "good inclination" in the constant struggle with one's "evil inclination." The person who trains himself in his youth to study Torah is never at a loss for something to do. He is never bored. Studying

Torah provides an avocation that meaningfully fills hours and days of leisure or years of retirement.

"Every Israelite person is required to study Torah" is the law.[27] But instead of being a dry, religious duty, it is a pleasurable, uplifting experience that brings delight to the soul. That is why the study of Torah is actually forbidden on those days when all pleasurable activities are proscribed, such as on Tisha b'Av and during the week of mourning (*shiva*). In the popular view, the vision of heavenly bliss may be a fantasy of gourmet feasting and countless women providing endless physical pleasures to their faithful. In the Jewish tradition, the fantasy of ecstasy consists of endless immersion in the study of Torah which provides exciting spiritual joy to the faithful.

The joy of Torah study may not be discovered at the superficial level. But, "the more one studies it, the more relish one finds in it." [28] It is very much like discovering oil. The initial search and the constant digging into the earth or the seabed is hard and tedious. But once oil is struck, it gushes forth in a constant stream. One needs controls to contain it. A successful strike is worth all the effort.

Finally, while Torah study has its beginning in early childhood, it has no end. While there are stages of study and levels of achievement, there is no point during one's lifetime at which it can be said to end. As water is to the body, Torah is to the Jewish soul.

To Cherish Eretz Yisrael

At the heart of the Jewish faith and heritage, and emanating directly from the study of Torah is the bond between the Jewish people and the land which came to be known in biblical times as Eretz Yisrael, the land of Israel. The historic relationship of the Jewish people to the land of Israel was always more than a nationalistic sentiment. It reflected a deeply religious attitude that saw Israel as an integral part of God's Covenant with the Jewish people and as an opportunity for a deeper relationship with Him than was possible anywhere else in the world. To the Jew, the land was holy from the very beginning of creation. The existence of an entire body of religious duties that apply only to those who live in the Holy Land highlighted this view. The themes of almost all the religious holidays are built around the land of Israel, as are so many of the daily and Sabbath prayers. The belief in the coming of a Messiah who would usher in a Messianic era marked by the moral perfection of all mankind and the harmonious coexistence of all people free of war, fear, hatred, and intolerance was always related to the establishment of Jewish sovereignty over the soil of Israel, the ingathering of the Jews to their ancestral home and the restoration of Jerusalem to its spiritual glory. The spiritual vision of the future was seen by Isaiah as including the prospect "that out of Zion shall go forth the Torah and the word of God from Jerusalem" (Isaiah 2:3).

According to many of the sages, to live in the land of Israel is one of the biblical commandments incumbent upon Jews to fulfill.[29] So much importance was attached to this religious duty that, like Torah study, some held the merit of observing it to be equivalent to the observance of all the other religious duties combined.[30]

And if all Jews living in countries around the world do not uproot themselves to return to their ancestral home, their feelings of solidarity and support for the modern State of Israel reflect the depths of their convictions about the spiritual centrality of the land of Israel in the faith of the Jewish people.

To Love Justice

Emanating directly from the study of Torah is the Jewish emphasis on justice. This value existed among Jews from the very beginnings of its history, from the very challenge thrown to God by the father of the Jewish people. In pleading for the fate of the cities of Sodom and Gemorrah, Abraham assumes the presence in those cities of a community of righteous people and cries out: "Shall not the Judge of all the earth deal justly?" (Genesis 18:25). Many of the commandments of the Torah are intended to effect a social order based on justice and righteousness. Sensitivity to injustice is found throughout the writings of the Hebrew Prophets who fought for the poor, the widowed, and the orphaned. One cannot study the Jewish sources without becoming sensitized to this value. The emphasis on justice is applied not only to obvious areas as fair trials and honest judicial decisions, to the use of fair weights and measures and honest business practices, to the mutual obligations of employer and employee, to the responsibilities of society to the less fortunate, but it is applied even to such interpersonal relations that require one to give another the benefit of the doubt and to judge others on the scale of merit. The Torah commands: "In justice shall you judge your neighbor" (Leviticus 19:15). The passage "Justice, justice shall you pursue" (Deuteronomy 16:20) gave rise to the rabbinic thought that the Torah intended to teach us that not only must justice be the goal in all human endeavors, but the means by which those goals are achieved must also be just. Such is the meaning assigned to the repetition of the word "justice."

To Be Compassionate

In addition to justice, compassion is one of the basic human qualities that study of Torah stresses. Rabbinic scholars have gone as far as to insist that it is not only an important feature of the Jewish moral system, but is in fact at the very heart of Jewish faith and living.

The biblical call to walk in the ways of God has been regarded from earliest times as a signal for people to imitate the Divine qualities of compassion and kindness: "And now Israel, what does God require of you, but to revere Him. . . . and to walk in His ways" (Deuteronomy 10:12). As to what constitutes *the way of God*, ancient sources teach us: "Just as He is gracious, so be you gracious; just as He is merciful, be you too merciful . . . just as He is full of kindness and truth . . . so you too." [31] The prophet Micah also says it clearly: "He has told you what is good and what God requires of you, but to act justly, to love kindness, and to walk humbly with your God" (Micah 6:8). Rabbi Israel Meir Hakohen (1838–1933), better known as The Chafetz Chaim, emphasized that the "entire Torah is permeated by this [kindness] concept." [32] "If a man shows no mercy," says an ancient source, "what difference is there between him and a beast which can callously stand by and not feel the anguish of its fellow creature?"

When the Talmud notes the qualities possessed by Israel it says: "Three characteristics does the [Jewish] people possess: they are merciful, modest and perform deeds of kindness." [33] Jews who lacked these qualities were considered unworthy members of the people. Maimonides went so far as to declare that "there is reason to be suspicious of the Jewish credentials of one who is cruel." [34]

It is only where compassion perverts justice or perpetuates wickedness do we find that Israel is cautioned against allowing that sentiment to prevail. While tradition required justice to be tempered by mercy, the latter was not expected to pervert justice and upset the delicate balance between the two.

The quality of compassion and mercy, the "good heart," was not to be a mark of weakness and cowardice, but of strength of character and a disciplined will.

To Show Civic Responsibility

Throughout Jewish teachings, there permeates a sense of importance about participating in the life of the Jewish community. The Mishna quotes Hillel as having taught: "Do not separate yourself from the community." [35] One cannot live a Jewish life nor fulfill oneself as a Jew if one isolates himself from the Jewish community. And while in the view of other faiths the highest spiritual moments are best achieved in isolation and solitude, Judaism emphasizes the presence of other people as the way to spiritual heights.

The central and most momentous experience of the Jewish people took place in the midst of *all* the people at Mt. Sinai. The Torah instructs Moses to "gather the people—men, women, children" (Deuteronomy 31:12) for the purpose of teaching them the word of God. The wisdom of the book of Proverbs adds that "in the multitude of people is the glory of the King" (Proverbs 14:28). Although it is perfectly permissible for a Jew to fulfill his prayer obligations alone, Jewish law clearly insists on the preferability of *public prayer*. The principle set down is that "all matters that involve holiness require a quorum" (a *minyan*) of ten.[36] The basis for ten as the quorum is the biblical passage in Numbers 14:27, where the ten scouts are called a community. The joyous occasions of life are also best expressed in the midst of a community and not in privacy. The requirement of a *minyan* at a wedding for the recitation of the Seven Wedding Benedictions is due to the reference in those prayers to joy, *simha*, which cannot be expressed except in the presence of a community.

An extension of this same value is the importance assigned to communal service (*tzorkhai tzibbur*). The prayer book contains a special prayer recited every Sabbath morning that asks for God's blessing upon those "who occupy themselves in *faithfulness* with the needs of the community." Such involvement is deemed to be in the category of fulfilling a Divine commandment (*mitzvah*) that merits special reward.

The emphasis on public service extends also to the general community. Jewish thought stresses responsible citizenship in the city and country where one resides. The prophet Jeremiah taught: "Seek the peace of the city where I have caused you to be carried away . . . and pray unto the Lord for it" (Jeremiah 29:7). The tendency of Jews to become deeply involved in civic activities is in the finest tradition of the Jewish heritage. In doing so however, concern for the welfare of the Jewish community should not be diminished.

To Be Creative

Inasmuch as Jewish study is apparently so deeply oriented toward the past and particularly toward the study of fixed texts, it might be thought that Judaism does not encourage creativity or independence of thought. This is certainly not true of the authentic Jewish tradition, nor is it true of the spiritual giants of the Jewish people throughout the generations. On the contrary, the texts themselves convey the lesson that an essential aspect of the spirituality of the Jewish people depends on its continued creativity.

Man is seen as an active participant in "a continuing process of creation." He was mandated by God to fill the earth, to develop it, and to gain mastery over all that had been created. Judaism does not stop its adherents from striking out in new areas of knowledge and research in order to reveal the secrets of the unknown. The concentrated presence of Jews and their record achievements in all fields of endeavors could not have resulted from a basic value system that stifled thought.

Nor did the Jews hesitate, from the very depths of faith and not without a sense of reverence, to challenge even God Himself. The very first Jew, Abraham, set the example by challenging the justice of the Divine decision regarding the destruction of the cities of Sodom and Gemorrah. Job, while steadfastly refusing to deny God, hurled accusations. The Hasidic Rebbe of Berdichev, who lived but several centuries ago, gained fame as one who did likewise. Jewish scholarship plumbed the ancient texts to gain new insights, to challenge and debate their predecessors, to find flaws and reconcile differences. Every Jewish scholar takes special pride in his capacity to come up with *hidushim*, which can be defined as "original or creative scholarship." While Judaism rests on the acceptance of several faith principles as axioms and seeks conformity to certain basic rules of behavior, there is no denying the encouragement it manifests toward original thinking and creative efforts in every area.

In summary, a person who recognizes and reveres the values discussed in this chapter, and whose life reflects these values, is surely the kind of person Judaism seeks to develop. Is this the kind of person you would like your child to become? A sound Jewish upbringing consistent with the tradition is essential in the acquisition of these values.

CHAPTER

3

~~~~~~

The Ideal Jewish Education

Education of the Whole Child

JEWISH EDUCATION at its best is concerned with the total personality of the child. It influences his character, it shapes his values, it fashions his life-style. It imbues him with wisdom and understanding, it makes him self-sufficient and responsible, and it encourages him to good works. Clearly we cannot ask any school curriculum, no matter how fine, to do all this for us. The ideal Jewish education is achieved only when the home, school, and total environment interact to prepare a child to take his place in the world as a productive, cultured Jew, aware of and committed to his heritage. Jewish education at its best teaches the child to think, to question, to inquire, and to analyze. It encourages strong physical habits and contributes to sound mental health. It provides a sense of significance and self-worth, a feeling that there is purpose and meaning to one's life, and the satisfaction of belonging to a people which constitutes an historic religious-national community. Jewish education addresses itself to the intellect, it touches the emotions, and it affects behavior.

The essential goals in the upbringing of a Jewish child are:

To instill those spiritual convictions and behavioral disciplines that are the common heritage of the Jewish people and that are crucial to the preservation of our people as a faith community;   .

to train the child in those traits of character, morality, and ethics that are rooted in the teachings of the Jewish faith and that are reflective of authentic Jewish life;

to give the child a knowledge and understanding of the Jewish heritage by study of Torah, Talmud, and other writings and to teach the child to relate to it in a positive and meaningful way;

to provide the knowledge needed to understand the nature of man and society and to appreciate all fields of human endeavor; and

to provide the basic skills needed to later choose a *satisfying* profession, trade, or business in line with one's interests and talents.

In educating a Jewish child, we cannot dispense with any of these goals. They constitute an harmonious blend that caters neither to the assimilationist-Jewish orientation which dispenses with the Jewish-oriented goals, nor to the isolationist-religious orientation which discourages any Jewish integration into the larger society.

Learning: A Never-Ending Pursuit

Jewish education has its beginning in early childhood, but it has no end. While there are levels of study or achievement, there is no point at which it can be regarded as completed. The education of a Jewish child means conveying the lesson that the study of Torah is a continuing lifelong process. The ideal Jewish education is one that never stops but keeps growing and keeps being reinforced.

The sages well understood the psychology of learning. They taught: "He who does not increase his knowledge, decreases it." [1] The curve of forgetting, taught by educational psychologists, shows how rapidly one forgets material learned if there is no continuity and no reinforcement. To emphasize the spiritual death that was sure to follow in the wake of neglecting to study, they added: "He who does not study deserves to die." The tendency to procrastinate was also challenged: "Say not 'when I have leisure I shall study', perhaps you will never have leisure." [2]

Many American Jews seem to believe that Jewish study is only for the very young or the very old. If only the long-range nature of Jewish education were appreciated, children's entire Jewish upbringing could be put into an entirely different perspective. A boy would no longer go to Hebrew School just "to become Bar-Mitzvah," but simply because it is incumbent on Jewish people to study their heritage. Formal Jewish schooling would at least go through the secondary level. Although it is desirable for such schooling to be continued beyond high school into schools of higher Jewish learning, even where children do not continue, they would be encouraged to exploit all available opportunities for informal Jewish education. Time for reading and study in the privacy of his own home would be set aside. He would choose to attend classes or study groups offered at most synagogues, educational institutions, or by various fraternal and Zionist organizations. For however pursued, a good Jewish education means the unending pursuit of God's word for the refinement of man's outer and inner worlds.

A Total Education: What It Consists Of

Torah Studies and Religious Training

Rabbi Abraham Isaac Kook wrote:

> The main aim of education is to mold man into his civilized form. . . .
> Man is civilized if he acts justly and honestly; to educate man to live in that framework is the supreme aim of Jewish religious education. The surest way to achieve this aim is not through an ethics-divorced religion, but through a thorough religious grounding. Without God and religion, any system of ethical education will lack a solid base and constitutes an unreliable instrument for civilizing man.[3]

The basis for all Jewish religious education is the study of Torah. Although in its narrowest sense, Torah refers only to the Five Books of Moses (Written Torah), it also means the Oral Torah as embodied in the Talmud (Mishna and Gemara) and all the commentaries and codes built upon it. Torah is the source of Jewish ethics and morality. It is the basis for the unique Jewish way of life. It is the Covenant between God and Israel. Religious instruction without the study of Torah is not seen as possessing much merit. The Talmud teaches: "The ignorant person cannot be truly pious." [4] Only superstitious attitudes and practices result from ignorance. Genuine piety and scrupulous observance of the precepts can only come about through thorough study and sound knowledge of Torah.

Torah was not to remain the domain of a spiritual elite, of a select few. It was the inheritance of all the Jewish people. It was Torah knowledge the sages had in mind when they said: "There is no one so poor as the man who is wanting in knowledge." [5]

A Torah education provides the cement that builds Jewish people everywhere into a single national entity. Separated from one another by national boundaries and proclaiming political loyalty to different native countries, speaking many different languages and coming from many diverse cultures, it is the Torah that ultimately provides the unifying element which inculcates a feeling of common ancestry and common destiny. Study of, and adherence to, the Torah provides both the memories and the aspirations that made possible the Jewish national revival in our day as represented by the State of Israel. The Talmudic principle that "all Jews are responsible one for another" emanates from and is an integral part of Torah education.[6]

The biblical commandment "and you shall teach them diligently to your children" (Deuteronomy 6:7) refers to a Torah education. In addition to the spiritual values inherent in the very study of Torah, its superior importance is that it could "lead to doing," to the fulfillment of all the other precepts of the Torah.[7] Torah study that does not lead to proper actions in man's relationship to God and to humanity fails in its goals.

The problem of studying Torah for reasons other than for the purpose of fulfilling the precepts was solved by the ruling that a man should always engage in the study of Torah, even if not for its own sake, in the hope that it will yet be done for its own sake, i.e., for the proper motives.[8]

At this time, leaving aside the very real problems that many might have of how this might be achieved, let us set forth what a good *minimum* Torah-religious education should involve. While we project this as an *ideal* minimum, there are literally tens of thousands of American Jewish children who are receiving just such a training.

By the time a child completes his *elementary* education at about the age of fourteen, he should be completely familiar with the prayer book (*Siddur*) and should be able to easily participate in all religious services. He should have studied the basic laws concerned with the observance of the Sabbath and all the festivals, the prayers and the blessings for all occasions, and the laws that pertain to charity and the acts of loving-kindness toward other people. These should be studied with the view of keeping them. He should have completed all of the Five Books of Moses—Genesis, Exodus, Leviticus, Numbers, and Deuteronomy—at least once, for these books testify to the Jewish people's Covenant with God. Along with the text itself, he should have studied selected passages from the Rashi and other commentaries to provide him with a Jewish understanding of the Scriptures. He should have studied most of the books of the Early Prophets: Joshua, Judges, Samuel, and Kings. Here he will encounter the early history of his people and the drama of its early kings and prophets. He should have studied selected chapters of the Mishna from a variety of Talmudic tractates. No understanding of Jewish legal thought as reflected in the Oral Torah can be attained without knowledge of the Mishna. He should have started on the study of Gemara (Talmud), which carefully analyzes passages of the Mishna, and studied perhaps twenty to thirty pages of it. More important than the amount of Talmud text studied at this stage is the acquisition of the technique of studying the Talmudic text.

Cultural Education

There are several subjects that are not specifically designated as Torah study, or classified as religious education, but which nevertheless constitute essential components in every good Jewish education. One of these subjects is Jewish history; the other is Hebrew language. There are also Music and Art. While these subjects may be studied from a totally secular view, even with an attitude completely lacking any sense of Jewish identification, they can also be studied with the goal of increasing religious devotion, of deepening religious faith, of enhancing a sense of Jewish peoplehood, and of enriching one's Jewish—Hebraic cultural values.

JEWISH HISTORY

The Torah itself first stressed the importance of knowing history and of understanding its lessons: "Remember the days of old; understand the years of ages past" (Deuteronomy 32:7). Samson Raphael Hirsch, in his monumental work *Horeb*, writes that a knowledge of history provides "a useful companion study for the study of Torah." [9]

While loyalty to one's country or people is usually regarded as the main purpose for the study of history in the education of every nation's youth, the Torah takes this for granted and instead sees the main lesson to be derived from history as loyalty to God rather than to the people. Knowledge of history could help deepen one's appreciation for the Divine role in the historical process and strengthen one's faith in the special role that the Almighty carved out for the Jewish people. Knowing and understanding past history could help a nation or a people meet contemporary challenges and plan its course for the future.

Jewish history is not limited to the events related in the books of the Hebrew Bible. While biblical literature covers a period of more than 1,000 years, the Bible period ended over 2,500 years ago. A long and exciting history of the Jewish people took place since then. It included much travail and suffering, but also many achievements and victories. It is a history of challenges that were met and overcome.

The Arch of Titus in Rome is a monument erected to commemorate the final defeat of the Jewish people in the year 70 C.E.; but a modern visitor to that arch may see a defiant hand carving of relatively recent origin which reads most eloquently: *Am Yisrael Hai*, the Jewish people still live. The civilizations of the victorious Hellenistic and Roman Empires are long gone, but Jewish civilization, while it suffered great and tragic losses, is alive and vibrant. It is important for Jews to know that history, if only to better understand themselves in relation to their surrounding cultures.

By the time a child is fourteen years of age, he should have acquired some familiarity with all of the major periods of Jewish history and should have acquainted himself with the outstanding events and personalities of Jewish history till the present day. On the secondary and higher levels, the history of each period should be studied in greater detail and depth.

HEBREW LANGUAGE

Hebrew language is the key to a knowledge of Torah and of all the religious classics of our people. Torah study is impossible without it. It is only through the Hebrew language that one can give expression to or adequately comprehend many uniquely Jewish ideas and concepts. In translation, many words lose all the nuances of their historic or spiritual meaning. Hebrew is the language which gives expression to the Jewish prayers; the language needed in the ritual practice of Judaism. Learning to read, write, and understand Hebrew, at least in its classical forms, is the basis for all of the above and has, therefore, always been a traditional component of beginning religious instruction.

However, the studying of Hebrew grammar and learning to speak the language has not always been equally stressed. Inasmuch as Hebrew is today the living language of the modern State of Israel, it is desirable that a Jew also acquire conversational fluency in the language. Considering the closer contact today between Ashkenazic and Sephardic Jewry who never spoke Yiddish, and the loss of Yiddish among younger generations of Ashkenazic Jews, only Hebrew can become the universal tongue common to Jews throughout the world. Command of Hebrew provides invaluable assistance to all religious studies; it helps one to appreciate and adapt so much more easily to the Hebraic culture of the Jewish people; it enhances communication and understanding between the Jews of the diaspora and those of Israel.

By the time a child completes his elementary studies, his reading of Hebrew should be fluent and his understanding of the language should enable him to understand most biblical passages and grasp the meaning of most of the prayers. The ability to read Hebrew newspapers designed for young people and to engage in simple, but grammatically correct Hebrew conversation should also be achieved at this time.

MUSIC AND ART

Jewish cultural education cannot be complete without music and art. While the language of music and the arts is universal, being neither Jewish nor Gentile, religious nor secular, the specific expressions of these languages do reflect specific cultures, specific moods, and even specific religiophilosophical orientations.

The Jewish attitude toward music and the arts is rooted in the Torah. Artistic talent is not treated as just another skill, but as the infusion of a Divine spirit that inspires and enables one to fashion and to create. Bezalel, son of Uri, was picked to execute the plans for the construction of the Tabernacle. His associate was Oholiab, son of Ahisamach. They and all the anonymous artists who worked with them were called *hakhmei-lev*, "the wise-hearted," whom God filled with the "spirit of wisdom" (Exodus 28:3). "I have endowed him with a divine spirit of skill, ability and knowledge in every craft; to make designs for work in gold, silver and copper, to cut stones for setting and to carve wood . . ." (Exodus 31:3–5).

Musical instruments were used as part of the ancient Temple service and the Levites had to be trained in their use. Singing, vocal music, was a way to worship and praise God. The ability to sing is listed by the Talmud as one of the skills the Messiah is expected to possess. Hasidic rabbis were famous for their talent in composing melodies and for their emphasis on song during their gatherings and in their worship.

Jewish law stresses the merit involved in the aesthetic refinement of the *mitzvah* (the ritual duty) by striving to beautify the religious act and the ritual items in use. Much of the ingenuity of Jewish art has indeed been centered on the many ritual objects used for religious purposes. Among Jews, it was not the ceilings and walls of buildings that were the prime focus for paintings and drawings, but rather books and manuscripts.

The Jewish people's predilection for what is called the cultural pursuit is deeply rooted in its own heritage, although opportunities to pursue it were limited during long periods of poverty and oppression, when major effort had to be concentrated on the problems of survival.

The well-known fact that Jews avoided sculpture because of the biblical prohibition against the making of "graven images" did not deter their pursuit of other art forms. Art had to reflect the moral criteria of the faith and contribute to elevating the spiritual essence of the human being as he strove to beautify the sacred. Art, too, was seen as having to serve the ideals of Torah.

Music and the arts do open up avenues of personal and cultural enrichment. While those who show a native talent in these areas should be encouraged to develop it, some exposure to such cultural experiences can and should be made available to every child.

The vivid image of King David, the sweet singer of Israel, sitting at his harp playing and singing the inspirational words of the Psalms has its counterpart in the contemporary young Jew wearing a knitted skullcap, cradling a guitar between his hands, playing and singing the same songs of faith and hope.

While I regard an education limited to Torah alone as inadequate for the contemporary Jewish person, and consider Jewish history, Hebrew language, and the arts to be essential to a good Torah education, I regard a purely cultural or Hebraic education disassociated from its roots in Torah not just in terms of its *inadequacy*, but in terms of its long-range *ineffectiveness* to sustain the uniqueness of Jewish life and the permanence of its value system. Knowledge of the Hebrew language and of Jewish history and the appreciation of Jewish music and art does not alone lead to a Jewish way of life and to a Jewish way of thinking, nor does it provide the commitments essential to the survival of the Jewish people. There are tens of thousands of Christians and Muslims living in Israel and outside it, who possess such knowledge. Yet they are not Jewish and perhaps not even friendly. Jews who live in the diaspora surrounded by a dominant non-Jewish culture certainly cannot depend on the cultural components alone to create the Jewish personalities that only Torah study can fashion.

Character Training

Character training is built into the very fabric of a good Torah education. Rabbi Israel Salanter (1810–1883), in launching a movement that emphasized the profound ethical content of Judaism, wrote: "The ethical teachings of the Torah are a most important part thereof and in practical life we must train ourselves so . . . that we may follow them with the natural bent of our desires." [10] He was critical of those pietists who meticulously observed the ritual teachings of

Torah but were lax in keeping the ethical teachings, when in truth both are derived from the same source and are studied from the same codes of law, and the trespass of one is no less serious than the trespass of the other. Indeed violation of the ethical is regarded with greater severity.

The teacher must inculcate such training from the lessons of the Bible and its commentaries, from the codes of law, and from the personal influence he exerts. *Mentschlichkeit* was always regarded by Jewish parents as an essential and inseparable part of *Yiddishkeit*. To become a *guter mentsch* (literal meaning: a good person) continues to be a prime goal of raising and educating children. This is most effectively done in a religious environment. A child raised to abide by Torah would not think of challenging a parent with the belligerent words: "Who said I have to listen to you?" The Torah says so!

Most parents probably think of Jewish education as concerned only with training for religious observances, or with enhancing Jewish identity and promoting Jewish loyalties. It is however no less concerned with developing the best human qualities and the best human potential within each individual. It is no less concerned with the refinement of the social relationship between people. As a matter of fact, Jewish parents throughout the ages who took religious observances and Jewish identity for granted, considered their children's character development as the aim of education and the most important result of religious instruction.

Although today's secular educational system still thinks of character training as one of its aims, all serious attempts to instill such training have largely disappeared. The contemporary ethic is that "each one does what is right in his own eyes"; secular ethics today are situational, and no higher moral code is recognized. Nonconformist behavior is seen as an honest expression of one's own personality, of one's "true self," and is not to be challenged. Secular educators have little to go on. What is wrong today may be right tomorrow.

Jewish education has again become the sole resource outside the home for being exposed to such guidance. Jewish schools of whatever orientation, whose teachers or curricula ignore this component, are failing in their task.

Some of the personal qualities toward which Jewish character training is directed include the following elements: courtesy, honesty, integrity, truthfulness, even-temperedness, clean speech, courage, kindness, patience, self-discipline, modesty, and a sense of responsibility.

These qualities ought to be enhanced by respect for parents and reflected in the entire range of ethical-moral laws that the Torah sets forth to guide our relationship with humanity.

General Studies

It is in no way out of place to include general studies, sometimes called secular studies, as a component in a *Jewish* education. If Jewish education is said to be concerned with the *total* education of the whole child, then general studies fits into every philosophy of Jewish education. The disagreement is only to what degree. On the elementary level, this certainly means learning to read and write the native language and the study of arithmetic; it also means learning about the world, the country, and the community in which the child lives; it means learning the basic principles of the sciences so as to understand the natural world about us. The secondary level involves a deeper and more sophisticated study of these same basic subjects that are broadly classified as the natural sciences, the social sciences, and the humanities.

Some people regard these areas as the basic substance of education and the only areas of knowledge really worthy of pursuit. However, Judiasm views these general studies as but one component of a child's total education. Furthermore, such studies are not to be regarded as a deterrent to faith, but as a companion to faith. They are valuable in helping the committed Jew win respect for the teachings of Torah, function more effectively in the world, and fulfill the Divine mandate for humanity to become a partner in the continuing process of creation. General studies also provide the child with additional opportunities to develop his own interests and unique skills; a basis upon which to later build a satisfying livelihood.

The Talmud advises Jews to "know what to answer" the atheist, the agnostic, the unbeliever.[11] To be able to defend one's own faith requires knowledge of the other person's point of view and the ability to draw upon all sources for support. A good general education can help the committed Jew "know what to answer" those who would question or challenge him concerning his faith and its practices.

Jewish circles who fear that the general knowledge of the Western world can undermine one's faith in Judaism have little confidence in the ability of Judaism to hold its own against all other ideologies. Judaism can certainly meet the challenge.

The harmonious interaction of general education with Torah education, striving to bring the insights of one to bear upon the other, is the essence of the philosophy of *synthesis*, pioneered in America by Yeshiva University, but whose roots extend deep into earlier creative and dynamic periods of Jewish history. Samson Raphael Hirsch wrote:

> Give your children a well-balanced education in *all* subjects. . . . Try to apply the ancient principle . . . which ties religious and secular education closely together and makes one conditional on the other . . . for the field of Jewish learning is not . . . isolated from nature, history or real life. . . . These two components of education [Torah and general studies] strengthen and support each other.[12]

Though many great religious masters reflected this combination of Torah and "general wisdom," it met with opposition—on one side, from those who disparaged or feared general learning and, on the other side, from those who disparaged or feared Torah learning. Yet, it is precisely this combination that is needed to enable Jews to successfully function in contemporary society while preserving their Jewish selves and their Jewish heritage. "Pursued hand in hand [Jewish and general studies], each enhances the value of the other and produces the glorious fruit of a distinctive Jewish culture which at the same time is 'pleasant in the sight of God and of man.' " [13]

Physical Education

The biblical teaching that "you shall guard your lives" (Deuteronomy 4:15), provides Jewish educators with a mandate for giving educational emphasis to hygiene and physical training. Rules governing the proper care of the body by cleanliness, proper diet, moderate habits, and the prohibition against any act that poses a danger to health or life were incorporated into the traditional codes of law. The Talmud actually mentions swimming as one of the skills a parent is obligated to teach a child.[14] In this instance, the reason is because it is a skill helpful to self-preservation when traveling on water. Similarly, any skill that helps preserve life or maintain physical health is looked upon as desirable. In the educational philosophy of Samson Raphael Hirsch, training the "physical powers" of a child by exercise is stressed as a basic parental responsibility.

Abraham Isaac Kook, the great mystic philosopher of this century, even regards bodily health and physical fitness as a necessary condition to spiritual power. He writes: "The body needs to be healthy and whole for the purpose of spiritual rejuvenation . . . the more strength the body achieves, the more it enhances its spiritual power." [15]

In any all-inclusive Jewish educational program, physical training must have an established role.

Occupational Training

The Talmud teaches:

"A man is responsible to teach his son a trade." [16] Later authorities applied the ruling also to daughters. The term "trade" here is used to mean marketable skills that can earn one a livelihood. The knowledge and skills that can help one become self-supporting in any profession, craft, or business comes within the fulfillment of this trust.

The Talmud gives an ethical reason for insisting on this component in the total education of a Jewish child. If not, it says, one is in effect teaching a child to steal. If a person does not possess the training needed to earn an honest living, the person will be tempted or forced to resort to criminal means to sustain himself. The sages furthermore stressed that "all study of Torah that is not accompanied by work is futile." [17] A person has to be trained to support himself by his own labors and not become a burden to society.

That occupational training was seen as an integral element of *religious* purpose, and not as a purely secular matter, is indicated by the fact that the permission the sages granted for making educational arrangements for one's child on the Sabbath, because it was in the category of "the affairs of Heaven," i.e., religious duties, included the arrangements "for teaching him a trade." [18]

Since occupational training seems to be the underlying goal of *all* education in America, the intent here is not to emphasize the importance that Jewish tradition attaches to it, which it does, but to project the more balanced perspective in which Jewish tradition places it.

Occupational training is only one of the many responsibilities Jewish tradition imposes on parents, but certainly not the only one or even the most important one. What is the good of being able to *make a living* if the knowledge of *how to live*—as a Jew—is lacking?

At a certain stage in the life of the child, one must become concerned with preparing him for a suitable livelihood. But for most children, this is surely not before the end of the secondary school level. In fact, the best guarantee for developing the skills that will reflect the most satisfying potential within each person is to train him for *living*, not only for a *livelihood*.

Jewish Identity and Mental Health

While some people provide their children with a Jewish upbringing simply because it is part of a whole pattern of religious duties they live by, and others do so out of a sense of loyalty to the Jewish people, it also carries benefits of quite another sort—that of mental health. Professor Kurt Lewin, a pioneer in the field of Group Dynamics, came to the conclusion a long time ago that "an early build-up of a *clear* and *positive* feeling of belongingness to the Jewish group is one of the few effective things that parents can do for the later happiness of their children." [19]

The key words here are *clear* and *positive*. The sense of belonging and of having a strong Jewish self-identity is not achieved by merely telling the child "You are Jewish," and then letting him wonder in what way he is different from people who are not Jewish. Being different without himself being able to notice the difference and to be proud and happy about it can be very disturbing to a child. How often have we heard the complaint "I know I'm Jewish because I've been told so, or because all my friends are Jewish, but aside from that it doesn't mean very much to me."

An appreciation of difference is achieved by seeing and doing those things that are decidedly Jewish in character: observing Jewish holidays, learning Hebrew words of prayer, coming in contact with Jewish symbols, and feeling at home in a synagogue. These Jewish associations must provide warm and happy memories, to which there must later be added feeling about the worth and importance of Jewish life.

Child psychologists have noted that the very first group to which a child feels a sense of belonging is the family, but at a very early age, perhaps even at three or four, the child begins to show a need for identification with groups larger than its own family. The child needs to be a part of a nation, a faith, a people. If the child derives satisfaction from that association, it becomes psychologically armored against attack from without. One may challenge the worth of his group and get him angry, but one cannot provoke self-doubt and inferiority.

The best defense against psychological bruises and personality maladjustments when confronting instances of anti-Semitism is to have a clear-cut consciousness of identity. An interesting research project, undertaken by Kurt Lewin, studied two groups of young Jews on a university campus. One group had a good Jewish education and a strong sense of Jewish identity; the other lacked both. The young people in the group who felt nothing positive about their Jewishness felt anti-Semitism most keenly. The others were less troubled by it.

It is tragic when young Jews are identified as Jewish by all the world, yet nothing in their training or background gives them a feeling of their own Jewishness. Parents who fail to provide that guidance very early in a child's life are failing their children as well as the Jewish people.

A person does not choose to be born—nor to be born Jewish. But having been born, and having been born Jewish, the development of positive feelings about one's own group assists in the development of a healthy personality. Being sure of one's Jewishness and feeling good about it, contributes to a meaningful life, and is the greatest gift a Jewish parent can pass on to a child.

Part Two

TO RAISE
A JEWISH CHILD:
TRANSMITTING
THE VALUES

CHAPTER

4

Effective Child-Raising

Practices:

The Foundation Blocks

Aʟʟ the sages and scholars of traditional Jewish thought agree that creating a sound and healthy relationship between parents and their children is a primary goal of Jewish child-rearing. The finest formal Jewish education may be undone by a poor parent-child relationship. Psychological studies point to the connection that exists between the emotional relationship that one has with one's parents as a child and the attitudes that one later develops toward all authority, including religion.

Although the sages did not articulate it in contemporary psychological terminology, they did understand the effects of parent-child conflict. The Bible cites the case of "the rebellious and defiant son," the *ben sorer umoreh* (see Deuteronomy 21), whose parents have lost all disciplinary control over him. However, the sages related this defiance of parents to the defiance of religion and society. They used words that almost parallel psychological findings: "He rebels against the words of his father, and defies those of his mother; he rebels against the words of the Torah and defies those of the Prophets; he rebels against the words of witnesses and defies those of the Judges." [1]

The sages also noted that the Fifth Commandment "Honor your father and your mother," is traditionally related to those commandments that have to do with man's relationship to God rather than with the last five commandments that have to do with man's relationship to his fellowmen. Though clearly having to do with fellowman, the intuitive feeling expressed was that honoring parents was somehow related to honoring God; that a positive attitude to God depended on a positive attitude toward one's parents. The rejection of Jewish commitments is not necessarily the result of a rational process; it may result from conflict caused by some form of parental rejection. Striking back at a parent may well take the form of rejecting that which is or appears to be dear and sacred to them. Parents to whom the Jewish heritage is precious would be wise, for religious reasons, to pay much attention to this all-important relationship.

While it is not within the scope of this book to cite a multitude of specific situations that may serve as pitfalls to well-meaning parents, the basic principles that I feel ought to guide parents in most situations are formulated here. Although one may also read of these principles in many other books on child-raising or child psychology, my criteria in selecting those that I have was based on whether I found them to reflect the classical Jewish teachings and/or the common sense of traditional Jewish society.

Guide the Child

The Bible teaches us that parents bear the basic responsibility for guiding their children in developing a set of values and in choosing right from wrong in every area of life. The book of Proverbs (1:8) states: "Listen my son to the instruction of your father, and forsake not the teachings of your mother." Such guidance must begin early in life and continue throughout the growing-up period.

The best way to guide children toward a designated set of values is to set the example personally. The personal behavior of parents and the decisions that children watch you make in countless situations make more of an impact upon them than what is said to them directly. So also do the thousands of casual conversations children overhear between mother and father, between parents and their friends.

It is not what parents claim to profess, but what they do that is the real indication of their beliefs and values. Consistency is important. Children are very sensitive to discrepancies between parents' professed views and their actual behavior. One can emphasize the virtue of honesty all one wants and punish a child if the child is caught lying, but if that same child hears you boasting about how you told the police officer or the insurance company an untruth concerning an accident, or how tax reports are "fixed up," or how records are falsified to win a promotion, don't blame your child if he cheats on his school examinations or ends up lying about where he's been or what he's been doing. You may insist you've taught him honesty, but in reality that's not what he learned.

One may stress to him the importance of learning about his Jewish heritage, but he's not likely to be convinced if he sees that his parents lack such learning and show no interest in obtaining it. Loyalty to Judaism is not what he will learn from you if he doesn't see it practiced.

To avoid setting a bad example, the Talmud emphasizes that care must be taken even in what we promise children: "A person should not say to a child 'I will give it to you right away' and then not do it, because he thus teaches him to lie." [2]

What about parents who want to instill in their children qualities and virtues they themselves lack but which they believe are desirable? In that case, the deficiency must be openly acknowledged. Children must be made aware of their parents' sense of remorse about it, and appreciate the fact that some effort is being made to overcome it.

If children crave their parents' love and praise, they also crave their guidance and direction. While they don't want to be dictated to and ordered around, they do want to be told what's right and what's wrong. Even teenagers, despite all their protests to the contrary, appreciate a firm hand. They can be quite disappointed when parents surrender to their demands.

Dr. William Homan, a prominent pediatrician and a wise observer of child-raising practices, agrees that "the teenager needs and wants to have the whip cracked on matters of moral behavior," though he acknowledges that the teenager appreciates a measure of freedom on such other matters as personal care, clothes, and styles.[3] But even here, a parent need not be shy about expressing his feelings.

I recall an incident in our home when our daughter, then in her preteens, requested permission from her mother to go somewhere with some friends. Permission was denied and the reasons for the decision were explained. Our daughter kept insisting that she wanted to go and carried on with a continuous barrage of arguments. In desperation her mother finally said, "I wash my hands of it all. Do what you want to do." This was obviously not real permission nor did it indicate a change of mind, and to which our daughter blurted out: "But I don't want to do what I want to do. I want to do what you want me to do." While at that moment she desperately wished to go out with her friends, she was even more anxious that it be done with her mother's approval, or at least without her strong disapproval. Since that wasn't forthcoming, she finally accepted her mother's wishes in the matter.

Children are constantly testing the limits to which they feel their parents will allow them to go. An answer that indicates vacillation or generates a feeling that while parents may be saying one thing they really feel otherwise, contributes to the weakening of parental counsel in favor of outside influences.

One of the most devastating arguments children often use with parents is "but everyone else is doing it" or "so and so's mother is letting him do it." If a parent is convinced that the matter in question is not for their child, such arguments should be given no weight at all. The moment you say "I'll check with so and so's mother if that is really the case," you have lost. A meaningful response to a child who resorts to such arguments is to say: "In our family, we do it this way." It does not cast aspersions on the wisdom of the other parents, yet it acknowledges the legitimacy of differences and affirms family solidarity; it provides psychological support.

"Just because others are doing it, is no reason for you to do it" is another idea that ought to be instilled into the consciousness of every child. Indeed, it is a lesson that ought to be carried into adulthood. The Torah teaches: "Do not side with the many to do wrong" (Exodus 23:2).

A common error made by parents who themselves lack self-confidence is to criticize a child's misbehavior or failure because of "what will my friends say?" or "what will the neighbors think?" and not because they themselves object to it. The child who may be very concerned with what *you* have to say and with how *you* really feel about something, couldn't care less about the neighbors or your friends. Such a parental plea is bound to fall on deaf ears. A child must be impressed with the need to judge a set of circumstances in terms of the family's values and not on the basis of what others are doing or saying.

Some of the latest child-raising theories recommend a policy of nondirection as the best way to deal with children, particularly teenage children. These theorists advise that if a child comes to ask a parent's opinion about something, the parent should not give a direct answer. They advise the parent to mirror the child's feelings, reflect his concerns, and be noncommittal in responding to the child. As a parent, I heartily disagree. If a child asks, tell the child what you think, unless you honestly don't know. In that case, simply admit it.

The "nondirection" suggested is the application of a theory of nondirective counseling that is sometimes very effective in dealing with certain emotional problems. As a professional technique in psychological counseling, it has its place. In dealing with a child's *emotional* outburst, it can be helpful. Effective teachers have been known to use it in drawing a child along an avenue of thought leading to certain desired conclusions. For the average parent who is not a trained counselor, and who deals with the routine questions of normal children, the simple, honest, straightforward reactions are the most effective. Nondirective techniques in the hands of the average parent may become nothing more than the withholding of much needed parental guidance.

All that I have said about parental guidance presupposes that the parents themselves have a set of ethical-moral-religious values. If this is the case, providing direction and following a policy of firmness will help transmit these values. But where parents themselves lack values, they are hardly in a position to guide children. Where parents claim to profess certain ethical, moral, and religious values, but in practice equivocate about them, children will be the first to exploit that equivocation when it suits them to discard the professed values.

A final word of caution about guidance. No parent must expect to find himself entirely duplicated in his children. Although a child who is "a chip off the old block" may be a great compliment to a parent, attempts to create carbon copies of themselves are misguided. Within a framework of values in which parents function, the advice of Proverbs (22:6) is no less applicable today than when first written: "Train a child in his own way, and even when he is old, he will not depart from it." The most lasting results come from recognizing personality differences, different levels of ability, and varying interests. Each child is a unique work of art, to be appreciated, loved, and enjoyed for himself.

Love the Child

Love your child! What parent does not love his child? Yet it must be said, not for the benefit of those who may not, and there are such, but for all those parents who really do love their children, even profess that love, but may not communicate it. A parent may unintentionally say things to a child that will make the child feel rejected and convince him that he is in fact unloved. The most important thing in child-raising is that parental love be communicated to children. Children need to be aware of and feel secure in this love at every stage of their development from infancy on.

Physical contact helps convey the message of love. The mother who embraces her infant and the father who cuddles his child provide the child with nourishment as vital as milk. Milk nourishes the body; signs of affection nourish the soul. Both are equally necessary to sound health; the deprivation of either can be harmful to normal growth and development. Parents should, therefore, not hesitate to physically embrace their children, to give them hugs, plant kisses, place affectionate pats on their heads, and hold their hands. Such physical contacts, made spontaneously and for no special reason, speak louder than words and contribute to a warm feeling of being loved. It is neither unmanly nor inappropriate for fathers, as well as for mothers, to bestow such signs of affection on both sons and daughters even as they grow older.

There are many other signs and signals that convey the parental sentiment of love: sitting down on a child's bed in the quiet darkness of a room for a final "goodnight"; saying, for no apparent reason, "you're a nice kid; I like you"; making an effort to be present when a child is doing something that the child hopes will impress you—such as being in a school play or in an athletic contest. Love or the lack of it is also conveyed by the manner in which discipline is handled, by the way in which the child's personality is respected, and by the manner in which his self-esteem and independence are encouraged.

In a family where there is more than one child, it is important to avoid playing favorites, although each child likes to feel that he is the most loved. "Whom do you love better, Mommy?" can be a disquieting inquiry. To feel oneself less loved than a sibling is to feel a measure of parental rejection. The safest response is along the lines of "you are my best boy and you are my best girl" or "you are my best oldest child, you are my best youngest child, you are my best middle child (or my best second child, or third child)." Such assurances are usually enough to reassure all the children. Each one is "best" and "loved most" for their own place in the family, whatever it happens to be.

Parents should not make the terrible error of substituting gift giving for all other signs of love. While the donor of a gift may intend to show his love for a child, a child does not always get the message. Their gratitude is fleeting, if it is there at all. I frankly doubt whether children are capable of evaluating the emotional meaning an adult may attach to a gift. This is why children who come from homes where they are showered with gifts, and where their every whim and wish is granted, can also be heard to protest "but you don't love me."

Parents who have only learned to express their love for their children by buying them presents are candidates for blackmail. Children who want things they shouldn't have or that parents cannot afford, will sometimes say: "If you won't buy this for me, it proves you don't love me" or "If you love me, you'll get this for me." Such parents are in binds. If parents don't come across, they will fail the test of love, thus confirming the child's accusation. And if parents yield to the child's demands against their own better judgments, it only confirms the shallow basis on which their love rests. The parent who feels secure in loving one's children, who physically demonstrates that love from time to time, and who shows it in many other ways, doesn't have to prove oneself. The parent can reply to a child's extortionist demand: "It has nothing to do with love. You can't have it, and for the following reason." If a child insists on using love as a club, a parent will not be afraid to add: "Of course I love you, but if you think that my saying 'no' to you means that I don't love you, I simply don't care." A loving parent will not be afraid to say it because he feels secure that his child knows his true feelings.

A loving parent will also not be overly upset by the inevitable "I hate you, Mommy" or "I hate you, Daddy" that at certain age levels or in certain critical moments erupts from the depths of a child's emotions. I suggest that such outbursts be ignored.

The child who is loved for himself and feels it is also free to be himself. He feels free to do the things that lead to learning without fearing the consequences of failure. There is less need for evasion and concealment from parents. Furthermore,

> not the least of the factors that help him in learning to realize himself is that the loving parent also has a certain kind of freedom which the unloving parent is not so likely to possess, namely freedom to be himself in the role as a parent; he will not feel a need to put a false face on his feelings, to act as though he were always full of sweetness and light with a boundless amount of patience and an inexhaustible capacity for controlling his temper. He does not need to distort his personality by trying to live up to the impossible ideal of being a perfect parent. He will not feel a guilty need to grant the child's every whim or to indulge his every desire for fear that to do otherwise would threaten a precarious relationship between him and his youngster.[4]

While love for a child may be viewed by some as a natural manifestation of parenthood, the failure to convince the growing child that this feeling exists and that it is unconditional "is probably the single most important cause of personality deviation in later child-hood, in adolescence, and in adulthood." This failure has also been responsible in too many cases for undoing all the good that Jewish education is intended to do. Therefore, learn to communicate the love you feel for your children if you expect to see your efforts at child-raising bear fruit.

Discipline the Child

Discipline is an essential part of effective guidance. It means an attitude of firmness and the enforcement of the values and behavior patterns you care to develop in your child. The absence of discipline is tantamount to the absence of guidance.

Discipline is also the other side of the coin of love: "For he whom the Lord loves, He admonishes" (Proverbs 3:12). Discipline should and can convey a message of love. Whether it involves a stern look, a slap on the wrist, a good spanking, a sharp reprimand or the denial of privileges, it should carry with it the clear-cut feeling that you have your child's welfare and well-being in mind. The obvious point can be added that the reason for your lack of concern about the misbehavior of a neighbor's child is because you don't feel the same love for that child. You admonish and correct your child precisely because you love and care what becomes of your child.

The verse from Proverbs quoted above actually concludes with the words "like a father who appeases his son," suggesting that the punishment itself should be followed with a bit of love. "Just like a father whose only wish is to do good to his son and so he soothes and appeases him [i.e., speaks words of kindness and affection] after he hits him with the rod," is the way the Rashi commentary explains it. The Talmud suggests the same technique. In dealing with children, "let the left hand repel while the right hand draws near." [5] The idea that discipline should always be followed by warmth and love is found throughout Jewish religious literature. The child should not be permitted to interpret his punishment as a rejection of oneself, only as dissatisfaction with the *act* committed.

Biblical literature often expresses God's relationship to the Jewish people in terms of a father's relationship to his children: "You are our Father and we your children" (High Holyday Prayer Book); "Ephraim [a euphemism for Israel] is my precious child" (Jeremiah 31:19). And while Divine punishment is always threatened for disloyalty to God's teachings, it is always accompanied by the assurance that Israel is precious in the sight of God, and that God in His mercy and love would never permanently reject and abandon Israel.

This traditional Jewish approach is today widely understood by child-guidance experts. Dr. Homan writes:

> There would be absolutely nothing contradictory in correcting and criticizing a child's actions and behavior and at the same time letting him know how much you love him as a person, just because he is. To make this point in an *extreme* [emphasis mine] case, there is no inconsistency in knocking a child across the room for misbehavior, and then immediately picking him up, putting your arms around him, and telling him what a fine boy he is and how much you love him. Indeed not only are the acts not inconsistent, but in effect they convey the two notions that (a) "I bother to correct your behavior *because* I love you" and (b) "I disapprove of your actions, but I love *you* just as much, *regardless* of how you act.[6]

While the book of Proverbs expresses support for the practice of physical punishment: "Foolishness is bound in the heart of a child, but the rod of correction shall drive it from him" (22:15), it also shows an awareness that physical punishment must be restrained. Proverbs (19:18) says: "Chasten your son for there is hope, but set not your heart on his destruction." If you do administer a beating, don't do it in anger or with cruelty. The Talmudic sage, Rav, emphasized the balance that must be struck if and when punishment is called for: "When you hit a child, do not hit him with anything but the string of a shoe," [7] to which the Rashi commentary added: "In other words, a light stroke which can do no harm." While this advice is intended for teachers, with specific reference to the classroom, its applicability to parents is no less warranted. Furthermore, constant physical punishment can only diminish its long-term effectiveness and become a real stumbling block to constructive discipline.

Jewish law actually forbids administering physical punishment to a grown child. The term "grown" technically applies to any girl over twelve and any boy over thirteen, but it is also interpreted to mean a younger child who shows a certain maturity. This prohibition is based on the biblical injunction: "You shall not place a stumbling block before the blind" (Leviticus 19:14). By striking a grown child, one may invite him to strike back and to thereby violate a serious biblical injunction against striking a parent.

The Book of Proverbs (17:10) notes that other forms of chastisement may even be more effective, particularly when dealing with a child who has attained a certain maturity: "A rebuke enters deeper into a person of understanding than a hundred stripes into a fool."

While all punishment has its limitations, the absence of firmness and the unwillingness to discipline children are emphasized as the basic causes for rebellion against parents: "Because David did not rebuke his son Absalom, and did not chasten him, Absalom turned to an evil culture . . . causing him no end of severe troubles." [8] Most contemporary child-raising experts apparently agree with this Midrashic comment written over two thousand years ago.

Respect the Child

A good Talmudic guideline to parents and teachers alike is: "Let the honor of your pupil be as dear to you as your own." [9] All educators need to become sensitive to the importance of respecting the personalities of children, particularly as they emerge from infancy and become social beings. Although young and immature, children possess all the emotions and sensitivities of their elders. They may be helpless and dependent in a world that from their perspective is a world of giants, and so resign themselves to the authority of others. Where that authority is wielded with love and understanding, with wisdom and justice, children learn to accept it and to relate to it in a positive way. Where that authority is wielded with disrespect and insult, with harshness and cruelty, children feel the sting and resent the injustice. The immaturity of the child, his need to be guided and trained, and the parents' authority do not together combine to create a package that justifies disrespect and disdain. Children's personalities are considerably shaped by the degree to which this world of giants is sensitive to their feelings.

Never insult a child! Don't call him "stupid" even if he makes a mistake, if he doesn't understand some thing, or if he brings a poor grade home from school. If he isn't a stupid child, then you're guilty of lying. If he is, name-calling isn't going to help him get any smarter. It will only succeed in developing within the child feelings of inadequacy and inferiority or in conveying a message of rejection. It can only create resentment. Parents sometimes rely on name-calling as a form of shock-therapy to arouse an average or bright child from his "stupidity," or to "inspire" him to overcome the deficiencies that invited the disdain. While in some cases this may work and succeed in motivating a child to self-improvement, no parent should depend on it. It is more likely to encourage further "stupid" behavior that will conform to the expressed expectations of parents. The only purpose that name-calling serves is to vent a parent's anger or frustration. Patience, love, and understanding are surer routes to child improvement than deprecation.

Jewish tradition places great weight on the moral evil of publicly embarrassing others: "He who shames another in public is as though he has shed blood." [10] It is the moral equivalent of murder. There is no indication anywhere that the parent-child relationship is exempt from this ruling.

Never embarrass a child before others, not in front of your friends and certainly not in front of his. Even when you justifiably rebuke a child for some misdeed or error, and the child knows that he deserves it, the rebuke ought not to be made in the presence of others. Holding a child up to public scorn only builds up the kind of resentment which, if allowed to accumulate and fester, may someday lash out in open rebelliousness and defiance.

Respect for the personality of the child is also reflected in the way discipline is administered. Even when delivering a well-deserved spanking, the child's sense of personal dignity must not be torn down. It much not be done in a way that he regards as demeaning. If a facial slap is treated as humiliating, avoid it. The "discipline of the shoestring" not only implies a minimum of physical pain, but also a minimum of insult and embarrassment.

As children become teenagers parents ought to show increasing sensitivity to their opinions. Their children's views about family matters ought to be solicited; their wishes taken into greater consideration. Even where their views are not acceptable or their wishes cannot be granted, what they say or feel should not be dismissed out of hand, but should merit consideration and serious response. Take them into your confidence. By taking account of their growing maturity and treating them accordingly, you show respect for a child in a most important way.

Another subtle way of showing regard for their "adulthood" is to allow them to enjoy the privacy of their own rooms, uninterrupted by adult interference. If you knock before entering, you let them know that you respect their right to privacy and that you no longer regard them as little children.

Parents should remember that each child is different. Each one deserves the right to be judged on the basis of his own capabilities and not on the basis of what brothers and sisters have achieved or what friends may be achieving. Don't make comparisons. Show respect for the distinctive personality or capacity of each child.

A Hasidic story tells of a man called Zusya who once confessed to his friends his fear about being called to Judgment in the spiritual world-to-come. He said:

> It does not disturb me if the Divine Judge will confront me and say, "Zusya, why weren't you like Moses?" Nor even if Rabbi Akiva or Maimonides were set up as the examples by which to make the comparison. After all, I just never possessed the qualities to even come close to these great men. What disturbs me is the thought that the Divine Judge may say to me: "Zusya, why weren't you like Zusya, why didn't you reach the levels that you were capable of reaching?

The most we can demand of ourselves, or expect of others, is performing to the best of our respective abilities. The same consideration should apply no less to children.

Develop the Child's Self-Esteem

The Torah teaches: "Love your neighbor *as yourself*" (Leviticus 19:18). What is apparently taken for granted is that people do love themselves, and so they are enjoined to likewise love others. The biblical commandment may also be implying that before one can love others, one must first be able to love oneself. Interestingly, psychologists have established that people who do not like themselves can hardly be expected to sincerely feel friendship and love toward others. Such people are said to lack self-esteem.

Self-esteem is the quality of thinking well of oneself, of being happy with who and what one is. It is the quality of liking oneself. This is not to be equated with selfishness or conceit. The latter qualities are in fact usually associated with a lack of self-esteem. They arise as a cover-up for a poor self-image. Bragging, alibiing, applepolishing, and die-hard approaches are other symptoms of this deficiency.

Self-esteem is probably the most crucial personality ingredient a person can possess. It determines how effectively a person will use his skills and his aptitude. It contributes much to achievement and success, but even more so, it is the key to personal happiness. Without it, no outward success in life is gratifying and adult therapy to correct it is no more than palliative. Its importance in the total personality structure is evidenced by the fact that the National Institute of Mental Health used self-esteem in children as a valid index of the child's total psychological well-being.

Of course, there are many people who affect a child's self-image—teachers, friends, members of the family. Psychological studies have shown that the greatest determinant of adult self-esteem is the way one was treated by one's parents as a child. Studies have also shown that this quality is not at all dependent on height or physical attractiveness; that it is only weakly related to social status, academic performance, or material success. That is why one can find highly successful individuals who have attained great wealth or fame but who still suffer from a lack of self-esteem. Their successful achievements have never allayed their deep-seated anxieties about themselves.

Parents must communicate love to their children in order to build up their self-esteem. But there are other things too. Be free with your praise, in matters both great and small. Children crave their parents' approval and their respect. How else to explain a child's tendency to "show off" a newly learned skill in front of parents: "See, Mommy, I can do it! . . . Daddy, watch me, watch me!" In the playground and on the ballfield, in the swimming pool and on the monkey bars, it's the same. Children are so anxious to impress you. They want you to think well of them. They want *your* praise, *your* respect, and *your* admiration more than anything in the world. If a child has a part in a school play or is to receive some award at a school assembly, a thousand people in the audience do not matter to him as much as the presence of two special people, his own mother and father. Having parents share his moments of glory is the only thing he truly cares about. Have you ever watched children's eyes light up when they notice their parents at some event in which they take part. Take the time to share your child's joy. Learn to express your admiration for a newly acquired skill, no matter how trivial it may appear to you. Don't minimize the child's smallest achievements. Some parents have a tendency to belittle their children, to carp on their weaknesses and their failures, and to ignore praising them for their successes and achievements. The sensible way is the reverse.

Convey to your child a feeling of your confidence and pride in him. "You can do it," are words of encouragement that should come easily. Even if the child does not make it, don't ridicule him. Minimize his mistakes and failures—at home, in school, and on the ballfield. The child usually feels badly enough about them anyway, without your snide remarks about how "inept" or "dumb" or "careless" he may be. Praise him for trying. And, if you really feel it is within his ability, encourage him to try again.

Point out to your child the things he does well. Help him understand that even those whom he holds in greatest esteem—you, his parents—cannot do everything equally well; that when you were small you, too, did not always succeed in everything you tried; and that even now, you make mistakes and can't do everything. In any event, do not permit your child to feel that you think any less of him because he failed in some specific task.

To build up self-esteem, try to plan experiences or tasks that are within the child's ability to handle. While an occasional failure will be overcome and may even have a sobering or stabilizing effect, constantly setting goals that are unattainable is the surest way to destroy his self-esteem. Find opportunities for him to demonstrate his competence and success, and to function at levels that he sees as adult activity and that invite adult praise. In this respect, it should be noted that Jewish religious life offers children many such opportunities, both in the synagogue and at home.

Develop the Child's Self-Reliance

Jewish religious tradition clearly emphasizes the desirability of self-reliance and independence as a mature characteristic. Children are encouraged to gradually become independent of their parents. Jewish religious law entrusts children with the performance of adult religious duties as soon as they understand what they are doing and are capable of doing it, even though they have not yet reached their religious maturity; girls at twelve, boys at thirteen. In many congregations, children from the ages of seven or eight are invited to lead selected portions of the service that liturgical regulations permit them. The charge delivered by David, King of Israel, to his son Solomon, though already mature in years at the time, was in terms of: "Be strong and show yourself a man" (Kings I, 2:2). Hillel advised: "In a place where there are no men, strive you to be a man." [11]

The urge for independence is found in every child, and reaches a high point during adolescence. The natural tendency of teenagers to assert their independence from parents will be less rebelliously expressed if there has been a gradual but steady growth toward it all along. Their sense of growing up must be paralleled by encouraging self-reliance, a quality that also contributes to self-esteem. The child's need for guidance suitable to his age need not be compromised when letting go of the reins and permitting independence to emerge.

While no child will assert his independence before he is ready for it, fearful and overprotective parents can surely hinder its development. Although parents must protect young children from potentially dangerous situations and a child cannot be permitted to do as he pleases, the parent who is always intervening to make things easier for his child or to protect him from unpleasant consequences is not always doing the child a favor. In this respect, the parent who is "too good" may not be good at all.

Extra solicitude from a parent may be seen as a form of "I have no confidence in you" or "I don't consider you capable." Overprotectiveness undermines the natural reaching out for independence and destroys a child's self-esteem.

Encourage children to do things for and by themselves. Teach them to care for their own rooms, to make their own beds, to set a dinner table or clear it. Teach them to make their own sandwiches and to prepare simple dishes. Invite a child to help you in your workshop and occasionally in your place of business. If the activities are not simply unpleasant tasks that parents slough off onto children, doing them become part of growing up and makes a child more self-reliant.

Parents should certainly assist children with their homework. But this kind of assistance can be overdone, if the child is never encouraged to work out the answers on his own. The parent may be contributing to a better grade, but also to a reduced level of self-reliance. Do not eliminate the challenges the child is called upon to face in his day-to-day activities.

On the other hand, don't let independence for the child become a fetish. It can be overdone if all support is withheld or if children are pushed into situations or experiences for which they are not emotionally, psychologically, or physically ready. This may boomerang and have the very opposite effect than what is desired. The child may react with fright and withdraw into himself; he may interpret it as a form of rejection. It is responsible independence that we are after. This grows only in an environment where the child feels confident of parental support.

Do set goals for children to strive for. Do confront children with challenges to overcome. In affluent circles, this presents a major problem. After physical wants are satisfied and financial security is assured by the parents' fortune, what struggles are left for the children? I suspect that a contributing factor to the disaffection of some middle-class contemporary youth during their adolescent and postadolescent years, and their almost frantic search for new thrills, comes from having come to believe that no major hurdles were left for them to conquer. While a sense of security is a great thing, it can be very depressing to feel that life requires no serious efforts.

The rare child who wants to become a great musician, scientist, or even athlete is not the problem. Our concern is with the child who grows up in a relatively affluent family that has already "made it," but that denies to its children the need to also "make it" on their own. This, too, is a type of lost independence.

Instant attainment, while providing a great momentary thrill, is depressing in the long run and counterproductive. It destroys initiative. Imagine presenting a youngster starting out on a stamp collection with a complete set of stamps, a collection that might otherwise have taken him years to accumulate. His joy would be immense, but only for a while. The thrill of finding new stamps to put into his collection would be gone; gone would be the sense of achievement, of continuous growth. The youngster was given a whole stamp collection, but he was robbed of the excitement and the joy that comes with collecting them.

It is not only in terms of long-range career aspirations that there are goals to work for and aims to aspire to. They can be found in the routine course of a child's daily life at home and in school. For a Jewish child, the goals should also include the religious hopes and aspirations of the Jewish people.

CHAPTER

5

~~~~~~

The Home and Neighborhood: Creating an Environment

Parents As Teachers

THE Hebrew word for parents (*horim*) and for teachers (*morim*) are similar. They sound the same. They mean the same. Both words mean to instruct, to teach. Parents and teachers are listed together in the same passage of the Confessional recited on Yom Kippur (*Al Het*): "For the sin that we have sinned before Thee is belittling parents and teachers." They are listed together, not to save space, but because the Jewish heritage has traditionally linked their roles. The parent's role as teacher of his children is continuously stressed in Jewish sources. There has even arisen the custom of adding the words *mori* (m), or *morati* (f), my teacher, whenever the word for my father, *avi*, or my mother, *imi*, is used in any formal designation, as when saying the grace after meals. The correct form is, therefore, *avi mori*, meaning my father my teacher, or *imi morati*, my mother my teacher.

Judaism thus emphasizes the parent as the principal teacher of his children. The Torah commandment: "And you shall teach them diligently to your children . . . when you sit in your home" (Deuteronomy 6:7) is directed to the parent. Indeed the very first school to which any child is exposed *is* his own home; his very first and most important teachers *are* his own father and mother. It is parents who play the dominant role in the formation of the child's personality and way of life. Parents are the ones who provide the atmosphere from which the child derives a set of values and a set of assumptions about life. Though part of their children's education is turned over to and shared with many teachers, parents are still the most effective educational force in the lives of their children. They educate in many ways: by the direct guidance they give; by the examples they set; by the environment they create at home; by the neighborhood they choose to live in; by the schools they select for the formal education of their children; and by the informal experiences they expose their children to.

If Judaism is to become a source of steadfast faith throughout one's adult life, it is important, from early childhood, to receive and retain warm and precious memories of the Jewish way. Judaism must be a source of pleasure from the very start. And, if so, then even the restrictions of the faith will not be burdensome. They will instead help refine the child's character, raise a more self-disciplined human being, and contribute to the overall Jewish commitment.

Some well-meaning parents choose to expose their children only to the happy Jewish experiences, neglecting the ritual disciplines. They stress the positive commandments but ignore the negative commandments.* Others so emphasize the disciplines that they thrust the more pleasant religious experiences into the background, leaving the child with a view of Judaism that is defined by a framework of "thou shalt nots." Neither extreme is desirable; the first is shallow and the second is dangerous. The first lacks substance; the disciplines that are essential to and characteristic of Jewish living are missing. On the other hand, an exclusive emphasis on rigor and discipline invites rebellion and rejection of parents and faith by the children at a later age. Jewish scholars throughout the ages have consistently

---

* Jewish law is divided into two major categories. The first category consists of those laws that require the active performance of certain duties or rituals. The other category proscribes or forbids certain activities. The first is called the positive commandments as it consists of the "do's" (*mitzvot aseh*). The second category is called the negative commandments as it consists of the "do nots" (*mitzvot lo ta-aseh*).

underscored the importance of simultaneously pursuing both methods and of creating a sensible mix between them.

Only parents are able to provide early Jewish training in an atmosphere of joy and security. Such training at home should not be put off until the child begins his formal schooling. Jewish education in the truest sense must begin from the moment the child starts to become aware of his environment; it must become part of his natural surroundings, of his normal experiences.

Raising Jewish children requires that parents themselves lead Jewish lives. Formal Jewish affiliation, joining a synagogue, is totally meaningless unless it is accompanied by an association with the only "denomination" that really counts, *Experiential Judaism*, whose basic philosophy is simply that Judaism must be experienced, it must be practiced for it to be loved and best understood. The home is the key. If the seeds have not been planted at home, and the soil is not constantly watered, not much should be expected to grow. Sometimes a parent is heard to say: "We don't observe much at home. That's why we feel our child's religious education is so important." If parents really felt the child's religious education to be so important, they would make an effort to "observe much at home." The ideal Jewish mother is not the one who is caricatured as pushing food into her children *"ess, ess, mein kind"* (eat, eat, my child), but the one who conscientiously provides the atmosphere for spiritual nourishment.

What To Do

During the Preschool Years

HEBREW PRAYERS

The training of a Jewish child should begin at a very tender age—at about the age of three or four, depending on the child's development. As soon as the child learns to talk, he should be taught to recite the following Hebrew passages:

Hear O Israel, the Lord our God, the Lord is One.

שְׁמַע יִשְׂרָאֵל יְיָ אֱלֹהֵינוּ יְיָ אֶחָד.

Shema Yisrael adonai elohainu adonai ehad.

Moses commanded us the torah, the inheritance of the Jewish people.

תּוֹרָה צִוָּה לָנוּ מֹשֶׁה, מוֹרָשָׁה קְהִלַּת יַעֲקֹב.

Torah tzeevah lanu Moshe, morasha kehilat Yaakov.

Teaching these verses and the blessings that follow serves several purposes. It introduces the child to the use of the Hebrew language and makes the child familiar with its sounds. The child is taught Torah at its most elementary level by his own parents. The child is trained to observe some religious duties. Here are a few simple blessings to teach your children.

For bread: Blessed art thou Lord our God king of the universe, who brings forth bread from the earth.

בָּרוּךְ אַתָּה יְיָ אֱלֹהֵינוּ מֶלֶךְ הָעוֹלָם, הַמּוֹצִיא לֶחֶם מִן הָאָרֶץ.

Barukh ata adonai elohainu melekh haolam,
hamotzi lehem min ha-aretz.

For wine: Blessed art thou Lord our God king of the universe, who creates the fruit of the vine.

בָּרוּךְ אַתָּה יְיָ אֱלֹהֵינוּ מֶלֶךְ הָעוֹלָם, בּוֹרֵא פְּרִי הַגָּפֶן.

Barukh ata adonai elohainu melekh haolam,
borai pri ha-gafen.

For fruit: Blessed art thou Lord our God king of the universe, who creates the fruit of the tree.

בָּרוּךְ אַתָּה יְיָ אֱלֹהֵינוּ מֶלֶךְ הָעוֹלָם, בּוֹרֵא פְּרִי הָעֵץ.

Barukh ata adonai elohainu melekh haolam,
borai pri ha-etz.

For cookies and cakes: Blessed art thou Lord our God king of the universe, who creates various kinds of food.

בָּרוּךְ אַתָּה יְיָ אֱלֹהֵינוּ מֶלֶךְ הָעוֹלָם, בּוֹרֵא מִינֵי מְזוֹנוֹת.

Barukh ata adonai elohainu melekh haolam,
borai mee-nai m'zonot.

For water, juice, candy: Blessed art thou Lord our God king of the universe, by Whose will everything was created.

בָּרוּךְ אַתָּה יְיָ אֱלֹהֵינוּ מֶלֶךְ הָעוֹלָם, שֶׁהַכֹּל נִהְיֶה בִּדְבָרוֹ.

Barukh ata adonai elohainu melekh haolam,
she-hakol nee-yeh bidvaro.

When eating a meal with many different types of food, only the blessing for bread need be said. When in doubt about the appropriate blessing, the one for water should be used. That blessing is the most inclusive. Although traditional practice is to avoid pronouncing God's name as *Adonai* (Master, Lord), except when the occasion calls for the actual recitation of the blessing, it is perfectly permissible to do so when the purpose is to teach the blessings to children.

JEWISH STORYBOOKS

In addition to the usual fare of children's books, it is recommended that parents read to their children books of Jewish content. These may be about historical Jewish heroes, Jewish festivals, or experiences of other Jewish children. Such stories contribute to the strengthening of the child's Jewish identity, give him a sense of the larger group to which he belongs, and teach him something about the Jewish culture of which he is a part. Consult Appendix A for some recommended titles, and where to secure more information about children's books of Jewish content.

JEWISH RECORDS

It is also recommended that parents acquire children's records of simple Hebrew songs or English songs that tell about the festivals or other Jewish themes. As with Jewish storybooks, records of Jewish content give a child happy early associations with the Hebrew language and with subjects and ideas that he will later study formally in greater depth. A great variety of records suitable for different age groups is now available. Consult Appendix A for the names of the firms or institutions where these records can be ordered.

EDUCATIONAL TOYS

Educational Jewish toys for the very young, such as Hebrew letter blocks, are also available. Picture games and coloring books that depict religious items, such as a *tallit, tefillin,* a *shofar, lulav* and *etrog,* or scenes of the various holidays, can also be purchased. While such pictures are no substitute for the direct experience with or the actual seeing and touching of the objects themselves, they do provide additional support for recollection and for reinforcement. They are excellent educational tools for the preschool child. In this delightful way, it is a relatively simple matter for children to learn the Hebrew names and basic themes of all the Jewish holidays and of the many ritual objects identified with them. Thus the shofar is identified with Rosh Hashanah, the sukkah and the lulav and etrog with Sukkot, the eight-branched menorah with Hanukah, the *Megillah* and noise-makers (*gragers*) with Purim, matzah with Passover; a Torah scroll and the Ten Commandments with Shavuot; and the Star of David and the Western Wall with Israel Independence or Jerusalem Day. Scenes from Israel can provide early awareness of a land where most of the people are Jewish and where all the Jewish holidays are also the national holidays.

Although storybooks, records, games, and picture books make up the content of every good Jewish nursery or kindergarten, it is important that parents provide this early training at home and that children identify this instruction with their parents and their home environment. If children will come to Jewish nurseries already equipped with this type of background, parents can rest assured that Jewish educators will be thrilled to upgrade and enrich the nursery and kindergarten curricula so that they supplement and not duplicate home training.

OBSERVING THE SABBATH

The most Jewishly impressive impact that can be made on any child is to give him a taste of the traditional Sabbath, the Shabbat. Properly observed, the Shabbat can quickly become the high point of the very young child's weekly experiences. The festively set dinner table, the lit candles, the dressing up for Shabbat, the recitation of the Kiddush and the sip of wine that follows, the special *hallot* on the table, the singing of songs and prayers—all of this is an eagerly awaited occasion, sometimes mystifying and filled with wonder, always happy and gay for the child. To the child, it is an exciting family party. The whole family is together. The child comes to realize that on this particular day his father will always be at the dinner table and have time to play with him. There are only a very few games that children usually play that are not appropriate for Shabbat. Home games such as chess or checkers and similar activities are permitted on the Shabbat. For older children, that lost art of conversation and visiting friends can be revived and encouraged. And, of course, the most appropriate activity for the Shabbat, studying Torah together, can never be started too young and is never outgrown.

Those activities that children should be restrained from engaging in on the Shabbat, such as coloring or cutting, will be accepted with little or no resentment if they find security, love, and tranquility reflected in the rest of the Shabbat experience. The discipline gained from learning not to do something forbidden is also of great value in developing the child's personality.

The Shabbat should be given an aura of "specialness" by making it a "TV-less" day. This is probably the most difficult thing to do, even more so for the parents than for the children. If children sense the discipline that governs the parents in this matter, they too will readily respect it. I recall that in our home there were daily problems of getting our children to turn off the television set to come to dinner, to go to bed, or to finish their homework. Their answers were always "after the program." A determined parental response to "turn it off *now*" was invariably accompanied by moans and groans and resentful submission. But not so on Friday evenings! "OK kids, it's candlelighting time" was the magic formula for them to jump up, turn off the television, no matter what point the program was at, and to make their last-minute preparations for Shabbat.

From Kiddush on Friday night through the recitation of the Havdalah after nightfall on Saturday night, the special nature of the Shabbat as a sacred day different from all other days must be empha- sized. Attending Sabbath services at the synagogue will contribute to that feeling. Enjoying a few additional hours of sleep in midafternoon is no less part of the traditional Sabbath pleasures. It is a good day for reading and studying, preferably matters that will add to your family's Jewish knowledge. Visits with friends in the neighborhood may provide an opportunity for joining together for the closing Havdalah service. The Shabbat adds a measure of love, warmth, and fellowship to Jewish family life.

BLESSING THE CHILDREN

A particularly impressive ritual of tremendous value in establish- ing a sound parent-child relationship is "blessing the children" every Friday and festival evening, just prior to the recitation of Kiddush. It is usually done by the father, but may also be done by the mother. It is a ceremony that can be continued until the children grow up and marry. The ceremony enhances the parent's role as a spiritual guide to his children. A child who steps forward each week to receive a blessing from his parent is also bound to relate to his parent in a more respectful manner.

While the child of three may not be fully aware of what the ceremony is all about, he eventually learns to attach great meaning to it. And as he gets older, he will hardly permit himself to miss being blessed even if he may, for whatever reason, be acting up at the time. The ritual of "blessing the children" is best introduced when the child is very young. To wait until children are appreciably older will only interfere with the naturalness of the whole ceremony and introduce a sense of awkwardness on the part of parents and children alike. "How come, suddenly, something new?" is not a question designed to imbue a sense of reverence into a meaningful ritual.

The ceremony is performed as follows: Instruct the child to stand before you with a slightly bowed head and place both your hands on the head of the child. If two children are blessed simultaneously, place one hand on the head of each child. Then in Hebrew or English say:

To a son(s): May God make you as Ephraim and Menasseh.*

יְשִׂמְךָ אֱלֹהִים כְּאֶפְרַיִם וְכִמְנַשֶּׁה.

Yesimkha elohim k'Efrayim v'khiMenashe.

To a daughter(s): May God make you as Sarah, Rebecca, Rachel, and Leah.†

יְשִׂמֵךְ אֱלֹהִים כְּשָׂרָה רִבְקָה רָחֵל וְלֵאָה.

Yesimaikh elohim k'Sarah, Rivkah, Raḥel v'Layah.

Either of the above sentences is then followed with:

---

* Ephraim and Menasseh were the sons of Joseph who received the blessing from their grandfather, Jacob. That blessing has become a favorite among Jews: "The angel who delivered me from all evil, bless the lads, and let my name and the name of my fathers Abraham and Isaac be named in them, and let them grow into a multitude in the midst of the earth" (Genesis 48:16). Tradition credits Ephraim and Menasseh with retaining their religious loyalties though raised among the Egyptian aristocracy.

† Sarah, Rebecca, Rachel, and Leah were the founding Matriarchs of the Jewish people. They are associated with the virtues and meritorious deeds considered ideal for Jewish womanhood.

May the Lord bless you and protect you; May the Lord make His countenance to shine upon you and be gracious to you; May the Lord favor you and bestow peace upon you.

יְבָרֶכְךָ יְיָ וְיִשְׁמְרֶךָ ; יָאֵר יְיָ פָּנָיו אֵלֶיךָ וִיחֻנֶּךָ ;

יִשָּׂא יְיָ פָּנָיו אֵלֶיךָ וְיָשֵׂם לְךָ שָׁלוֹם.

Y'varekh-kha adonai v-yish-m'rekha
Ya-ehr adonai panav ay-lekha v'huneka
Yisa adonai panav ay-lekha, v'yasem l'kha shalom.

If a parent wishes, he may add whatever additional prayers he may be moved to say in his own words. There is no reason to resist the natural impulse to conclude the blessing with a kiss.

SPECIAL ACTIVITIES FOR THE FESTIVALS

There are many special occasions during the year in addition to the Sabbath that provide extra excitement, intensify the Jewish experience, and tie the heart of the Jewish child to his family, his people, and his God.

Even the preschool child can help decorate a sukkah and enjoy the novelty of eating in it. On Hanukah, he can help you light Hanukah candles after reciting the blessings and then join in singing some of the holiday songs he learned from his records. Purim is the time to have the child masquerade as one of the principal characters in the story of Purim. For the Passover seder, you don't have to wait until the child starts school to teach him to ask at least the first line of the Four Questions:

Why is this night different from all the other nights?

מַה נִּשְׁתַּנָּה הַלַּיְלָה הַזֶּה מִכָּל הַלֵּילוֹת?

Mah nishtana ha-lailah hazeh mikol ha-laylot?

And if the child can manage to learn the entire first question, teach the child the rest of it:

All the other nights we may eat bread or matzah, this night only matzah.

שֶׁבְּכָל הַלֵּילוֹת אָנוּ אוֹכְלִין חָמֵץ וּמַצָּה,

הַלַּיְלָה הַזֶּה כֻּלּוֹ מַצָּה?

She'b-khol ha-laylot anu okhlim hametz u'matzah, ha-lailah hazeh kulo matzah.

Children can be involved in other parts of the seder too. Such playful games as having a child "steal" or "find" the afikomen are customary. Parents can prepare the children for the seder with the help of a Passover Haggadah, records, and sheet music of the holiday songs.

GOING TO THE SYNAGOGUE

The time to acquaint a child with the synagogue is during the preschool years. I don't recommend that very young children be taken to the synagogue if it is difficult to keep them from disturbing the services. But beginning at about the age of four or five, a start should be made in bringing them to the synagogue on the Sabbaths and festivals, even if only for brief periods of time. This is the time to impress upon them a sense of reverence for the synagogue and the importance of proper decorum during services. It is interesting to watch young children insist on taking a prayer book in their hands and, though they still cannot read, go through the motions as though they are deeply engrossed in prayer. Perhaps in their own way, they really are!

Parents who bring preschool children to the synagogue *only* on the nights of Simhat Torah and Purim are not giving them the right kind of synagogue experience. If the child is already familiar with the synagogue and has attended the synagogue on other occasions, these excursions into "happy bedlam," when the decorum of the prayer service is waived, provide exciting variations to the synagogue experience and in the celebration of the festivals. They highlight the joy of Simhat Torah and the gaiety of Purim. If, however, these occasions constitute the child's *only* experience with the synagogue, it must surely come across in a most distorted light, one not conducive to the development of a serious attitude to the synagogue. The child learns to see the synagogue as a "children's fun palace" that he eventually outgrows instead of learning to relate to the synagogue as a sacred place where prayer to God and study of His word takes place.

During the Elementary School Years

START THEM EARLY

It is important to give the child an early start on formal Jewish studies. It ought not be postponed till the age of eight or nine or later. Hebrew reading and writing are the basic skills needed for any program of Jewish education that intends to go beyond a purely superficial level. There is usually no reason why instruction in these skills should not begin at the same time the child learns to read and write English. Some parents deliberately delay the study of Hebrew out of fear that it might adversely affect learning to read and write English, inasmuch as the two languages are read and written in different directions (English—from left to right, Hebrew—from right to left). The experience of the day schools over many decades has convincingly shown such fears to be unjustified when dealing with the normal child. In fact, the opposite appears to be true. Educators find the ages of five to seven to be the ideal period for the acquisition of a second language. Learning to read, write, and speak a second language, rather than confusing a child, often acts as a catalyst to an even quicker grasp of his native language.

There is still another reason why learning to read and write Hebrew, which requires rote learning, should begin as early as possible, preferably with the first grade and no later than the second grade. The rote practice in pronouncing isolated syllables, or even of whole words, that is necessary when learning to read and to develop reading fluency is enjoyable to the very young child. As the child gets older, such exercises become increasingly boring. The sooner such skills are developed, the quicker one can progress to the study of more challenging texts and more exciting material. One reason for the disinterest that is quickly developed toward Hebrew studies by many children in the afternoon schools is that at the ages of nine, ten, and eleven they are still struggling with exercises that are better suited to the level of the six and seven year old.

STUDY WITH THEM

If a child's Hebrew studies are to become meaningful to him, he must feel that they are an important aspect of his becoming an adult. The best way to give him this feeling is for him to know that the skills he is learning are also possessed by his parents. If they are not, it will not be too long before he stops to take those studies seriously. After all, "Mom and Dad are Jewish and they don't know all this." It is, therefore, important that parents who themselves were denied an elementary Hebrew education, or who have long forgotten their early studies, make an effort to fill that gap in their knowledge. It is simpler than you think. An average adult with no background at all can master the rudiments of Hebrew reading in about ten to twelve hours. Fluency of reading then depends on practice and repeated use. Most synagogues in the United States offer a one-hour-a-week, ten-to-twelve-week course in Hebrew reading, in addition to other courses covering all facets of Jewish living. An increasing number of schools are now sponsoring courses designed specifically for parents. If your school doesn't have adult courses in Hebrew education, you may want to speak to the rabbi, principal, or educational director about inaugurating such programs.

Parents who make an effort to correct their own deficiencies in basic Jewish knowledge signal to their children the value they attach to Jewish studies, thus encouraging a positive attitude in the child. If attendance at such courses requires some sacrifice from the parents, such as giving up the weekly game of bowling or the weekly game of cards, missing a favorite television program, or going out to study when obviously tired from work, the example set for the child is a good one.

Parents who do not lack the basic skills or the basic information should also participate in Jewish study programs. Parents at all levels of Jewish knowledge should seek to join a regular class or a study group in some area of Jewish learning. It can be a marvelous experience to share together with your child the joy of learning and of acquiring new Jewish insights. It can only serve to inspire a child with a respect for learning and whet his appetite for knowledge.

The parent who possesses a basic background in Jewish studies can also help a child with his Hebrew school homework and can assume in the eyes of the child the rightful role of "my father my teacher, my mother my teacher."

RELIGIOUS TRAINING

The ideal period for the child to become familiar with and proficient in religious practices is during the elementary school years. This is the time when the child should be taught to perform all those religious skills that every adult Jew should be able to do. While a child is technically not required to perform religious duties until the age of Bar- and Bat-Mitzvah, the religious precept that requires training children to enter responsible Jewish adulthood, *hinukh*, imposes duties and restrictions at an earlier age. During this period, the religious experiences discussed in connection with the preschool child should be continued. The child can also assume greater responsibility in observing the Sabbath, Passover, Sukkot, lulav, tallit, and tzitzit.

The elementary school boy can be asked to recite the Kiddush (the Sabbath prayer of sanctification said over a cup of wine) every Friday evening together with or *after* his father recites the blessing. The practice of assigning the task of reciting Kiddush entirely to a son under thirteen years of age, however well-meaning, is incorrect and demeans the importance of the Kiddush as an *adult* duty. It is precisely as an *adult* duty that Kiddush is important to the child, and gives him a sense of importance when saying it. While he may be thrilled with the opportunity to occupy the center of the family stage, he will not be impressed with the fact that he also has to say it when he grows up. That lesson derives only if he sees his father say the Kiddush. In a household where there is no father, due to death or divorce or when the father is temporarily away, the mother should make the Kiddush.

Likewise, a girl should light the Sabbath candles with her mother, with the two reciting the blessing together. In this way, a young girl is taught to become proficient in a ritual that she is not required to perform until she herself marries or unless she moves out of her parents' home and lives alone.

Beginning at the age of about eight or nine, children should be taught to fast on Yom Kippur. The first year, children should be encouraged not to eat or drink anything at all throughout the evening of Yom Kippur. The following years, the hour for breakfast (breaking fast) can be pushed further and further ahead—till ten o'clock, then twelve o'clock, then two o'clock, then four o'clock. By the time a girl has reached her twelfth birthday and a boy his thirteenth, they are required to complete the entire fast.

Perhaps the word *allow*, rather than *encourage*, partial fasting for children on Yom Kippur, would have been more appropriate. It is usually unnecessary to encourage children. Children who see their parents fasting regard the ritual as a mark of maturity and are anxious to prove their endurance and grown-up status by maintaining the fast for as long as they can. Except for children under the age of nine, parents should not be afraid to permit their children to show off a bit in this regard. They will not perish of hunger or malnutrition.

Attending services at a synagogue is one of the things American

Jews do least. While parents are often happy to send their children to the synagogue, they themselves stay at home or drop them off and go elsewhere. Lacking parental examples only serves to make the child await the day when he too grows up and can also stop going to the synagogue. That "growing up" takes place very quickly.

Yet, apart from all religious considerations, going to the synagogue with one's children can contribute immensely to cementing the parent-child bond. A passage from Genesis (22:6, 8) that has made a lasting impression on me since first studying it in childhood is the twice-repeated phrase that struck me as an idyllic scene: *Vayailkhu shnaihem yahdav* "and the two of them walked together." The passage describes Abraham and Isaac walking together on their way up the hill toward the altar where Isaac was to be bound as an offering to God. At that point, the Torah teaches us that God did not demand, indeed he forbade human sacrifice in contrast to the prevailing practices of that time. But those three simple Hebrew words leave a powerful impact. They still conjure up a vision of father and son walking together, sharing a common goal. Its vision is the very antithesis of a "generation gap."

The precious moments when this vision takes on the cloth of reality is when parents and their children walk hand in hand to and from the synagogue on the Sabbath. Sometimes this walk is accompanied by intimate and precious conversation, sometimes by equally precious silence that establishes a communication that reaches far above the level of words. I have heard many parents express their delight with these moments, as they feel the bond between their children and themselves become stronger.

Parental responsibility does not disappear even within the synagogue where it is best to keep one's children at the side of a father or a mother. It is the parents' duty to supervise the decorum of their children, to teach them when to answer *amen*, to encourage them to participate in congregational singing, and to go forward to kiss the Torah as it goes by. Thus, the parent maintains the role as teacher even during services. It is also good for the child's self-esteem to be allowed to participate in these adult activities.

Contemporary synagogues often feature "junior services." While a separate service for adolescents may be desirable if it satisfies a desire for independence and provides children with the opportunity to participate in and to conduct all parts of a service, a separate service for the preadolescent is highly questionable. Since these services need to be conducted on a child's level, the challenge of gradually adapting to the longer and more demanding adult services is eliminated. Some children never seem to graduate from that level, and end up as impatient misfits in the adult services when they get older. It also eliminates the educational value in watching parents, the rabbi, and other adults at prayer.

ON OVERCOMING CAR POOL FRUSTRATION

The car pool is one of the inconveniences created by suburban life in the United States that parents have to learn to live with as it is essential to the operation of many Jewish schools.

You should try to avoid the temptation of expressing displeasure about the onerous burden of having to drive or car pool your children to the Jewish school. Though heavy traffic and bad weather conditions might cause any person to express disgust with having to make daily trips or more than one trip a week, children might interpret such parental remarks to mean that you'd be a lot happier if they were also rid of their Jewish schooling. Parental flexibility in yielding to a child's disinterest in continuing beyond Bar- or Bat-Mitzvah is very often subconsciously influenced by the relief from car pooling that parents too would enjoy.

SHOW INTEREST

It is important to show the same interest in the child's Jewish studies as in his general studies. A child will get the impression that you are less concerned about his Jewish studies if you appear to regard the grades he gets in his Jewish studies with less concern than his grades in the general subjects; if you seem more eager to pull him out of Jewish studies classes, to attend to various necessary chores (medical appointments, shopping, special lessons, and so on), than you are to pull him out of general studies; and if you request to have him excused from Jewish studies for reasons that he knows you would never tolerate as an excuse from general studies. If you wish to create a home environment that encourages your child's Jewish schooling, be careful of all the subtle hints that may cause loss of interest and sabotage a good Jewish upbringing.

During the Adolescent Years

Adolescence is widely regarded as a most difficult period for parents. There is a popular Yiddish saying that "little children, little problems; big children, big problems." The physical and emotional changes that take place within each child during adolescence, the transition from childhood to adulthood, the overwhelming influence of the peer group, plus the child's personal fears, hopes, and frustrations, certainly make it a period requiring greater tact and understanding than the elementary school years. If the foundation of a good parent-child relationship had been set during preadolescence, this period should be easier to cope with and less problematic. A good parent-child relationship should help natural adolescent rebelliousness and self-assertiveness express itself in more acceptable and creative patterns.

Although asserting their independence, adolescents are very much in need of a family's protective security. Parents who may, therefore, be tempted to disrupt the family unit at this stage of their children's lives by divorce or separation should be very wary of shaking the very foundations of their children's world. Shock, despair, cynicism, and antisocial behavior are not uncommon reactions to family breakdown. Good children sometimes take drastic steps if they feel it will help them cement the family unit back together and prevent the loss of one or both of their parents.

Children of this age cannot be forced to do things, go places, or learn things that they do not care about. The "come, let us reason together" approach, on a basis of equality, is the most effective way to deal with most problem situations during this period. However, parents should be wary of the issues they select for confrontation. Not every behavior deviation is worthy of becoming an issue.

One should always answer the questions that children ask. This is true at every age level, but it is critically important during adolescence. When children are small, answers should be as simple and as brief as possible. Involved, complicated explanations are usually uncalled for. During adolescence, more sophisticated answers should be given. Patience must always be shown even if a question is repeated many times. If you don't know the answer, don't hesitate to admit it. Either direct your children to people who might provide the answer or tell your children you will find the answer out for them. Don't hide the fact that you don't know everything. Children soon find that out for themselves! Your children should learn to respect you for the things you do know, for the wisdom you do possess, for the experiences you have had, and for the honesty to admit what you don't know.

Good advice to parents of teenagers is simply to be available to your child as much as possible when your child gets home from school. Even the preadolescent will find a parent's presence at that time encouraging. It is the moment when a child may wish to ask a parent's opinion, vent an emotion or frustration about the day in school, that parents' support and security, in the face of some problem situation, are welcomed. One cannot put up a "hold" sign when a child is ready to confide. If the "moment of truth" passes by, it may never again surface. This does not mean that parents must always be housebound. This may not be possible. It does mean that as a rule a child should expect to find at least one parent awaiting his return and showing a readiness to listen and to talk. Even working parents can sometimes manage to arrange their schedules to accommodate this need. The youngster may not often wish to talk, but that is fine too. Your mere presence provides a sense of security, a feeling that you care. It is important that children have that feeling. In some families the dinner table provides that opportunity daily.

Parents should be very sensitive to the great influence that peer groups have on adolescents. Perhaps the greatest contribution that parents can make to the Jewish development of their children during this period of their lives is to try to bring the youngster in contact with acceptable peer groups and to minimize as much as possible the opportunities for contact with objectionable peer groups. The kind of school a youngster attends, the type of summer camp he goes to, and the institutions with which the family associates are all important factors in the way an adolescent develops. If parental influence during this period cannot be exercised directly, indirect influence can still be immense. These influences will be discussed more fully in Chapter Six.

In discussing the adolescent period, I am assuming that a Jewish way of life has already been created by the family, and that the Jewish spirit generated during the elementary school years has been carried over into the child's teen years. Even so, attitudes, convictions, and commitments can be strengthened during this time by the extent to which parents articulate their concern for the future of the Jewish people, voice their convictions about the meaningfulness and importance of Jewish life, and by their consistency in doing the practical things that reflect their stated concerns. These are important influences on an adolescent.

But what if a family has done very little before, and it is only when children have reached adolescence that parents become awakened to the dangers of intermarriage, or for more positive reasons now want to begin to make their children's lives more Jewish? What are parents to do? Should parents become better acquainted with the Jewish heritage? Allow the Sabbaths and festivals to play a greater role in their lives? Start adhering to some of the religious disciplines? When children are small, they fit right into the pattern that parents set for them. When they are older, this is no longer possible. The adolescent may not be sympathetic to changes; the adolescent may be quite happy with his life-style and has peer-group support for it.

It is surely more difficult, but it may not be too late for some Jewish impact. A family conference with the children can become the forum for a full discussion of the parents' emerging fears, of their basic convictions, past omissions, and future aspirations. It may be that the children will respond very positively to all their suggestions. If they do not, parents should not impose themselves on the children. Parents should proceed to do all they can to create a Jewish home environment *for themselves* and with the hope that the children will slowly be drawn into it. Support can be sought from other institutional and human resources the community provides, bearing in mind the many suggestions offered above and those to be discussed in Chapter Six.

One crucial decision most Jewish adolescents make concerns the selection of a college or university. It is a decision that parents can help their children make. The academic reputation of an undergraduate school and its potential contribution to one's professional advancement should not be the sole criteria. One ought to also ascertain the opportunities available in the campus community for maintaining Jewish values, for making Jewish associations, and for continuing Jewish experiences. Increasing attention should be given to the Jewish colleges in America, Yeshiva College (for men), Stern College (for women), and Touro College (coed), although these can accommodate only a very small percentage of Jewish youth who attend college. As a rule, a university that is located in or very close to a large Jewish community, or that forms part of a cluster of colleges with large Jewish student bodies, should be the most sought after schools as some of these have reputations for having vibrant and dynamic Jewish student groups or for offering opportunities in Jewish studies.

The type of university one attends is the final sensitive area in any Jewish upbringing. It may be a source of potential spiritual danger or an opportunity for developing a person's sense of Jewish responsibility.

Selecting a Community: Factors to Consider

The Neighborhood

"The Master said to them, 'Go forth and see which is the right way to which a man should cleave.' Rabbi Jose said, 'A good neighbor.' " [1] These words of wisdom come from the Ethics of the Fathers.

When a family chooses to relocate in a new neighborhood or move to a different city, many factors usually go into their choice of area: the quality of the schools, the distance to public transportation or of convenient travel routes to one's place of work, the availability of easy shopping, and the social desirability of the area. Once an area has been chosen with one or more of the above reasons in mind, attention is then turned to the size, quality, and cost of the home desired. If no area or home is found possessing all of the desired features, then the family's scale of priorities determines what are for them the "nonnegotiable" conditions and those on which they are prepared to compromise.

Unfortunately, many Jewish families contemplating a move overlook or fail to give consideration to those factors that could help make Jewish living easier and assist them in the Jewish upbringing of their children. This does not mean one need seek out an exclusively Jewish area. But it does require proximity to a synagogue; it does require a good Jewish school of the type preferred; and it does require the availability of kosher food supplies. It is also very important to have several neighbors with positive Jewish interests and a peer group for the children that reflects a positive orientation to Jewish living. The fact that a neighborhood may boast of many Jewish residents does not necessarily mean that all, or any, of the desired criteria exist. It is quite possible for a family with a positive Jewish orientation to feel isolated even in a densely populated Jewish area. A Jewish community is much more than a group of homes occupied by Jews. It is easy to overlook the Jewish criteria when choosing an area in which to reside, only to realize much later the difficulties encountered in providing children with Jewish experiences outside the four walls of the home.

The Synagogue

"Get yourself a teacher," is the advice offered in the Ethics of the Fathers.[2] The local synagogue can be a most powerful ally in realizing the Jewish aspirations you have for yourself and your children. You should join a synagogue, not only because it is the Jewish thing to do, and not only because you will need to make use of its facilities, but because, through the person of its rabbi, you "get yourself a teacher," and you acquire a personal religious counselor. The synagogue can serve as a lighthouse even for persons far removed from traditional Jewish life, as a reminder of Jewish values and teachings, and as a gauge by which to measure one's own level of Jewishness. If we agree that a synagogue has potential impact on a family's standards and values, and if there is a choice, the quality of the particular synagogue should be a consideration. Without descending into a fruitless discussion of denominational differences, it is fair and accurate to say that some synagogues, by virtue of the caliber of their rabbinic and/or lay leadership, set religious, moral, and ethical expectations for a congregation and others do not.

Parents should be interested in more than a building where they can participate in religious services. They should seek out a congregation that will help them maintain religious standards and grow spiritually. Many families are afraid of just that and often do just the opposite, seeking out congregations where they feel they will not be expected to do more than they are now doing and where they will not be challenged to greater religious commitments. They feel more comfortable in a less demanding environment. Undoubtedly so! Yet parents deeply concerned with raising Jewishly committed children will pay heed to the atmosphere and the mood of expectations generated by the synagogue and welcome the challenge to more intensive Jewish living and greater Jewish study.

The location of the synagogue should also be a factor to consider when choosing a neighborhood. For the Sabbath observer, the presence of a synagogue close enough to walk to on the Sabbath (usually no more than a mile away), is a "nonnegotiable" condition in one's scale of priorities. The readiness of those not committed to traditional Sabbath observance to move away from the synagogue should be seen as affecting much more than the religious issue of driving to services on the Sabbath. Moving a distance away from the synagogue makes it inconvenient, if not difficult, to take advantage of all the programs and services that take place at the synagogue. Children cannot get there on their own, even during the week, and so instead of becoming a familiar and inviting place to go to, the synagogue is reserved for special occasions.

A community living around its synagogue has a certain cohesiveness, and a wise and energetic synagogue leadership can exploit that cohesiveness to strengthen Jewish values and to enrich the quality of Jewish life. "Keeping up with the Joneses" (or the Goldbergs, for that matter) is much more than an observation on the crude materialistic competition that affects society; it is a very insightful comment on the subtle influence that neighbors and friends have in determining a family's "needs." This influence exists not only on the materialistic level; it exists also on the spiritual and moral levels. It can be a force for bad; it can also be a force for good. "Keeping up" with one's neighbors is an element today in the problems of divorce, alcohol, and drugs; but it can also be effective positively, in setting standards for Sabbath, kashrut, and Jewish education.

Where the Jewish community is scattered and Jewish families spread out at great distances from their synagogues, the influence of the synagogue and its rabbi is felt less strongly, the social pressure for conformity to the values represented by the synagogue is reduced, and the cohesive quality of that community is lessened. Fewer memories about the synagogue are left with the growing child. To depend on formal membership in the synagogue to provide the same influence on a family as does living within its proximity and attending it with greater regularity, is like saying that buying meat and keeping it in the freezer provides the family with the same protein requirements as though they ate the meat.

One cannot say enough about the importance of the synagogue, and of living within proximity to the synagogue, as a factor in raising a Jewishly committed family. When moving to a newly developing area, it is important to find out whether there are any plans for the founding of a congregation and the establishment of a synagogue.

The Jewish School

It is common knowledge that the quality of the local public school system is a prime consideration, if not the critically determining one, for Jewish parents when choosing a new community. Jews have been known to uproot themselves from well-established homes and neighborhoods, sometimes at great financial loss and at great inconvenience to themselves, only because the educational quality of the schools in their area have deteriorated.

Why then isn't the type and quality of Jewish schooling available also one of the major factors in deciding whether and where to relocate? Sometimes it is hard to escape the suspicion that when it comes to Jewish education, "anything at all" will do. Families move out to areas from where transportation to a Jewish school may be exceedingly difficult and burdensome. Even car pools, so familiar to the suburban scene, become a problem when traveling time becomes too great or there are not enough people with whom to share the driving. This being the case, children end up attending nowhere, or are enrolled in the closest Jewish institution without regard to its type or quality.

Parents who regard Jewish education as an integral part of their child's total development, and who are no less uncompromising with their Jewish upbringing as with all other aspects of their upbringing, will very carefully consider the proximity and the quality of the Jewish schools when selecting a new community.

An evaluation of the different types of Jewish schools and the ideological variations among them, discussed in Chapters Eight and Nine, should be helpful to parents in making their decisions in selecting a school.

CHAPTER

6

Peer Groups: Leisure=Time Education

I T is the rare adult who can maintain beliefs and customs which contrast sharply with those around him. How much more difficult it is for the child. What is in style bestows a legitimacy on modes of behavior that may previously have been looked upon as religiously or morally unacceptable. Often, the relaxation of religious disciplines and changing moral values are more the reflection of environmental and peer-group influences than of any intrinsic change in the religious moral codes.

Forewarned is forearmed! Knowing this, people who wish to develop or to maintain Jewish values and religious sensitivities should seek out social circles that will lend support to the life-style they wish to maintain. This is not to imply that deep and lasting friendships ought not be established with those who do not share one's life-style and views, be they Jews or non-Jews. They certainly can and ought to be developed. People should be judged for the human qualities they possess, on the basis of their personalities and by their ethical deeds. Wide-ranging friendships can only add to the richness and scope of one's own life, and contribute to broader understanding of people and issues. This is the best reason for living in a religiously and racially mixed neighborhood.

Loneliness is a terrible burden. To be the only one or one of the very few in a group, neighborhood, or town who wishes to pursue a Jewish way of life is difficult. While some families have succeeded admirably in affirming their Jewish individuality even under such circumstances, it is not easy to do. It is particularly hard for children. In the face of many environmental influences that draw one away from Jewish living and Jewish values, it becomes especially important for adults and children to be able to create satisfactory social relationships with at least some friends who share the same Jewish interests.

Such friends may be drawn from among neighbors, worshipers in the same synagogue, and groups of parents who send their children to the same Jewish school. The day school in an area especially serves not only to educate children, but, equally important, to bring together families who share similar Jewish values. A subcommunity is thus formed that supports and strengthens the traditional values possessed by its individual members. You are no longer alone. There are others like yourself. For most people this is terribly important.*

The reality of peer-group influence, susceptibility to which reaches its height during adolescence, imposes a special responsibility on the parent. It means steering children away from contact with undesirable peer groups and creating opportunities for them to come in contact with desirable peer groups. Dr. Homan makes the point emphatically:

> I know that few children of less than high-school age can forever maintain their vocabulary, social values, educational standards, sexual viewpoint, and value scale against a concerted assault by a solid phalanx of their peers. Therefore I conclude that it is the parents' responsibility at least to see that their child has the opportunity to select his friends from a group which contains individuals with whose

---

* One of the major problems that many sincere proselytes to Judaism confront is the lack of contact with observant Jews with whom they can associate and from whom they can learn. The secular life-style of Jews with whom they do associate is not conducive to helping newcomers to the faith adapt to patterns of authentic Jewish living.

views his family expectations will not clash. . . . A child is old enough to be relatively immune to the teachings of his peers when his own personality is not adrift and after you have taught him to have a firm confidence in the integrity of his own values. Until this point is reached . . . you cannot allow your child to select at random his constant companions.[1]

Even after children have become too old for parents to have control over their choice of companions, parents still have opportunities to select environments from which their friends will be drawn. You are very fortunate if you are able to select environments that are even spiritually superior to what you can provide at home. The Jewish school where you send your child, particularly if it is a day school, is one way of providing a desirable environment. But school is not the only place where peer-group contact is made, or is it the only avenue for instilling Jewish values and transmitting Jewish knowledge. We have now become far more sensitive to the importance of leisure time in the Jewish upbringing of children and to the need of properly exploiting it for educational purposes. Regardless of the type of formal Jewish schooling that children receive, no parent can afford to be oblivious to the opportunities offered by the summer camp, a visit to Israel, and youth organizations.

The Summer Camp

Jewish parents have long understood the opportunities for personality and social development offered by the overnight summer camp. The potential it has for Jewish training and for Jewish growth is not as widely appreciated by parents. The summer months, when the child is relaxed and free of school pressures, provide a great opportunity to intensify the Jewish experiences of the child and to meet some of the child's spiritual needs. The right kind of summer camp can do much to help develop committed Jewish personalities.

A good Jewish camp is one that creates a Jewish atmosphere, imparts Jewish knowledge, motivates commitment to a Jewish way of life, and demonstrates the relevance of Judaism to daily living.

For a child who comes from an observant Jewish home and an intensive Jewish educational background, a good Jewish camp complements and strengthens his year-round experiences. For a child who comes from an environment where he has had less experience with Jewish living, a good Jewish camp can stir new feelings and create within the child new interest in his Jewishness, make the child more serious about pursuing a Jewish education, and give the child a taste of what Jewish living can be like. A seven-to-eight week stay at a good Jewish summer camp is educationally more worthwhile and spiritually more meaningful than a year at a poor afternoon Hebrew or Sunday school. A good summer camp provides more Jewish living experiences in two months than a year of typical class instruction.

Next to the impact made by the day schools, summer camps with an educational and religious content have contributed enormously to strengthening children's ties to the Jewish people, adding immeasurably to their Jewish knowledge, and in many instances to reinforcing their religious commitments.

The history of Jewish educational camping can be traced back to 1919, when the Central Jewish Institute in New York sponsored a summer camp. Over the past several decades, a number of such educational camps have written an impressive chapter in the effort to raise a young generation of Jews.

Camp Yavneh, a Hebrew language camp, sponsored by the Hebrew College of Boston, was the first of these. In addition to the usual athletic activities, it features cultural programs oriented to Zionism, Israeli history, and geography. Camp Morasha, sponsored by the Community Service Division of Yeshiva University, devotes a few hours of each day to informal study sessions in a relaxed atmosphere, sitting on the grass or around tables. Talmud, Bible, or Jewish philosophy are studied, and campers are assigned to groups reflecting their vastly different backgrounds in Jewish education. The chain of Ramah Camps, sponsored by the United Synagogue of America, stresses the use of Hebrew conversation. There are many good educational summer camps sponsored by various schools and Yeshivot as extensions of the school's year-round educational programs, and by the Hasidic Lubavitch movement.

The weekly Sabbath day in these camps assumes a special character that reflects a mixture of special joy, extra rest, and reverence. In the city, it is easy to remain unaware of the fast of Tisha b'Av, the day of mourning that commemorates several major tragedies in Jewish history, which falls during the summer months. In camp, it becomes a rich, unforgettable, spiritual Jewish experience, for those who keep the fast as well as for those who do not.

There are also camps sponsored by various Zionist youth groups. The Zionist camps differ markedly in their religious orientation—some highly religious, some peripherally traditional, and some militantly anti-religious, reflecting the spectrum of the Israeli kibbutz movement. They are united in their dedication to Israel and to the ideal of *Aliya*. Camps sponsored by the Union of American Hebrew Congregations, though lacking kashrut and traditional Sabbath observance, do succeed in creating new Jewish interest and instilling positive feelings of Jewish self-identity in their campers.

The "Non-Jewish" Jewish Camp

Unfortunately, the "Jewish" camps to which most Jewish children have been sent is a far cry from what I have been talking about. The "Jewishness" of these camps is usually defined by its Jewish ownership, its Jewish clientele, and its Jewish staff. A perfunctory and attenuated Friday night "service" makes its "Jewishness" official. Yet, the education that these "Jewish" camps transmit to their campers via color-war themes, music, dramatics, and other cultural programming consists of American Indian folklore, Greek mythology, and whatever other themes counselors or directors may prefer. Jewish themes are not deliberately off limits. It is just that counselors and program directors are usually so uninformed on Jewish matters that they have nothing to draw upon.

Except for the brief Friday evening service, there is usually little in the life of the camp during the other six days and twenty-three hours that distinguishes it from a gentile camp. Often kashrut is also dispensed with, thus defeating the efforts of all Orthodox and Conservative religious leaders to encourage Jews to abide by these disciplines. The fact that the food served might even be kosher in some camps does not appreciably change the picture. The moral atmosphere usually reflects the latest views of the youth culture with no attempt to convey some of the traditional Jewish standards in boy-girl relationships. The staff is often so lacking in all Jewish commitments, and may even be antagonistic to Judaism, that they set poor examples for the young put in their charge.

The tragedy is not only that such "Jewish" camps—which are mostly privately owned but may also be owned or sponsored by a local Jewish community agency—lose an ideal opportunity to advance the cause of a Jewish upbringing. It is my contention that such "Jewish" camps actually do irreparable damage to the children's Jewish upbringing. Jewish educators try to stress that Judaism is a way of life intended for all seasons, for vacation periods as well as for periods of work. Two months at such a camp should dispel that notion. The totally secular life of the "all-Jewish" camp is itself the most devastating argument against the relevance of their Jewish heritage. In eight weeks, such camps succeed in undoing every ounce of religious commitment that the synagogues and the Hebrew schools have labored to instill during the previous ten months. What the Jewish community spends a fortune on to achieve from September through June, it spends another fortune on to counteract during July and August.

Parents should view the camp environment, despite its primary recreational aspect, as an extension of the home environment. A child *lives* in the summer camp and the totality of the experience exerts an influence that is closest to the home. That it lasts for only four to eight weeks does not mean that its potential impact can be treated casually. Anyone who has ever stood by and watched the tears and emotions of children on the day that camp breaks up, and watched them separate from friends to return to their own homes, cannot but be impressed with the overall impact of the experience. Since counselors and camp officials become the child's surrogate parents for this period of time, it is important to ascertain the atmosphere of the camp and the caliber of the personnel. Do they reflect the values you wish to instill in your child? Remember that a counselor spends more time in direct contact with a child in two months than a parent might in several years. The choice of a camp is worth the most deliberate and informed care.

A Visit to Israel

In the past several decades, Jewish parents have been given an additional educational resource in the Jewish upbringing of their children: The visit to Israel. The confrontation of an American Jew with a whole country where the vast majority is Jewish—where Hebrew is the spoken language, where streets are named after famous events and persons in Jewish history, where one walks the very places where once walked our biblical forefathers, where once preached the Hebrew prophets, where the Jewish heroes of the past and the present fought, and yet where all the complexity and technology of a modern state and a contemporary culture are to be found—has always had a very strong emotional impact on a young person.

To gaze out over Mount Moriah where the Temple once stood; to pass by the ancient well in Beersheba, which is believed to have been dug by Abraham; to walk around the hill where archeologists tell us Jericho once stood; to visit the Cave of Machpelah in the city of Hebron where Abraham and Sarah, Isaac and Rebecca, Jacob and Leah lie buried—all make the Torah come alive. King David and King Solomon, the Prophets Elijah and Isaiah take on a reality that mere textual study does not transmit. Jewish history assumes a new dimension just as does a visit to Valley Forge or Gettysburg to a young person studying American history. That the Jewish experience extends back for and is measured in terms of thousands of years, and not just in hundreds, only adds to the awe. In this way, religious education assumes a new significance; ancient roots and a several millennia-old heritage assume new meaning.

A visit to Israel usually adds to one's sense of Jewish pride and arouses many latent feelings of Jewish interest. The trip often takes on the qualities of a spiritual experience.

While even a two- or three-week tour of Israel is a worthwhile experience, the greatest impact on young people is made by the six-to-eight week tours that include some instruction in the geography and history of the country, that relate the youngster's experiences to biblical events of the past, and that provide for *opportunities to personally experience Jewish living.* Of even greater merit are the long-term study programs of six and twelve months' duration sponsored by different institutions for youths of high school and college age. These programs, of the "year abroad" type, are generally accredited so that they dovetail with the youngster's high school or college program in the United States. Young American Jews are often more amenable to Jewish learning in Israel than when they are in their own communities.

A word of caution: Israel is not the magic cure for Jewish apathy and indifference. It does not automatically inject Jewish knowledge or a renewed commitment to Jewish living. As a matter of fact, there are some Israeli programs for American teenagers that do nothing to inspire them to look with fresh vigor on their Jewish heritage and to involve them in the experience of total Jewish living. The sensitive American youngster who is searching for a measure of spiritual inspiration and for a more intensive Jewish experience might well experience a certain letdown from a trip to Israel that limits his contact to the secular side of Israeli life. Such an American youngster is looking for one's roots. A totally secular experience dressed in Hebrew language does not provide it.

Therefore, it is important that trips to Israel be carefully selected for their Jewish content and for their responsible supervision. Price and quality should not be the only considerations. Consult Appendix A for where to get information concerning summer tours in Israel with a Jewish content and about formal study programs of one or two semesters on the high school and college levels.

Youth Organizations: The Shabbaton or Weekend Retreat

Closer to home than the summer camp or the visit to Israel are the youth organizations sponsored by local synagogues or national Jewish organizations. Jewish youngsters may become devoted to the Jewish people and the Jewish faith as a result of their involvement with such groups. *If* the local youth group has good leadership, it can provide effective peer influences to offset the surrounding non-Jewish influences.

Except for the fact that each youth organization formally follows the philosophy of its sponsoring body, it is extremely difficult to make fair and accurate evaluations of their strengths and weaknesses. Obviously, the official aims espoused by each of them are all couched in superlatives. Realistically, the impact that any group succeeds in making on its young membership depends much more on the caliber of each group's local leadership, at any given time, than on the official goals or the organization's national leadership. The quality of the leadership and the activities of local youth groups tend to change every few years as the young people in them come and go.

One may also discover that, happily, these youth organizations sometimes reflect an idealism that surpasses that of their elders and often have a surprising clarity of direction. I once heard the seventeen-year-old president of a youth group in Detroit proclaim that it was the purpose of the organization "to put Judaism back into the Temple." That an adolescent was able to see the problem of contemporary Judaism in those terms is a promising sign for the future.

The most effective program sponsored by the various youth organizations has been the "weekend retreat" or the Shabbaton. It sometimes takes the form of a national conference or a regional seminar. During this brief period, the youngster is placed in a total Jewish environment and is exposed to as many Jewish experiences as possible. These include prayer and the observance of the Sabbath, washing for meals and reciting grace, periods of concentrated study or serious discussion of Jewish themes, and gay singing and happy dancing so characteristic of Jewish religious celebrations. The Shabbatons intensify the youngsters' Jewish feelings, strengthen their Jewish convictions, and provide them with peer-group support.

Even children who come with very little Jewish background get caught up quickly in the excitement. They easily adapt themselves to the routine of the Sabbath and to the religious code in force during the period. The Shabbaton is invariably an exhilarating experience that serves to inspire the teenagers, both intellectually and emotionally, and encourages many to continue their Jewish studies or to begin to take them more seriously. At the very least, it leads to a greater appreciation of their Jewish heritage. Much of the impact is made by the Jewishly well-trained young counselors and rabbis who staff these retreats, and to whom the youngsters are quick to relate.

The Shabbatons have also proven very worthwhile for youngsters who attend day schools or who come from religious homes. It is important for them to share intensive Jewish experiences with hundreds of other youngsters outside the formal framework of the classroom.

Parents would be wise to seek out programs such as those described and encourage their children to participate in them. Although scholarship assistance is often available, these programs do involve costs and parental support is essential. But whatever the expense, it is one of the best long-range investments one can make on behalf of one's children. Encourage them to try it. They may find that being Jewish can be very much to their liking.

CHAPTER

7

Cases from a Rabbi's Study:
Coping with
Contemporary "Situations"

Tʜᴇ troublesome situations that confront an average family over the years may vary. Those dealing with the raising and education of children are often the most perplexing. As rabbi of a quite typical suburban Midwest congregation who devoted a great deal of time to family counseling and Jewish education, I had occasion to become sensitive to many contemporary problems that call for some comment. I know that most parents want to do the right thing and try to do the right thing. Therefore, I want to share with you the essense of many discussions I have had with parents in the privacy of my study or at small gatherings. I have selected a sampling that I believe has wider application and is pertinent to many families. It is my hope that the "cases" discussed will be helpful to parents in avoiding potential pitfalls or in guiding them toward solutions of matters important to them.

• Don't Always Ask Your Child

A *faux pas* that very often arises among parents who send their children to Sunday or afternoon Hebrew school is that when the child is about ready to begin his formal Jewish studies, they ask him if he'd like to go. Perhaps it is a harmless question. It is intended to produce a "yes" answer. But a question like that implies that there are two legitimate answers—yes and no. What do you do if he says "no"?

Going to school to study the Jewish heritage must be treated as one of the facts of life to which there is no alternative. No one ever seriously asks a child if he'd like to go to public school; that's always in terms of "when," not "if." No one ever asks a child if he'd like to go to the doctor for his periodic examination or injections. You simply tell him about it and take him to the doctor. Once in Hebrew school, a child can be asked how he likes it, how he enjoys his Jewish studies, but never if he'd like to go or if he'd like to continue. Such questions only plant seeds of doubt in a child's mind.

If resistance is met to starting a supplementary program of Jewish schooling (for the same psychological or emotional reasons that make the first days in public school difficult for some children), or if some legitimate problems arise at the Jewish school after the child has been in attendance for some time, don't resort to the promise "you only have three or four or five years to go." That makes it sound like a jail sentence and only confirms his fears about its inherent unpleasantness. Instead, find the specific cause of the problem and try to solve it.

• If Your Child Likes Hebrew School, Don't Spoil It

Your child likes Hebrew School? He enjoys his Jewish studies? Don't spoil it by announcing to your friends and to others in the family in the presence of the child: "You know, my child likes Hebrew school, my child *really* likes it, isn't it wonderful," or by boasting, "I don't have to force my child to go."

While you are expressing approval and admiration, you are also expressing, whether or not you realize it, your surprise at your child's positive reaction. You are subtly signaling him that one normally is not supposed to like Hebrew school, and that he's different. Sooner or later, your child may come to the conclusion that there is something abnormal about his taste for Jewish studies and decide to revert to what he now knows you regard as "normal." After all, he likes public school too. Yet, he never hears you express your amazement that "he *really* likes public school," or "I don't have to force him to go."

It is fine to express your joy at *how well* your child may be doing in Hebrew school, but not that he likes it unless it's said in a framework that relates equally to his general studies or to the public school. Treat your child's attendance at the supplementary Jewish school as something you also take for granted.

• If Your Child *Doesn't* Like Hebrew School, It May Not Be Your Child's Fault

Your child doesn't like Hebrew school? It is, of course, quite possible that objective school factors are responsible—a poor teacher, material not geared to the child's academic level, a personality clash with either a teacher or classmates. This could happen in any school. The problem should be discussed with the teacher and the principal and as soon as possible corrected. The solution may involve changing classes or even schools. But it is also possible that classroom problems are invented by the child if not actually caused by him, or that insignificant situations are magnified out of all proportion to their seriousness because you have yourself sown the seeds of distaste. If so, the child's real aim is to rid himself of burdensome studies that cut into his hours of leisure and no solution is likely to work.

If you are taken aback at this acusation, think back. What expectations did you unconsciously develop in your child? Statements such as those discussed above do their share in contributing to negative attitudes. But there are others too. Are you as concerned about your child's absenteeism from Hebrew classes as you are about those from public school classes? Do you treat the homework assignments your child brings home from Hebrew school with the same sense of urgency as your child's homework assignments from public school? Even parents of day school students are cautioned to treat Jewish studies assignments and grades with the same seriousness as they do the general studies if the value of that education is to be preserved.

If you don't, you are telling your child in very clear, though unspoken, words that you don't really regard progress in his Jewish studies to be as important as in his general studies. You might possibly have been even more direct and said, "it doesn't matter . . . he won't be a rabbi, anyway" as though the only reason for pursuing a Jewish education and for doing well in it is to qualify for a profession. Such signals or statements are not lost on the child. The child receives the message and reacts accordingly.

• Don't Discriminate Against Daughters

You wouldn't think of discriminating against daughters, you say? Yet many parents are known to take the view that Jewish schooling for their daughters is somehow less vital. Daughters deserve just as good a religious education as sons. Everything in this book applies equally to both sons and daughters. While there are still differences of opinion in traditional circles about whether or not the Talmud should be included in a curriculum intended for girls, Jewish law clearly requires that daughters be given a thorough religious education that includes the study of Torah and of Jewish law.

The discriminating practice may in part stem from the fact that one Talmudic passage was taken to mean that it was actually forbidden for girls to study the laws of the Torah and so it became the practice for many centuries for the devout to ignore the formal Jewish education of their daughters.[1] In more recent times, this prejudice may have resulted from the fact that since there was no formal Bat-Mitzvah ceremony to prepare for, and girls were not required to recite Kaddish for the dead, the urgency of providing elementary training in Hebrew was diminished. This was particularly true among the immigrant generation in America. Home education, many felt, was enough.

As long as homes reflected strong Jewish commitments, and the local community was overwhelmingly Jewish, the informal education of daughters in the home may have sufficed. It may not have been enough to raise knowledgeable Jewish women or to make them comfortable in a synagogue, but it did serve to instill some Jewish values. But as the non-Jewish environment became increasingly overpowering, as exposure to secular education became more commonplace, and as homes became less Jewish in content, the homes failed to do even that. The widespread neglect of Jewish education for girls contributed much to the assimilation that is now taking place.

If the Jewish people are to survive, the education of daughters may be even more important than that of sons. It is the woman who usually determines the spiritual character of the home. It is the mother who is most often called upon to answer her children's daily questions. It is the extent of the mother's faith, the strength of her values and beliefs, that plays the dominant role in shaping the spiritual character of the next generation. One classic rabbinic opinion credits the redemption of the Children of Israel from slavery in Egypt to the presence of righteous Jewish women.[2] When a girl receives a sound Jewish education with strong commitments to her heritage, one can be fairly certain about the Jewish character of her home when she marries. When the same Jewish education is given to a boy, one cannot be sure about his future home unless he has an unusually strong personality. Much depends upon whom he marries.

In an age when women's roles are increasingly expanding, and when their influence is increasingly felt in every area of life, we cannot afford to compromise in any way with the quality of their Jewish upbringing.

• The Bar-Mitzvah: A Deterrent to Jewish Education

If your son asks you the reason for his having to go to Hebrew school, *please*, never say "in order to become Bar-Mitzvah." I cannot think of a worse reason for giving a child a Jewish education. Unless the child comes in contact with an exceptionally inspiring teacher, who will succeed in imbuing him with a real love for Jewish knowledge, this reason is bound to boomerang.

Why? First, it practically closes the door in advance for studying beyond Bar-Mitzvah. If your son's only reason for going to Hebrew school is to prepare for a Bar-Mitzvah ceremony, then your son is led to believe right from the start that nothing beyond Bar-Mitzvah is important or necessary. Later, if parents wish to encourage the youngster to continue, they will usually find that he has developed a strong resistance to further Jewish studies.

Second, it is not long before the youngster comes to realize that he really doesn't have to know that much for the Bar-Mitzvah ceremony itself. Children are quite capable of quickly learning the necessary blessings and the biblical chapter by the Prophets (the Haftarah) by rote and of reciting them "beautifully." If the Bar-Mitzvah ceremony is the goal, the mere ability to read Hebrew, which the child learned to do during his first year in Hebrew school, supplemented by a five- or six-month training period consisting of one hour a week is all the training he needs. Why then work hard at learning to speak or understand the Hebrew language, why struggle with Bible and Jewish history, or why spend time on laws and customs? At the age of seven or eight, he may not yet realize that most of what he is learning is not essential for the actual Bar-Mitzvah ceremony. But, by the time he is ten or eleven, that will suddenly dawn on him. At this point, the Hebrew school teachers, even the best of them, become the worst, and parents begin to hear the child's daily complaint that he is learning absolutely nothing. The subtle and nagging campaign to drop the more demanding school program in favor of a convenient one-hour-a-week Bar-Mitzvah training lesson begins this way. He will begin to insist that he will learn more with a private tutor than in school.

If preparing for the Bar-Mitzvah ceremony is the only reason for going to Hebrew school, then the private tutor is indeed preferable. That is why most Hebrew schools use a one-to-one tutorial system in teaching the Haftarah. But it is *not* preferable if we are concerned with a total Jewish upbringing and with an entire Jewish studies curriculum.

So please don't focus in prematurely on his Bar-Mitzvah. Tell him the reason he is going to Hebrew school is because he is a Jewish child and must learn about the Jewish people, about the Jewish religion, and about the Jewish way of life. Explain to your child that every Jew must study Torah and the more one knows and studies the better off one is. Let him know that he has to go to a Jewish school until he grows up and that Jewish study is a necessary part of life.

While we, like most other families, were compelled to reserve a date for our son's Bar-Mitzvah at the synagogue almost five years in advance, that fact was never mentioned directly to him or in his presence. We never discussed becoming Bar-Mitzvah with him until about the time he turned eleven years old. Then he raised the subject himself, and inquired as to what plans we were making for his Bar-Mitzvah. Only then did we tell him that we had a date reserved, and what that date was. As to any other details concerning the celebration, we said that we didn't know yet. Surely, becoming Bar-Mitzvah was part of growing up as a Jew. But what he had to learn for the Bar-Mitzvah would be only a small part of his Jewish schooling.

As important a moment as it is in the life of every Jewish male child, the Bar-Mitzvah is certainly not the goal of the child's Jewish studies or is it the peak of the child's Jewish experiences.

• The Jewish Dropout: "He's *Been* Bar-Mitzvah'ed"

While on the one hand, the Bar-Mitzvah is widely credited as being one of the major incentives for whatever Jewish education most children do receive before the age of thirteen, it has also become the most common excuse for terminating their Jewish education. "He's *been* Bar-Mitzvah'ed. He's had enough." Usually the child shares this feeling. This has created the problem of "the Jewish dropout."

It is precisely during the post-Bar-Mitzvah years, between the ages of thirteen and eighteen, that a youngster matures, that his lifelong views begin to crystallize, and that the values instilled by his parents are tested, either to be confirmed and absorbed, or revised and discarded. It is during these years that questions of substance regarding faith and morals, philosophy and science, interpersonal relations and public problems, begin to interest him and, perhaps, to trouble him. It is a very important time for him to remain in regular contact with a rabbi, with Hebrew teachers, with the synagogue, with leaders of Jewish youth organizations, and with all who are able to react to and respond maturely to his questions. It is a most important time for him to be exposed to Jewish ideas and values, both for the positive contribution they can make toward the development of his personality and character, and for the balancing influence they can provide for the non-Jewish, secular, and agnostic influences that dominate his general schooling and culture.

After all, a good elementary Jewish education is only a building block designed to prepare the child for serious Jewish study. To stop after elementary Hebrew school is like teaching a child to read and then refusing to give him books! Furthermore, without reinforcement, the process of forgetting sets in and, before long, the youngster regresses to the first or second grade level.

Even the more intensive program of study provided in a day school cannot possibly address itself to many areas that are unsuited for study by younger children, to many issues that simply call forth no interest at an earlier age, and to many questions that simply do not arise on the elementary level.

If the first five years of a child's life are crucial to the development of his lifelong personality, then the teenage period is as crucial to the developent of his lifelong value system. Both crucial formative periods of a person's life need to be filled with meaningful Jewish experiences and significant Jewish influences. The years from five to thirteen are the quiet, middle years. They are devoted to learning the skills on which a good postelementary education can be built, but which do not and cannot provide the crucial lasting ingredients.

• "Why Did My Child Learn So Little?"

"My daughter went to Sunday school for ten years, and my son to afternoon Hebrew school for five years, but they learned so little! It was supposed to be a good school, but they don't know anything!"

116

Many well-meaning parents who feel they have quite properly insisted that their children go to Hebrew school for years have expressed their sad disappointment with the results. Some bitterness may be expressed in later years by the students themselves. This happens to parents who have high expectations but who never understood the built-in limitations that face Sunday schools and afternoon Hebrew schools. Even the best of them have very limited goals. Most parents don't know or choose to ignore this and would like to think that a very substantial part of Jewish history, religion, and culture will somehow be magically transmitted to their children in a few hours a week.

So little was learned because so little time was spent in learning. A Sunday school usually offers two hours a week of instruction; an afternoon Hebrew school about six hours a week. As a school year consists of approximately thirty-five weeks, the Sunday school provides seventy hours of instruction and the afternoon school 210 hours. In ten years the Sunday school provides 700 hours of instruction; the afternoon school provides 1,050 hours in five years. If one thinks that this is a lot of learning, it should be remembered that a regular public school program provides, 1,050 hours of schooling in just one year.

It is not realistic to expect that the equivalent of one year or less of full-time school should be able to cover and do justice to an entire Jewish liberal arts program in Hebrew language; Jewish history; Hebrew Bible; Jewish laws and customs; prayers and synagogue skills; holidays and festivals; Jewish current events, which includes the study of the American Jewish Community and the State of Israel; and Jewish music. All this is in addition to assemblies, holiday programs, and other routine but necessary school functions.

Since all of these subjects are included in every afternoon Hebrew school program it is naturally impossible to do more than touch base superficially with each of them in the course of a six-hour week. The problem is even more pronounced in the Sunday school where the schedule is curtailed and does not permit more than one or two of these areas to be included in the curriculum.

While this issue will be discussed at greater length in Chapter Nine, parents should be realistic about the limited attainments possible in such programs of supplementary Jewish education. If expectations are truly greater as they should be, parents should either consider the day schools or make an effort to implement the suggestions on page 180. Under present conditions, if a Sunday or afternoon Hebrew school manages to inspire a student with a commitment to Jewish living or to continue his Jewish education elsewhere on higher levels, it has succeeded in its task.

• "I Need a Rabbi for the Children, Not for Me"

"I need a rabbi for the children, not for me!" Rabbis hear such comments time and time again. One might imagine it to be said by people so well versed in Judaism that there is little they can learn from the average rabbi. But, it is most often said by people who possess a meager understanding or knowledge of Judaism. Unwilling to admit Jewish educational shortcomings, they "protesteth too much" about their own need for a teacher.

Jews well grounded in Judaism feel the need to have rabbis and teachers not only for their children, but also for themselves. Rabbis teach them Torah, decide their religious questions, and guide and counsel them. Furthermore, while a good schoolteacher may suffice for the children, ordained rabbis are needed by the adult community. As a matter of fact, the more learned a community, the greater should be the rabbi whom they invite to guide and instruct them. The advice of the Ethics of the Fathers is apt: "Get a rabbi for yourself." Where adults do not acknowledge the importance of the rabbi for themselves, they compromise the rabbi's effectiveness with the young.

• "Teach Them To Be Jewish, Not Religious"

The above sentiment is sometimes heard from parents who possess strong feelings for the Jewish people and for the State of Israel, but who do not abide by the religious traditions and, perhaps, also cannot accept the basic principles of the Jewish faith. While anxious

118

to instill Jewish cultural and national loyalties in their children, they recoil from the possibility that their children may take to those religious aspects of their Jewishness that they themselves have long discarded.

Since the emergence of the Jew into Western society during the past few centuries, there have been a number of Jewish educators both in Europe and in America who have tried to create educational programs to transmit the rich cultural heritage and the high moral values of Judaism minus the weight of the religious disciplines. Such goals seemed possible for a generation that had itself been brought up in dynamic contact with a vibrant religious community and for one such generation this may work. However, experience has shown it to fall apart, not only in the diaspora where the dominant non-Jewish culture makes the greatest impact, but also in Israel where Bible and Jewish history is taught in every school and where national life is dominated by Jewish cultural patterns. For even Israel is no longer an island unto itself. The influence of mass worldwide communications is felt.

There is abundant historical evidence to show that in the absence of a religious base, the cultural accoutrements eventually wither away. The problem generated by this attitude is discussed in greater detail in Chapter One, where there is an additional analysis of the question raised.

There is also a measure of irony to the request. Parents turn mostly to the synagogues and to other religiously led schools for their children's Jewish education. Can one really ask the principals and teachers in such schools to agree to do the very opposite of what motivates them to engage in Jewish education in the first place? If they could not teach the faith of Judaism itself, most would not be teaching at all and most such schools would never have been launched.

The other side of the same coin is the claim that "we're not Orthodox," which is often given as a reason for not giving a child an intensive religious education or for not adhering to one or another of the traditional observances. While such a remark may be a statement of the fact, it is hardly a reason. For in the very essence of being a Jew, one has duties and one's fellow Jews have every right to call upon one to partake of the spiritual experiences of the Jewish people and to assume the disciplines and duties of Jewish "citizenship."

• "I Want Them To Choose for Themselves"

"I want to let my children make up their own minds about religion." Such comments are sometimes used as arguments against a traditional Jewish education. It is naive or self-deceptive to believe that one can be truly neutral and exert no influence one way or the other. Furthermore, no child is given a choice when it comes to values or behavior expectations about which the same parent feels strongly. Parents are constantly telling their children what is "nice" and "not nice," restricting their behavior when it is "dangerous" or "bad for them" or that runs counter to parents' set of ethical or moral norms. If, in the area of religious practice, parents do not offer such guidance, and do not permit others to do so, that in itself says something to the child.

When a child from a nonobservant environment is denied religious training, he is in effect being denied a choice. The doors to religious experience are closed to him. Separated intellectually and experientially from religious contact and influence, he is denied the information on which to make his choice and truly "make up his own mind."

If nonobservant parents are honest about wanting to give their children a real choice in the matter of religious commitments, they should seek to offset their own negative or indifferent views about Judaism with someone else's positive views. They should choose to balance their own nonreligious environment with a strong religious one. It can never be a fair match anyway because the home's influence is always much stronger. But, having come in contact with both, the child is at least given some basis upon which to later make a choice, either intellectually or emotionally.

• "I Don't Want To Be a Hypocrite"

Parents whose children ask that they begin to practice at home a religious observance learned in religious school sometimes defend their reluctance to do so by saying they don't want to be hypocrites.

The remark is also heard in response to a rabbi's plea for greater religious observance in general.

Hypocrisy is indeed a bad thing and nobody wants you to be a hypocrite. It occurs often enough without our using the word inappropriately and applying it too indiscriminately. Hypocrisy is not when one does not act in accordance with one's *feelings*. It is when one does not act in accordance with firmly held *beliefs*, when one preaches one set of values while personally behaving in accordance with a contrary set of values.

It is *not* an act of hypocrisy to observe a ritual because your child asks you to do so, even though you personally do not derive any satisfaction from it or believe in its importance. You do many things for your children that you might not do for yourself. You go with them many places you would not go to yourself because you don't enjoy them. Is that hypocrisy? You attend many meetings or functions you do not regard as important, yet for one reason or another feel a duty to be there. Is that hypocrisy? You pleasantly receive and show courtesy to people who bore you or whom you actually dislike. Is that hypocrisy or politeness?

Courtesy and consideration are hardly hypocritical. On the contrary, such thoughtfulness reveals that one believes that *politeness* and *civility* are preferable to rudeness, even if being rude is truer to one's inner desires at the moment. In the other examples, it is an *authentic* expression of one's belief that duty to the community take precedence over one's own pleasures; that it is important to bring gladness to the heart of a child, even if it means participating in some activity that one wouldn't ordinarily enjoy or want to do for oneself. The parent who introduces some traditional observances to satisfy the wishes of his child is being anything but a hypocrite. Parents' sincerity lies in acting on their desire to satisfy a child's innocent wishes and in their belief that it is important to provide one's child with Jewish experiences and direction. Who knows? The experience may move the parent to more positive feelings about his own faith and its way of life.

It is also not hypocritical for a person in religious doubt to try to observe as much as one can in any specific area of the Jewish faith. Nonobservance is not the only alternative to perfect observance. Ten percent is better than zero, forty percent is better than ten percent, and eighty percent is better than forty percent. In keeping kosher only at home, for example, one cannot be regarded as a kash-rut-observing person. It's what goes into the stomach that counts, not what goes on the dishes in one's kitchen.[3] But one is observing it *more often* than he would be if he did not have a kosher home, and that is a good thing. A man who puts on tefillin only once or twice a week cannot be called a tefillin observer, but it is certainly preferable to not putting them on at all.

Although faith in God is the basis for the entire Jewish faith, it is not hypocritical if in the presence of doubt, or in the absence of perfect faith, a person continues to live by Jewish values. A person may be acting in accordance with his conviction about the importance of the survival of the Jewish people, or in accordance with his belief that in this way he is preserving moral and ethical values he does regard as vital. That this is preferable to permitting the lack of faith to be reflected in non-Jewish behavior is indicated by the Midrash which credits the Almighty with the view that: "Would that they leave Me if only they kept My teachings." [4] By keeping the teachings, the possibility for a wholehearted return remains an ever real hope.

• On Staying Out of School on the Jewish Holidays

Jewish children and their parents constantly confront the problem of "staying out of school on the Jewish holidays," since many of the sacred days on the Jewish calendar fall during midweek when public schools are in session and the rest of America goes about its regular work.

Children attending the day schools do not have this problem because the day school calendar takes the Jewish holidays into consideration. But, for children in the public schools it can be a source of stress and inner conflict.

On the one hand, the rabbi and the child's religious schoolteachers urge the child to celebrate the holiday by staying out of school and coming to the synagogue for services. On the other hand, there is the pressure of missing schoolwork or important examinations. The conflict is even further aggravated if there is no holiday atmosphere at home to which the child can relate—the father is off to work and the mother is about her daily activities. Some parents even insist that their children attend school on these days, some because they are genuinely concerned about the child missing schoolwork, and others because having the child home all day interferes with whatever else they had planned.

Children of course are mostly delighted to listen to the rabbi in this matter and at the opportunity to legitimately skip a few days of school. It is a delight that should not be denied to them even if it means missing important schoolwork. Schoolwork can be made up. By staying out of school on these days the child is taught to assign priority to his religious commitments and to assert his Jewish self respect in an overwhelmingly non-Jewish society. It is an expression of Jewish dignity. Of course, the additional delight of rejoicing in the Jewish holidays themselves should not be denied them. Celebrating the holidays enriches the child's Jewish experiences and helps define his Jewishness. Staying out of school on the holidays is most meaningful if the entire family observes the festive occasion at home in the appropriate manner and attends services at the synagogue. Where this is done, absence from school on these days is seen as proper and necessary by both parents and children.

In the context of this discussion, it should be said that Jewish children who do attend school on these days make it harder for those who do not, especially in schools with large Jewish student bodies. When practically all Jewish children absent themselves on Rosh Hashana and Yom Kippur and on the first days of Passover, teachers are impressed with the religious significance of these days and take the expected absences into consideration when organizing their lesson plan. When only a small percentage of the Jewish students show similar conscientiousness toward the equally important biblical holidays of Sukkot and Shmini Atzeret (Simhat Torah), Shavuot, and the last days of Passover, teachers are apt to question the legitimacy of the religious claim by pointing to the greater number of Jewish children who have shown up. The teacher interprets such widespread attendance as evidence of the holiday's minor significance. It should be explained to teachers that either these other children come from homes that are not observant of the religious traditions, or possibly, in the case of the second day of each of the holidays, that they come from a Reform congregation where only one day of each of the festivals is kept. The advance cooperation of the teacher to avoid giving examinations on these days should also be obtained.

• What to Do About Christmas

Absolutely nothing! Jewish parents would do well not to get so upset at the very real holiday spirit that pervades all of America during the month of December. Recognize it for what it is—an important Christian holiday. Since most Americans identify with Christianity, the penetration of the holiday into the secular domain is inevitable. Don't try to fight it by going overboard on Hanukah, or by trying to imitate Christmas within the Hanukah framework. You don't have to harbor a sense of guilt about enjoying the holiday spirit of a neighbor. Feel free to extend wishes to your non-Jewish friends and neighbors so that they may have an enjoyable Christmas holiday. But, as for your own family, it's simply not yours to observe.

If you fear the impact of Christmas, the best way to counterbalance it is to provide your children with the excitement of all the Jewish festivals all through the year. Jewish children have very colorful and gala festivities on Passover, on Sukkot, on Simhat Torah, and on Purim, as well as on Hanukah. They are not in dire need of celebrating a Christian holiday.

Parents err when they try to build up Hanukah as the Jewish equivalent to Christmas. First of all, Christmas and Hanukah are not on the same level of religious importance within their respective traditions. Christmas is one of the two *major* Christian festivals; Hanukah is one of several *minor* Jewish holidays. Furthermore, in the American environment Hanukah cannot possibly be made as exciting to your children as they sense Christmas to be. Hanukah's observance is confined to the home and religious school. Christmas is in the public domain. Why should parents try to make the equation and have Hanukah pale by comparison?

Synagogues unfortunately contribute to this exaggerated buildup and to Hanukah's distorted weight in the Jewish religious calendar.

Synagogues annually publish the blessings for the lighting of the Hanukah candles in their bulletins, but they do not regularly publish the blessings for other rituals such as for the Sabbath candles, the lulav and etrog, the tallit and tefillin, the Kiddush, the Havdalah, and so on.

Some parents strive to offset the influence of Christmas by giving their children gifts on all eight days of Hanukah. This is very expensive and totally unnecessary. It suggests to the child that the Jewish way is preferable because gifts are more plentiful! In its own modest way, Hanukah can be plenty of fun if you plan family celebrations or special activities.

The celebration of Christmas in the public schools is another aspect of the problem. Parents should request that their children be excused from participating in the singing of carols or from acting in school plays that reflect beliefs that are contrary to their Jewish faith. Uncompromising supporters of Church-State separation insist that public schools are not the place for the celebration of any religious holiday—neither Christmas nor Hanukah. The pressures on the public schools usually result in the compromise of adding Hanukah to the school celebration. I'm not happy with this compromise because the incorporation of Hanukah into the public school framework minimizes the importance of the other more important Jewish holidays that are not celebrated in the schools. Still, some feel that the addition of the Hanukah theme to that of Christmas probably does give the Jewish child in a public school an important psychological lift and provides the child with a welcome alternative in an otherwise uncomfortable situation.

• The Adopted Child

Three questions arise: Should parents tell the child if their son or daughter is adopted, and, if so, at what age? And, what should a parent do if the adopted child's natural mother is not Jewish? Does legal adoption by a Jewish family automatically grant Jewish status to the child according to the Jewish law?

My own answer to the first question has always been a decisive "yes," and that the child should be told in as loving a manner as possible at the earliest possible age. The desire to hide that information from children is full of danger. They are bound to find out sooner or later and then the discovery could have a deeply unsettling effect. Also, a parent should not wait until the child reaches adolescence in order to tell him that he is adopted.

While I would not advise parents to make a special point of always telling people about the child being adopted, I would not treat it as information to be withheld should the subject come up.

From the very start impress your child with the idea that *being adopted* means *being chosen*. Your son or daughter was chosen to become your child, forever.

It is the parents themselves who may cause a problem by treating an adopted child with a kind of supersensitivity and caution that they would not have for their natural offspring. This can interfere with proper disciplining of the child. This may especially be the case if there are also natural-born children in the family. Love for children cannot be proven by more permissiveness.

From the religious point of view, a person who raises the child born to another is "as though he gave birth to him." All the duties that a child has toward one's natural parents, an adopted child has toward one's adoptive parents.

The dictum "as though he gave birth to him" does not, however, extend to the point where religious law confers the status of the parents on the child. Thus, if the adoptive father is a Kohen or a Levite, the adopted child does not assume that status. If the status of the natural father is not known, the child is treated as an Israelite, which is the status of the majority of Jews.

If the natural mother of the child is not Jewish, raising the child in the Jewish faith is not sufficient to confer the status of Jew on him, nor is it conferred by simply giving the child a Yiddish or Hebrew name, or blessing the child in the synagogue. It is necessary that the adopted child formally undergo the ritual of conversion. For a male child, this consists of circumcision and total immersion in a mikveh; for a female child, it is just the immersion in a mikveh.[5]

It is best to have this ritual of conversion take place as early as possible. While I would hesitate to undertake an immersion before the child is one year old, I have found the ages of one to three to be ideal. Properly done, the momentary immersion is swift and safe. The officiating rabbi can provide instructions on how to hold the child while the child is being immersed. Although it can also take place a few years later, when a child is able to swim a little, the child then requires an explanation. The child may want to tell his friends about it. Since it is assumed that the child knows that he is adopted, he can then simply be told that this is a ritual that Jewish law requires of all adopted children as a confirmation of their Jewishness. That Jewishness will be reconfirmed, they can be told, when they become Bar- or Bat-Mitzvah.

• A Death in the Family

Upon a death in the family, questions invariably arise about whether or not to take a child to the funeral and how to explain what happened. The tendency of many families to shield children below adolescence from the experience of attending a funeral service or going to a cemetery is in my opinion unwarranted and unwise. If the child is not permitted to go the child will think that it is because the adults are afraid to expose him to the "horror," and so the child's mind invents scenes that are more disturbing than if the child actually went and saw with his own eyes what takes place. The reality is surely less frightening to a child than the fantasies he can conjure up.

While children of three or four are too young to even realize what is going on, and it is probably best to leave them at home, I would have no hesitation in taking children beyond that age to a funeral service; and from the age of eight or nine, even to the cemetery. There is no harm in letting children see adults cry or grieve over the death of a loved one. It teaches children how to cope with a tragic loss. It is an opportunity for them to express their own emotions and release pent-up feelings.

If the child is moved to tears about what has happened, let the child cry it out. Crying is better than telling him not to cry and to restrain honest emotions. A child cries about things far less significant or painful. If the deceased was a parent or someone else in the family particularly dear and precious to the child, it can be a great source of consolation to hear a rabbi's words of public praise about the deceased. The awareness that others share one's loss can provide a strong psychological support to the child. This awareness can be felt most keenly at the funeral services. Finally, attending a funeral may impress a child with the mortality of the human being and the preciousness of life——and with the importance of taking care of oneself.

Although minors under the age of Bar- or Bat-Mitzvah are not required to abide by the rules of mourning that are observed during and after the week of shiva (the week of mourning that follows the burial), they should not be kept from participating in the practices if they show an inclination to do so. They should certainly not be sent off to school during the week of shiva as though nothing happened, unless they express a desire to go to school. A period of adjustment is as important for the child as it is for anyone else.

In explaining death to a child, one should avoid explanations designed to hide the difficult truth, namely, that death is the end of life for the body. To explain it as a permanent "sleep" can only serve to frighten a child from going to sleep lest he does not wake up; "going to heaven" should not convey the idea that the body also ascends. What should be conveyed to the child is that there is "a world to come" in which the soul of man continues to live, a belief imbedded in Jewish tradition. It can be a source of consolation. In answer to a request for more specifics about the "world to come," you as a parent really don't know yourself and you don't have to feel compelled to make up answers.

Avoid the temptation to blame God, to make Him into the "thief" who robbed the child of a precious possession. While the belief that "the Lord has taken away" is rooted in the Bible and "act of God" is a traditional explanation, the first and last part of that same passage also should be remembered: "The Lord gave ... blessed be the Name of the Lord" (Job 1:21).

• The Single Jewish Parent

Children being raised by a single parent involves some considerations that relate to their Jewish upbringing. The single status of a mother or father, due to either death or divorce, should not be allowed to interfere with the development of a fully Jewish home atmosphere. In that respect, some questions may arise.

We have come to think of lighting the Sabbath candles as being in the exclusive domain of the woman, while the recitation of Kiddush and of the Havdalah as a ritual performed only by the man. While this is the way it is done ordinarily, Jewish law is not so limiting. In the absence of a woman in the house, it is the obligation of the man to light the Sabbath candles. A father raising young children should assume that duty. If he has a daughter over the age of twelve, he may assign that responsibility to her if he so chooses.

In the absence of a man in the house, there are no restrictions for a woman to recite the Kiddush on Friday evening and the Havdalah on Saturday night. She is equally obligated in the ritual and may recite the blessings for herself and her young children. If she has a son above the age of thirteen, the privilege of reciting the Kiddush and the Havdalah for the household may be turned over to him.

A mother who is at home alone with young children should not only prepare the food for a Passover seder but should conduct it as well. Three or more women over the age of twelve can recite the grace after meals using the traditional introduction (except that the first word *rabotai* is replaced by the feminine *gvirotai*). There is no reason why the full Sabbath and festival dinner ritual cannot be fully performed by a single parent of either sex.

What about the propriety of dating by a single parent? It is perfectly all right especially since it is traditionally regarded as desirable for the single parent to find a marriage partner. Parents should, however, adopt for themselves the same restrictions that they might impose on their own teenage children, in terms of keeping reasonable hours and in behaving with discretion.

Single parents must also take the Fifth Commandment very seriously: "Honor thy father and thy mother" (Exodus 20:12). In death, there is no problem since the memory of the deceased parent is cherished and the deceased parent's good qualities are remembered and even enhanced. In divorce, this is a problem for there is a tendency to discredit the divorced mate in front of the children. The fact that parents have divorced does not free the child from observing the biblical commandment. Where one parent undermines that duty, by prevailing upon a child to disregard it when relating to the other parent, it tears away the respect for both parents and neither comes out ahead. The tendency to do so should be strongly resisted.

• "She's Not Jewish, but We're Only Dating"

The question of interdating usually arises among high school and college youth long before there is any thought of marriage. The same youngster who might be inclined to avoid marrying a non-Jew, may think nothing of interdating: "It's only a date. We're just friends, that's all."

Whether or not dating couples consciously see dating in that perspective, it always has been and still continues to be a form of courting, a prelude to marriage. It paves the way for a possible permanent relationship. What may be "only a date" is in fact the strengthening of a social relationship that may unexpectedly burst into love. And from love to marriage is a short step. "He's a nice boy" or "she's a nice girl" is all the more reason for concern that the relationship might become serious. If the end goal of marriage is not rationally desirable, a youngster should be impressed with the fact that wisdom dictates refraining from the initial steps that emotionally lead to it. Understanding on the part of youngsters, and firmness on the part of parents, may avoid much family anguish at a later time.

Interdating is not so much a problem in large urban centers with dense Jewish populations as it is in smaller Jewish communities and on college campuses. Children in a small Jewish community are likely to be socially integrated with their non-Jewish peers to a great extent. At the elementary and junior high school age, the friendships that develop with non-Jewish children are a natural extension of the relationship between classmates or neighbors. Invitations to birthday parties and other social events are mutually extended, and to forbid young children to socially mingle with those with whom they have come in constant contact is unreasonable. As a matter of fact, it may not be wise for parents to raise the issue during the preadolescent period. Dwelling on a problem can serve to make "forbidden fruits sweeter."

Since the goal is not to forestall friendships with non-Jews, but to stop short of marriage, the point at which some restraint must be established depends on the circumstances and may be different for different children. The maturity of the child is certainly a factor.

The best approach is to create an atmosphere of love and of Jewish content at home. A home that is conscious of Jewish history and of Jewish obligations has the best chance of instilling an awareness in the young person about the potential dangers of youthful interdating. It is less likely that a youngster from a happy family that keeps the Sabbath and that successfully creates a special atmosphere on Friday nights will be drawn away from Judaism. One is more likely to seek out other youngsters with the same interests as one's own. On this issue, serious, thoughtful discussions between parents and children should be held.

If part of the problem is the unavailability in one's own circle of Jewish youngsters of the opposite sex, parents have an obligation to create the opportunities for their children to meet and befriend other Jewish boys and girls.

When the time comes for the youngster to be on one's own, away from parental supervision and control, it is only the extent of one's commitment to Jewish living and one's understanding of the relationships that lead to marriage that will restrain one from starting out on a path that may lead to intermarriage.

• Intermarriage: "Dad, Mom, I Never Thought It Would Matter That Much to You"

Many dramas in many Jewish homes today begin this way. The fact that the non-Jewish young man or woman your child may bring home is a fine and decent human being and a good person, whose friendship anyone can cherish, makes it difficult to raise objections on a personal level. It does not, however, alter the basic Jewish objections to intermarriage.

Couples in love regard their relationship as a totally private affair. Yet, when the time comes to crystallize these sentiments into the bonds of marriage and the responsibilities of home and family, it is not exclusively a private matter. It affects all the members of the respective families. One not only marries a single person, but one enters into a relationship with an entire family—parents, brothers, sisters, uncles, and aunts. This relationship affects the raising of children. It affects the nature and strength and, therefore, the survival of the Jewish community.

Opposition to intermarriage stems from Judaism's emphasis on the home and family as the heart of the Jewish religion. The home is the focus of the practice of Judaism, even more than the synagogue. It is not without reason that the home is referred to as a *mikdash me'at*, a small sanctuary. The home is the core of Jewish religious life. Among the basic aims of a Jewish marriage is the creation of a family where Jewish tradition and faith will thrive, where the Jewish heritage will be kept and transmitted to yet another generation. Where one of the partners is not Jewish, these aims are hardly attainable. "Be thou sanctified to me according to the Law of Moses and Israel" is the *key* phrase in a Jewish marriage ceremony. If the union is not in accordance with the Law of Moses and Israel, this legal formula is hardly applicable. That is why no religious sanction is attached to such "marriages" even when they are contracted by civil statute or solemnized by other than Jewish religious criteria.

The inclusion of non-Jews in the membership of the "small sanctuary," which is the home, is no more tenable than their membership in the "large sanctuary," which is the synagogue. In both cases the non-Jew is welcome only as a guest and cannot claim privileges or perform the duties reserved for the members of the faith community.

The Torah saw intermarriage as a risk to the retention of the Jewish faith: "Lest you take wives from among their daughters for your sons, their daughters will lust after their gods and will cause your sons to lust after their gods" (Exodus 34:16).

Opposition to intermarriage also rests on the legitimate Jewish desire for self-preservation. Widespread intermarriage by a numerically small group simply does not go hand in hand with the survival of the group, spiritually or physically. The long history of Jewish assimilation into surrounding cultures, and their gradual disappearance as Jews, is sufficient testimony that such fears are not without foundation. As far back as two thousand years ago, there were ten million Jews (not much less than today) who constituted ten percent of the then known world population. The smallness of the Jewish people today is not due solely to their oppression in hostile surroundings and to physical destruction by enemies; it also stems in part from the ease with which they lost their identities in sympathetic and nonhostile environments.

In far too many cases, young people who plan to intermarry do not think that their parents will have strong objections. They have, after all, been taught to relate with great tolerance to all people. If there is nothing particularly Jewish about their own home environments, then there are no special Jewish commitments that should rule out a person who is not Jewish. While parental objections may be quite sincere, in that this may be the last straw of Judaism to which an assimilated family is clinging, the young man or woman does not at all see it that way. The parents' sudden protestations of Jewishness are seen as a rather hollow claim, if not actually racist in character.

The objections to intermarriage cannot begin after a non-Jewish partner is brought home. The answer to intermarriage begins years earlier with the warm and loving relationship parents maintain with their children, with the pervasiveness of Jewish values in the home in which the child is raised, and with a Jewish education which instills pride and pleasure at the prospect of raising one's own Jewish family.

• Reacting to a Marriage with a Prospective Convert to Judaism

How should one react to the news that a son or daughter plans to marry a prospective convert to Judaism?

If a person sincerely accepts the basic principles of the Jewish faith and commits himself to the Jewish way of life and people, and follows through with the required ritual of conversion, such a person becomes a full-fledged Jew.[6] Despite the non-Jewish background of the proselyte, and the family problems that may arise as a result of it, the marriage is essentially a marriage between two Jews. While there may be much family unhappiness about it, there are no religious barriers to such a marriage, except that a male of priestly descent (Kohen) may not marry a convert.

Once converted, attention must not be called to the person's non-Jewish background lest it be a source of embarrassment to him. The convert must be treated with love and consideration. The Torah teaches: "You shall love the stranger" (Deuteronomy 10:19). The daily prayers include a blessing for the righteous proselyte, who is grouped together with the pious and the just.

If it is, however, obvious that the non-Jewish person has not developed Jewish religious convictions and has no intention of adhering to its tenets, but only wants to convert to Judaism in order to qualify for a Jewish marriage ceremony, the same objections raised to a mixed marriage apply. A conversion to Judaism that is not marked by a distinctive change in a gentile's way of life is not an honest conversion. A brief course in Judaism is no substitute for a commitment to Judaism. Every liberally educated Christian should have a cursory knowledge of Judaism, and many non-Jews study Judaism with no thought of ever changing their religion.

It often happens that the barrier to a fuller observance of Judaism by the prospective proselyte is none other than the Jewish partner. The non-Jew may have discovered in Judaism the source for potential spiritual fulfillment and is prepared for serious Jewish religious commitment. But the Jewish partner, in having adapted oneself to a non-Jewish life-style, is not anxious for one's mate to get too serious about Judaism. The Jewish partner's only interest is to have a rabbi provide the non-Jew with a formal and legal change of status.

Although one born a Jew cannot have that status taken away, even if one doesn't practice it (unless he renounces his faith and converts to another), Jewish law does not confer the legal status of Jew on a person not born into it except on spiritual grounds. To convert to Judaism in order to become like other nonprofessing or nonpracticing Jews is a paradox. The classic declaration of the convert is that of Ruth, great-grandmother of King David, who proclaimed: "Your people are my people, and your God is my God" (Ruth 1:16). Conversion to Judaism cannot take place without both elements: becoming part of the people and part of the faith.

I know there are those who feel that in order to be considered Jewish one should only have to proclaim oneself a Jew, or only be required to go through a quick symbolic ceremony. I would think that such a policy of "open admission," that makes no demands, only cheapens and endangers Judaism. Religious conversion cannot be treated as cavalierly as a switch in membership from one political party to another, or can it insist on less prerequisites than that required for joining many fraternal organizations, or for becoming a naturalized citizen of some country. If it means anything at all, conversion involves changes that affect every aspect of a person's outer life, inner soul, and future salvation.

If the Jewish partner is the real barrier to a meaningful conversion, then the Jewish partner, too, should be encouraged to undergo a "conversion" to Judaism by studying and spiritually returning to one's own heritage.

• Reacting to a Mixed Marriage: After the Fact

What does one do if a son or daughter goes ahead with one's plans to marry a non-Jew who has not converted in either a civil or non-Jewish ceremony? Should one at that point submit to the inevitable and attend the ceremony? Should one help the couple celebrate the occasion? What do you do if they confront you with a *fait accompli* —the marriage took place? You are upset and deeply shaken. Should you, however, make a reception for them?

That such questions are even considered today is indicative of the tolerance to intermarriage that has developed in the Jewish community. Not too long ago, Jewish families actually sat shiva and mourned as "dead" a son or daughter who married out of the faith. All contact with one's child was permanently severed. Kaddish was recited. This custom is not practiced much anymore. But, the alternative to this extreme practice need not go as far as to personally celebrate the event. There is, surely, a middle position.

The mere presence of parents at the wedding ceremony, however grudgingly they come, is interpreted as a sign of acceptance. It eases whatever qualms the children may still inwardly feel and relieves whatever guilt that may still be burdening them. Furthermore, participation in an event that runs counter to one's own conscience and commitments is nothing more than an act of surrender. Painful as it is, Jewish parents should not only refuse to make a reception when confronted with such a decision by a child, but should also not attend the marriage ceremony. Friends and family who disapprove of intermarriage, and who are invited to such a ceremony, should also not attend. They should not hide the reason for their absence behind some other pretext.

The thought of "not losing a child" may be the motivation behind the grudging and belated acceptance, and one can only sympathize with parents in such a dilemma. The best thing parents can do to "keep *their* child," in the deepest sense, is to maintain their own self-respect. Some long overdue firmness may in the long run be the most effective way of "getting their child back."

In contrast to the complete and irreversible severance that marked the traditional Jewish reaction in the past, conditions today encourage contact and dialogue so that the door for the children's "return home" may be left open. Children should know that a Jewish marriage and a return to a Jewish life would pave the way for parental reconciliation. One does not reject a son or daughter. One rejects only what he or she is doing. It is vital that they too are aware of and understand the difference. The difference is important.

• Television: The Distorting Image

Jewish attitudes toward many of the religious and social problems confronting our generation are more likely to have been shaped by one of society's most powerful educational tools—television—than by the norms of the Jewish heritage. In its serious as well as entertainment programs, television is constantly conveying values and molding opinions. It brings the non-Jewish culture in which we live, and of which we are keenly aware, right into our own homes. Sometimes it projects values that undermine the very foundation of what Jewish parents are trying to teach their children.

Parents should, therefore, become more sensitive to the impact of television. They should not permit indiscriminate television viewing, but should evaluate the suitability of programs watched by their children. They should encourage their children to watch programs that contribute to their knowledge and wholesome upbringing and discourage them from watching less desirable programs.

We are also faced by the effect of too much television watching even where the content is not objectionable. Watching television is a passive involvement and too much of it deprives a youngster from developing his own potentialities. Permitting children to become addicted to television, even when it's not interfering with their schoolwork, does them a great disservice though they would like nothing better.

After television watching seemed to get out of hand in our home several years ago, we instituted some new rules. Everyone in the family was permitted to watch only five programs a week. Newscasts were exempt from this limitation, as were special educational programs of classics that teachers might assign. At first, our children didn't know what to do with their new found time. They would complain: "But I finished my homework . . . I've done all the studying I have to . . . I have nothing else to do." "That's fine," I would answer, "do anything else you want—go out and play ball, ride your bicycle, take crayons and draw, use your pottery set, play games, read a book, lie down and do nothing, do anything but watch television."

The children eventually learned to keep themselves busy. They developed new interests, started new hobbies, learned new skills, read many books, and did things they otherwise would never have done, but which brought them many pleasurable and productive hours.

To impose such restrictions, however, requires that parents also abide by the same rules. The same beneficial results might well accrue to them.

Part Three

SELECTING THE RIGHT SCHOOL

CHAPTER

8

~~~~~~

The Ideological and Pedagogical Differences Among Schools

B EFORE parents decide whether they prefer a day school, afternoon school, or Sunday school, they should consider the deeper issues of the educational orientation of the school on a number of important questions. If they live in an area where they have a choice among schools, such awareness will surely help them in making a wise decision. If they don't have a choice, parents should at least be aware of what the issues are and informed about their school's stand on them.

As expected, some of the differences are a reflection of the divisions among Orthodox, Conservative, Reform, and secular groups. But, there is much more to it than that. Labeling a school along "denominational" lines does not pinpoint the profound differences that exist among the "denominations" or the differences that exist within the groups themselves. Orthodox-oriented day schools, for example, can be subdivided into several widely divergent orientations. While Conservative and Reform-sponsored schools present a more homogeneous image because of their respective national organizational unity, important differences will be found there too.

Even the so-called "nondenominational" schools sponsored by a community cannot claim to be "objective" or "neutral." There really is no such thing as a "neutral" education. The famous American educator, John L. Childs, once wrote: "A manifestation of preference for certain patterns of living as opposed to others . . . is inherent in every program of deliberate education." [1] Community-sponsored "nondenominational" schools mean only that they are not *formally* affiliated with any of the religious or secular groups. In an educational-philosophical sense, however, they cannot help but reflect a "preference for certain patterns of living" that corresponds to one or another of the ideological groups in American life.

A report on Jewish education sponsored by the Association for Jewish Education notes the similarity in the official statements of each of the groups:

> There is a striking similarity in the official statements of fundamental or guiding principles and aims in Jewish education made by all the Commissions representing the three main "denominational" organizations of American Jewry. There seems to be very little indeed in the statements of one group that the others can object to. Certainly this does not mean that their actual curricula and teaching are the same; for evidently very wide differences can and do arise from the spirit and the manner in which these principles and objectives are "spelled out" in educational activity. These differences in selection of materials, in method and in the spirit of instruction, can be very important. That such differences do *exist* is common knowledge. [2]

In view of this, it is important for the layman to be able to cut through the heavy layers of verbiage about "Jewish values," "appreciation for Jewish life," and "transmitting a heritage," and discover how these aims are in each case reduced to reality.

Since each school is really independent and may well represent a conglomeration of views, adopting different positions on different issues, I do not believe that it would be fruitful to approach the problem of clarifying the differences among the schools by repeating the *official* educational pronouncements issued by each "denomination." This can only further encourage parents to fit schools into formal categories, rather than help them think about the issues. For in the final analysis, it is not the "label" that counts, but what is really believed and practiced. I have, therefore, decided to avoid focusing on the official views of those national groups with whom the schools are formally affiliated. Instead, I think it will be more useful to indicate what the major religious and pedagogical issues of the day are, and then to explain where the different schools seem to stand in relation to these questions. Then, parents should decide how they themselves feel about these issues and make them a prime consideration in their selection of schools. Needless to say, the schools in all groups welcome all Jews, regardless of the family's level of religious observance, regardless of the "denomination" with which the family may or may not be formally affiliated.

Attitude to Torah

The Torah is the heart of the Jewish faith and gives substance to the Jewish people. Without Torah, there is no Judaism and the term "the Jewish people" has no meaning. It is the Torah that has sown the seeds for a unique and distinctive "faith nation." It is the Torah that is the source of the Jewish way of life, its values, and its ideals. It is the Torah that is the core of all Jewish education.

In its most specific sense, Torah is the Pentateuch—the Five Books of Moses, the heart of the Hebrew Bible. In the form of a scroll, it is given the central place of honor in every synagogue where it is kept in a Sacred Ark and where it is read as a key portion of every Sabbath and festival service. Torah is also the Oral Tradition which was long ago recorded in the Mishna and the Midrashic commentaries and which provides us with the Jewish understanding of Scripture. Why then should the attitude to Torah be an issue?

In the traditional normative view, the source of Torah has traditionally been set in God's *Revelation* to all the Children of Israel at Sinai and in subsequent Revelations to Moses and the Prophets. However one interprets the manner of these revelations, the traditional view is that all the teachings of the Torah derive from God, that the Torah laws were given to guide Jews in every generation, and that the laws are not subject to abrogation by the decisions of men.

Contemporary liberal theology ascribes the source of Torah to the spiritual genius of man. While insisting that it was written under "divine inspiration," it is no more "divine" than other great literary and artistic masterpieces. While the teachings of the Torah that suit the thinking and temperament in each generation are to be respected, the people in each generation have the right to alter, change, or entirely ignore that which no longer seems desirable.

According to the normative view, the child is taught that the Torah is eternally binding on all Jews and, even under changing conditions, people must adjust to its demands and abide by its basic teachings. According to the second view, the Torah is adjusted to the desires * of men. The teachings of the Torah are approached selectively with the authority residing in the people themselves.

According to the traditional view, we are to judge moral and ethical issues by the eternal standards of Torah. All other religious, political, social, and philosophical ideologies are rated good or bad, right or wrong, based on the degree to which they are compatible with what the Torah teaches. According to the second view, the truth of Torah is dependent on the degree to which it is compatible with the political, social, or philosophical views prevailing in society and to which one may be committed.

Nontraditionalists regard the traditional view of Torah as "unscientific" and as a barrier to accommodate society's changing social patterns. The traditional response is that Revelation is outside the realm of scientific investigation, and that the conviction of its truth is based on faith and the historical experience of the Jewish people. Traditionalists charge that the nontraditional view involves a rejection of one of Judaism's basic foundations, and that such rejection spells the erosion of Judaism and its eventual demise.

The theological disputes in the traditional camp about the nature of Revelation, and how one believes Revelation took place, should not be permitted to becloud the basic issue. Such disputes are not

---

* I use the term *desires* rather than the more compelling term *needs*, because except for such needs without which the body cannot function, all other "needs" are quite relative and determined by the social circumstances in which one lives.

new, and differences of opinion on the matter are to be found even among the great biblical commentaries. What really matters in this disagreement is the very bottom line, i.e., the conclusion drawn as a result of those views. Is the Torah seen as the will of God binding on all Jews in every generation or is it not so regarded? The answer to this question bears directly on whether Torah is taught as the ever-meaningful Word of God or as ancient Hebrew literature.

A nonobservant parent may feel dismayed at having one's child taught that the laws about keeping the Sabbath or avoiding certain prohibited foods are found in the Torah and reflect the Will of God. But, the traditionalists argue, if Torah is not taught in that spirit, then what compelling religious basis is there for keeping the law of "Honor your father and mother," and the entire range of the Torah's ethical and moral teachings? If the ritual commandments can be compromised to accommodate the changing mores of a society, so can the ethical and moral commandments. If part of the Torah is made subject to personal whim and not to a "higher code," it is inevitable that all the other parts will also be so subjected.

All shades of Orthodox opinion are united in their conviction about the divine basis of Torah. Their educational institutions convey this faith. Reform and secular opinion lack this faith and their educational institutions reflect that position. Conservative opinion varies. The specific orientation of a Conservative-sponsored school will to a large degree depend on the conviction of the rabbi or the principal in charge and of the teachers engaged to teach Torah.

While the issue as presented assumes that all but the secular group share a belief in God, the truth is that among those who regard Torah as human wisdom rather than divine teaching, there are also others who do so as a result of a still more fundamental disagreement: They do not believe in the existence of God in the first place.

Naturally, schools that reflect the secular philosophy function from this premise. And while the Reconstructionist movement, an outgrowth of the Conservative movement with whom many Reconstructionists still identify, uses the term "God," their understanding of God is radically different from the traditional one. God is not seen as a spiritual power beyond humanity and nature to whom man can relate. Although a belief in God is at the core of classic Reform theology, an exhaustive self-study of the Reform movement, known

as the Lenn Report which was completed in 1972, yielded the as-
tonishing information that twenty-eight percent of the Reform rabbinate saw themselves as either nontraditionalists, agnostics, or
atheists. Only ten percent believed in God, "in the more or less
traditional Jewish sense." If only those who were ordained after 1967
are taken into account, the percentages change to forty-two percent
and three percent respectively.[2a]

This report rather accurately confirms what was written by Jakob
J. Petuchowski, Professor of Theology at the training center for Reform rabbis, Hebrew Union College, several years earlier:

> The young rabbi [who openly proclaimed himself an atheist] merely
> admitted in all frankness to a mental attitude which he is by no
> means alone in representing, though several of his peers would pre-
> fer the more innocuous designation of "humanist" . . . One would
> normally assume that an ordained rabbi, wishing to join a rabbinical
> organization, is a theist of some kind. . . . That the assumption is
> no longer valid in 1965 has by now become obvious. . . . The time
> has come for the American Jewish community to be told and in so
> many words—that mere membership in the Central Conference of
> American Rabbis does not *ipso facto* imply commitment to what are
> commonly considered to be the religious affirmations of Judaism. . . .
> The community must learn to understand that the title "Rabbi" as
> used by members of the Central Conference is no guarantee for any
> definite and specific religious views which the community might ex-
> pect of the holder of such a title.[3]

Parents, too, must begin to understand that the contents and the
goals of any educational endeavor are greatly influenced by the
depth and nature of the educator's belief in God and Torah. This
varies greatly among those today engaged in Jewish religious
education.

Attitude to Acceptance of Halakha

A parallel issue that determines the character and the tone of a
Jewish education is the educator's attitude to *halakha*. Halakha is
the term applied to the final authoritative decision on any specific
question of Jewish law and practice; it is also the overall term for

Jewish law. Halakha involves a legal, judicial way of making decisions and solving problems. Although faith in God and in His Torah is the basis out of which Halakha grew and continues to develop, its major emphasis is on the correct way to implement all ritual, moral, and ethical teachings. Halakha translates the concepts and values of Judaism into everyday living. Within its scope are the commandments contained in the Torah, the wide range of rabbinic legislation, and the practices that through usage have been sanctified in Jewish life. The practical duties are collectively called the *mitzvot maasiyot*.

The crux of the issue is whether or not there is a basic acceptance of halakha as binding upon oneself, so that even laws that are clearly of rabbinic origin are accepted as no less binding than the laws passed by the Congress or the state or the city legislatures. Or does one see halakha, even the Torah commandments in the system, as entirely optional or voluntary in character? [4]

The attitude held by teachers and educators on this issue determines whether Jewish laws and practices are taught as rules to live by or only as information about customs and rituals practiced by some Jews. Parents should understand that Jewish laws and customs are taught along such widely divergent ways.

What should be appreciated are the profound differences between these two approaches. American educators understand the difference when they express their unalterable opposition to the introduction of religion in the public schools and yet do not hesitate to recommend teaching *about* religion. According to them, teaching religion means "securing acceptance of any one of the numerous systems of belief regarding a supernatural power." Where "securing acceptance" is eliminated as a goal, they have no fears in teaching *about* the historical highlights of respective faiths, about their basic doctrines, and the meaning of their various symbols. In this way, American children of the Christian faith might even be taught about Judaism just as Jewish children could be taught about Christianity. These educators would agree that the study of Jewish subject matter, or that of any religion for that matter, without the aim of "securing its acceptance" does not constitute *religious instruction*. Their views are valid. Parents should stop for a moment and consider if Jewish schools, whose stated aim is to provide Jewish religious instruction, are fulfilling their responsibility if the instruction is not intended to "secure acceptance" of what is being taught.

The rejection of the binding character of halakha is invariably a consequence of the nontraditional attitude toward Torah, discussed in the previous section, although it is possible for one to make a conscious and deliberate decision to accept halakha as binding even where one posits its source in human rather than divine authority. After all, the law-abiding citizen chooses to obey civil law knowing its "man made" background. A person does so as a matter of loyalty to the public good rather than out of special awe for the legislature or fear of the law enforcement agencies.

The rejection of halakha is characteristic of the Reform and secular groups and of some of the elements within Conservatism. All Orthodox opinion and a part of Conservative opinion is committed to halakha as the key to the perpetuation of the Jewish faith and its sanctified way of life.

While there are three, four, or even more so-called "denominations" in Jewish life today, they can all be reduced to two major camps, the traditionalists and the "progressives," depending on their attitude to this question of halakha. The traditionalists include all the Orthodox and some of the Conservatives. The others reflect the nontraditionalist approach. While the "progressives" may be quite sincere in wishing to perpetuate Judaism, and may indeed believe that it is possible to do so outside of the halakhic framework, the traditionalist camp insists that the rejection of the halakha starts the erosion of the Jewish way of life and is an open invitation to assimilation and intermarriage. Whether a child's Jewish education is oriented toward the traditionalist or the "progressive" view of halakha may, therefore, make a profound difference on the child's Jewish future.

Attitude to Application of Halakha

There is yet another issue concerning the attitude to halakha. This issue divides the traditionalists themselves, and the divisions are reflected in the educational process. This has to do with the relative flexibility or rigidity of halakha. Though sharing a faith in Torah as the revealed Word of God, and in halakha as the process by which that Word is applied to new conditions and circumstances, differences of opinion arise on many specific questions. In truth the opinions of religious scholars and masters of halakha have never been frozen into one mold. The Talmud itself provides sufficient evidence for the fact that within the halakhic framework, there is room for flexibility, for differences of opinion, and for lenient and stricter decisions. And it has been this way throughout Jewish history. Regarding these differences of opinion the Talmud says: "These and these are the words of the living God," ᵇ because all such opinions basically emanate from faith in God and out of a sincere desire to perform His will. Such opinions are not seen as being either "less religious" or "more religious." Opinions that reflect sound rabbinic scholarship on both sides of a question, and are capable of being defended under the accepted rules of halakhic interpretation, represent equally legitimate expressions of the Jewish heritage.

Today, as always, a wide range of opinion is found among those committed to halakha. At one end of the spectrum there are those who view any innovation even in local custom as inherently forbidden, for no other reason than because it is new. They see Jewish law as not tolerating any modifications in practice. At the other end of the spectrum are those who call for bold halakhic decisions by the Talmudic giants of our day. They emphasize the dynamic role of halakha as a decision-making system that has always risen to the challenges posed by changing circumstances. In between are those who would agree, but insist that the halakhic process, as all judicial processes, must be deliberate and avoid the far-reaching dangers that inevitably come in the wake of hasty decisions. Above all, they say, halakha must be wary of embracing the fleeting fads of society.

Schools within the Orthodox camp reflect views that range from the strictest view of halakha to the most lenient or liberal views. Conservative educators who share a commitment to halakha will be found alongside the latter group. Educational institutions within the same traditional "denomination" may differ depending on whose halakhic opinions their educators follow on any given problem. A number of issues which divide the traditionalist camp will be discussed later in this chapter.

In the ongoing struggle between the institutions of Orthodoxy and

Conservatism, it is natural to pick the most vulnerable position found in the opposing camp and attack that position as though it represented the entire movement. Conservative spokesmen like to charge the Orthodox with religious fundamentalism, "with little allowance for a creative human dimension," with thinking of Torah and halakha as a "finished and closed" system in contrast to its own approach which is then presented as one of progressiveness within the tradition. Orthodox spokesmen, on the other hand, charge the Conservatives with the same radical destructiveness of the tradition of which the Reform were guilty.

While there are indeed groups within Orthodoxy who represent such fundamentalist thinking, it is not characteristic of Orthodoxy as a whole where, as indicated, a great diversity of views coexist with the more literalist attitudes. And while there are elements in Conservatism today that are indistinguishable from Reform, in both their theology and their practice, that too is not characteristic of the entire movement, where the commitment to the tradition is certainly far stronger than in Reform, and where some reflect a commitment that is almost indistinguishable from liberal Orthodoxy. In any given Conservative school, one has to know the views of the educators before one can say with certainty whether the school is oriented toward the traditionalist or the "progressive" camp.

Attitude to "English" Studies: The Secular Arts and Sciences

As state law requires that a general education be given to every child, and every philosophy of Jewish education today makes provision for such studies, it may come as somewhat of a shock to learn that it is even an issue. Yet it is an important intra-Orthodox issue and it is the focus of major differences among schools they sponsor. In fact, it is an issue that has a long and honorable history. How does Jewish tradition view the study of subjects outside the realm of Torah? Is such knowledge essential or only peripheral? Is it desirable or only tolerated?

The differences of opinion that surround the study of worldly wisdom are based on Talmudic disputes where there are three basic approaches. One is a proscription against the study of "Greek wisdom," because it contained heresy and was potentially dangerous to the retention of the faith.[6] Another view does not regard such study as forbidden, but sees it as infringing on time that should be devoted to the study of Torah[7] and conforming with the verse in Joshua (1:8): "You shall meditate in it day and night." Still a third view justifies such study. Accordingly, the requirement of the verse "to meditate in it day and night" is met by setting some time aside each day and evening for the study of Torah.[8]

These basic differences have been with us ever since, except that the debate was extended to include not only the study of heretical philosophies, but also the general fields of human knowledge. Thus, Rabbi Moses Isserlish, whose glosses on the Shulḥan Arukh form an integral part of that Code of Law, permits the study of general wisdom only if it is limited to occasional study and if it does not involve a fixed or systematic program of learning, because that would infringe upon the obligation to study Torah.[9]

The Chafetz Chaim was even more restrictive. He came out against studying "outside books," meaning the literature and philosophy of the Western world, for fear that it paved the way to assimilation and for too much integration with the non-Jewish society.[10] Such views were characteristic of many Jewish scholars for many centuries and is characteristic of some religious circles to this day. Some think of general education as a threat to religious faith, others regard it simply as taking time away from the more important study of Torah.

On the other hand, there were always those who saw Jewish education as including general wisdom. Maimonides (1135–1204) clearly established the desirability of becoming well grounded in the general sciences[11] and had guided his own disciples in such a way. Such study possesses intrinsic value and merit in that it contributes to the greater understanding of Torah and of God.

Rabbi Baruch of Shklov, one of the disciples of Rabbi Elijah, the Gaon of Vilna (1720–1798), wrote in the preface to his Hebrew translation of Euclid, published 1780, that he was once asked by Rabbi Elijah, the renowned halakhic scholar, to translate into Hebrew as much worldly wisdom as possible so that he could make it available to Jewish readers and "increase knowledge among our people in Israel." Rabbi Baruch quoted the Gaon as having said that "according to the degree to which a person lacks information from the other wisdoms, he correspondingly lacks a hundred-fold in Torah wisdom, for Torah and Wisdom are fused together." In other words, Torah and general knowledge were not to be thought of as rival disciplines engaged in a struggle for supremacy, but rather as interdependent knowledge emanating from the same source. The Gaon was of the opinion, according to Rabbi Baruch, that the lack of general knowledge among Jews invites disdain in the sight of the nations and actually constitutes a "desecration of God's Name." This is given as one of the Gaon's reasons for entering upon the project of translating the wordly classics into Hebrew. He was starting with Euclid only because he believed that "it was the foundation upon which all the other wisdoms are built."

The case for general studies was also made most forcefully by Samson Raphael Hirsch in his well-known philosophy that saw the educational ideal in terms of "Torah with the way of the land" (*Torah im derekh eretz*). According to him, God revealed himself not only in Torah, but also in nature and in history—and their study was, therefore, also essential to attain religious understanding.

Isidor Grunfeld, the rabbinic scholar, wrote in his introduction to Hirsch's *Judaism Eternal:*

> If anything had been forced on the Jew, it was not adherence to, but his exclusion from, general culture and education. When at the beginning of the nineteenth century, the Jews again found their way into the world of science and general education, they came in reality back to their own. For the estrangement was not organic but superimposed. It had by no means arisen from the essential character of Judaism. Just the contrary was true, as the golden era of Jewish history in Babylonia and Spain had shown.[12]

During those periods, Judaism had embraced every facet of intellectual and spiritual life, with Talmudic learning interacting with all other learning. Spiritual isolation and intellectual withdrawal became dominant only as a result of increased persecution in the period following the Crusades in Europe. Furthermore, he wrote, "apart from the enormous support which the study of Torah, Mishnah and Talmud receives from secular knowledge, the whole task of the Jew as a servant of God in the world depends on his insight into the natural historical and social conditions around him." [13]

The existence of "wisdom" apart from "Torah wisdom" was first appreciated by the sage of the Talmud. The Midrash says: "If a person tells you that there is wisdom among the nations, you may believe it; if he tells you that there is Torah among them, do not believe it." [14] What better evidence that general knowledge was always held in high esteem than the fact that Jewish law provides that a blessing be recited when seeing a man, even a non-Jew, who is a great scholar in some secular field: "Blessed art Thou, O Lord our God who has shared His wisdom with mortal man."

Nonetheless, echoes of the struggle between those who welcome secular learning and those who resist it continue to be heard to this day. While all Orthodox day schools teach all the required secular subjects, and most place great stress on achieving excellence in the general program because they regard it as intrinsically desirable, there are some that do little to encourage the child to excel in them because they look with indifference upon secular studies. While most schools encourage their students to go on to university training, and their graduates have compiled a long list of achievements in both undergraduate and graduate studies, some schools are known to actively discourage their students from pursuing a university education. If this means bypassing professions that require a university background, so be it. Greater importance is attached to Talmudic scholarship than to middle-class American status symbols.

While these differences in orientation are not too evident on the elementary level, they become more pronounced on the secondary level where general "English" studies and Torah studies begin to compete more sharply for the available time. While most Hebrew day schools strive to strike a balance, some are known to lean more strongly in one direction or the other.

Attitude to the State of Israel

Another issue that has come to divide Orthodox-sponsored schools is, ironically, the result of their unusually strong feelings about the great significance of the Land of Israel for the Jew. The issue is not concern for the well-being of the State of Israel. Except for a small handful of extremists on the far right (ultra-Orthodox) and far left (ultra-Reform), Jews of all shades of opinion and belief are united in their desire for a sovereign Jewish state and in their support of Israel's struggle to survive. But among religious Jews, the dream of Zion redeemed does not end only with the restoration of a sovereign Jewish state upon the ancestral soil of the Holy Land. Theirs is a vision of a country ruled by the laws of the Torah, of a country where leadership is in the hands of the religiously faithful, and where the nation's entire way of life reflects the "kingdom of priests and the holy nation," "a light unto the nations," that Israel was meant to be. It is a far off spiritual goal perhaps, but it is this very spiritual aspiration that kept the dream of "Next Year in Jerusalem" alive for countless generations and that provided the basis for the restoration of modern Israel.

And while the Jewish state, which has been restored after a lapse of almost two millennia, reflects so much of the Jewish culture and faith, its basic institutions and national life are conducted as in any democratic secular state. It is not a theocracy. Its leadership and political parties reflect the entire spectrum of political and religious ideologies; its legal system draws upon the jurisprudence of Anglo-Saxon and other laws. The reality falls short of the religious ideal.

In reacting to this reality, there are those who, nevertheless, treat the restoration of the Jewish state, however imperfect, as a manifestation of the Divine Will and as the beginning of the process of redemption leading to the Messianic era. Yom Atzmaut, Israel's Day of Independence and the day of Jerusalem's liberation, are treated as religious holidays, marked by the recitation of the same special prayers reserved for other religious holidays. "Hatikvah," Israel's national anthem, which originated in the Zionist movement, is sung. This group is ever ready to work with all other Jews to advance both their own program and the common goals. In Israel this ideology is reflected in the political program and the educational system supported by the National Religious Party.

However, there is a powerful element in Orthodoxy for whom the religious imperfections of Israel are the decisive factor. While great numbers of those who share this view actually live in Israel, and others go there to study and even to settle, they assign no religious significance to contemporary developments, and are among the severest critics of Israel's government. They do not celebrate Yom Atzmaut or Yom Yerushalayim; they do not sing "Hatikvah." If they live in the diaspora, they generally do not regard it important to study the Hebrew language. In Israel, this ideology is reflected in the platform of the Agudat Israel which, though represented in the Israeli Knesset, never joined the Zionist movement, primarily because it disapproved of the secular orientation of the Zionist leadership, few of whom observed traditional religious practices. While it is safe to say that proponents of both sides of this issue educate children with deep Jewish loyalties and concerns, the issue does generate strong feelings and arouses heated controversy.

Inasmuch as there are parents who share strong feelings on this issue, and want their children to reflect either one view or the other, they should be aware that Orthodox-sponsored day schools tend to lean in one direction or the other on this matter.

Religious Qualifications for the Teacher: Must the Teacher Be Religious?

Must a teacher of Jewish religious subjects personally be a believing and practicing Jew in addition to possessing sound educational and pedagogical credentials? Each school sets its own policy, but the policy is a direct outgrowth of the school's ideological position. The answer depends on the objectives of the school. If the educational purpose is to convey information only, then the teacher's own beliefs and way of life are not pertinent. If, however, the purpose is to instill Jewish values, encourage a Jewish way of life, and inspire a measure of faith, then the teacher's beliefs and practices are very pertinent. The personal example set by the teacher is crucial to the child's spiritual development. A nonbelieving teacher cannot possibly teach religious subjects in a manner that encourages faith or that leads to religious commitments. A teacher who does not observe the Sabbath or the dietary laws, or attend the synagogue, cannot possibly encourage pupils to do so. A teacher that does not believe

155

or practice one's faith cannot be expected to teach others to believe or to practice that faith. The teacher's own lack of commitment is sure to surface.

Orthodox institutions have been quite uncompromising on this issue. They feel that teachers of Jewish subjects, and the figures of authority in a Jewish school's administration, must embody within themselves the educational and religious goals of the institution. Schools operating under Conservative auspices also indicate preference for such staff, but in practice have been flexible on this issue. Conservative schools often do engage teachers who fall short of the religious standards that they themselves strive to instill. Schools under the auspices of the other ideological groups do not consider personal religious practices or convictions a factor in the selection of staff. Community-sponsored schools are generally flexible on this issue.

The Curriculum: "Talmudic" or "Hebraic"?

Among Orthodox-affiliated day schools, above the elementary school level, there are wide differences in the curriculum of the Jewish studies program. There are schools that concentrate almost exclusively on the study of Talmud and its many commentaries. Others divide the time evenly between the study of Talmud and the study of such other areas as the Hebrew Bible,* the Codes, Hebrew language and grammar, Jewish history, and Jewish thought and philosophy. Still others concentrate more on the latter subjects and devote little time to the study of Talmud. Schools of the first type are sometimes referred to as "Talmudic." Schools of the second and third types are sometimes referred to as "Hebraic."

While such variations in Jewish studies curriculum usually distinguish entire schools from each other, there will be found some

---

* The Hebrew Bible consists of the following divisions and books: *Pentateuch* (Five Books of Moses)—Genesis, Exodus, Leviticus, Numbers, Deuteronomy; *Prophets*—Joshua, Judges, Samuel I and II, Kings I and II, Isaiah, Jeremiah, Ezekiel, The Twelve Prophets (Hosea, Joel, Amos, Obadiah, Jonah, Micah, Nahum, Habakkuk, Zefania, Hagai, Zechariah, Malachi); and the *Writings*—Psalms, Proverbs, Job, Songs of Songs, Ruth, Lamentations, Ecclesiastes, Esther, Daniel, Ezra, Nehemiah, Chronicles I and II.

secondary and higher schools of Jewish learning that provide these different tracks within the same school. The students themselves may have the choice as to the program they wish to follow.

The "Talmudic" curriculum characterized the European *yeshivot* and is still characteristic of the traditional *yeshivot* and schools of higher Jewish learning. To study Torah means to study Talmud. The Shulhan Arukh, the authoritative Code of Jewish Law, stresses the obligation to spend a third of one's time in the study of the Hebrew Bible, a third in the study of Mishnah, and a third in the study of Gemara (Talmud).[15] It is, however, a gloss by Rabbi Moses Isserles that gives expression to the tendency to limit Torah study to Talmud. He writes: "There are those who say that in the study of the Babylonian Talmud which is an admixture of Scripture, Mishnah and Gemara, one fulfills one's obligations to all the areas." In truth, one finds no rulings by either the Earlier or Later Authorities that make this restriction mandatory or that prevents the broadening of the sacred (*limudai kodesh*) curriculum. The contents of that curriculum differed in different periods of Jewish history and in different Jewish communities. All through the ages, scholars of great note have seen the need to include other studies that are part of, or relate to, the Jewish heritage. And so do many scholars today.

One cannot hope to attain true Jewish scholarship without an in-depth knowledge of Talmud. To the extent that study of Talmud is missing from a curriculum, or is only superficially touched on, there will be a serious gap in the understanding of the Jewish heritage. At the same time, the study of the Hebrew Bible, Jewish thought and philosophy, and other Jewish studies is essential to a full appreciation of Judaism's vast spiritual richness.

Hebrew Language or Jewish Religion?

While the day school may find it possible to pursue a number of educational goals simultaneously, the afternoon school is compelled, by virtue of its limited schedule, to concentrate on one of several possible objectives. It is in the afternoon school context that the question of priorities arises. Which goal should be given priority: (1) Hebrew language or (2) training in the skills needed for participation in the life of the synagogue?

For many decades, Jewish education reflected the influence of those who made Hebrew language the core of their educational philosophy. And while knowledge of Hebrew is certainly the key to the understanding of all the religious texts, the limited time that afternoon schools could devote to Hebrew language study makes it extremely difficult for students to acquire a satisfactory level of comprehension of the classical Hebrew found in the texts, or of conversational fluency in modern Hebrew. Except for a small handful who take to language study and are motivated to continue beyond the elementary level, the educational result of this approach leaves much to be desired. The average youngster is left with neither a working knowledge of Hebrew nor with the religious skills to serve him at home or in the synagogue.

Other afternoon schools make no pretense about teaching Hebrew, except for developing fluency in reading the language so that the child will be able to participate in the services of traditional congregations, and to recite the prayers and the blessings for the many home rituals in Jewish life.

This orientation has the drawback of leaving bright youngsters very dissatisfied at being unable to understand a language they are taught to read. Such schools are often condemned for failing to teach comprehension of the Hebrew language, although they do invariably teach hundreds of basic Hebrew words. Unfortunately, a good understanding of the classical Hebrew found in the prayer book and the Bible requires far more hours per week and more years of study than youngsters in afternoon Hebrew School are required to go. On the other hand, if one acquires fluency in reading, deficiency in understanding can be somewhat overcome by using books with English translations to provide a general understanding of the Hebrew passage.

A delicate ideological question hangs beyond the periphery of the issue. To what extent are the goals of Jewish education achieved by the study of Hebrew language only? Hebrew ideologists naturally maintain that Hebrew language study is the core of Jewish education and contributes to the achievement of its goals. Others view Hebrew as a necessary tool for Jewish education, as a useful key to the Torah and all the other religious texts and to the understanding of Jewish concepts. But in itself it does not constitute anything that by any stretch of the imagination can be called a Jewish education. There are after all many Israelis, Jews, and non-Jews alike, who speak Hebrew fluently and yet know very little about Judaism.

Language of Instruction: Hebrew or English?

Almost all day schools offer instruction in the Hebrew language. Yet, Hebrew is an issue that divides the world of the *day schools* even more than the afternoon schools, because fluency in the Hebrew language is a realistic goal in the day schools. Since comprehension and conversational fluency is best advanced by using it as the language of instruction in the entire Jewish studies program, it is around this question, rather than about courses in Hebrew, that there is a parting of the ways. Some day schools use Hebrew as the language of instruction for Jewish studies while others conduct their Jewish studies program using English.

Those who object to the use of Hebrew as the language of instruction do so from a number of considerations:

1. Since Hebrew is not the natural tongue of the American child, there is the feeling that there will be a deficiency in the comprehension of the subject matter the child is studying. Since the major goal is to make the youngster proficient in Torah and the other religious texts and to emphasize religious observance, there is a feeling that these goals will be compromised if the child's comprehension is not on as great a level as it is in English.
2. The greater amount of time that must be given to Hebrew in the earlier grades, if comprehension and fluency are to attain a satisfactory level, makes it necessary to delay the study of Humash (Pentateuch) by a year, or possibly two. Progress in the studies regarded as most important is, therefore, reduced.
3. Perhaps another unarticulated reason also plays a role in the objections. A great percentage of the teachers, qualified in every other

respect, simply do not themselves have sufficient command of the Hebrew language to speak it fluently, and so use a pedagogical rationale to justify their method. In the final analysis, this is a most compelling pragmatic reason.

Educators who strongly support the use of Hebrew as the language of instruction make the following points:

1. Agreeing that comprehension is important, educators maintain that once there is an adequate grounding in Hebrew language, there is no reason why comprehension in Hebrew cannot equal that of English for most class discussions. If, on occasion, the teacher feels compelled to make some complicated explanations or feels that the students' Hebrew is inadequate for some particular discussion, and any good teacher should be able to sense this, there is no reason why at such times English should not be employed. No one suggests inflexibility to the point where no English word may be uttered in the classroom by either the teacher or the pupil.

2. Overall proficiency in Hebrew is an extremely valuable tool for the study of Torah and all the other religious texts. It not only leads to added comprehension of the very subjects considered most important, but it also leads to quicker and greater progress in all those subjects. It enables a student to immediately get to the meaning of the text and to probe deeper, without getting bogged down and wasting time on word translations.

3. The delay in beginning the study of Ḥumash, caused by early concentration on Hebrew, is more than offset by the quicker progress that can be made in Ḥumash once there is a better grounding in Hebrew. Israeli children, for example, for whom Hebrew is their native language, are able to study the Hebrew Bible with a speed and comprehension and measure of depth that are years beyond their American counterpart. And the American child who gets a grounding in Hebrew, while he still cannot compete with his Israeli counterpart, can do substantially better than those who must continue to struggle with Hebrew word translations throughout their school careers.

4. The revival of Hebrew as a living language, the tongue spoken daily in Israel, makes it imperative that Jewish children everywhere develop its fluency. The very real prospect in this day and age that Jewish children will one day visit Israel for a longer or shorter period of time, and perhaps even choose to settle there, provides additional impetus for developing proficiency in the language.

160

The Hebrew Pronunciation: Ashkenazic or Sephardic?

The pronunciation of Hebrew words passed down through the centuries took two major forms: Ashkenazic and Sephardic.* The Ashkenazic pronunciation, with its several variations, was used by Jews throughout eastern, central, and western Europe. The Sephardic pronunciation, with its variations, was used by Jews stemming from countries along the northern and southern coasts of the Mediterranean, and from such countries as Yemen, Syria, and Iraq.

The differences between the two are not great but they are distinctive, very much like the differences in English between a Southern accent and a Bostonian accent. It is not a question as to which pronunciation is correct. Both are correct, except that to speak one in an environment where the other is being spoken sounds odd.

When the Ashkenazic European Jews settled in Israel at the end of the nineteenth century, and through whose efforts the Hebrew language was revived, had to decide which pronunciation they were going to use, they opted for the Sephardic. While the historic basis for their decision is open to question, they believed that the Sephardic pronunciation was closer to the Hebrew spoken in ancient Palestine. The new settlers also preferred the smoother, less harsh, and more melodious sounds of the Sephardic pronunciation. On the basis of their decision, the Sephardic pronunciation became the dominant pronunciation in modern Israel.

American Jewry who stem mostly from Ashkenazic European stock, learned to pronounce their Hebrew using the Ashkenazic pronunciation. Hebraists who immigrated to America, some of them great Hebrew writers, spoke a fluent and grammatically perfect Hebrew in the Ashkenazic pronunciation, but the development of Israeli Hebrew made the Sephardic dialect the universally accepted form. Those who had learned their Hebrew in the Ashkenazic accent learned to shift into the Sephardic.

---

* The two most distinct differences in the two dialects are: (1) The vowel pronounced in Ashkenazic "*aw*" is in most instances pronounced "*ä*" in Sephardic and (2) the *taf* letter of the alphabet is always pronounced *t* in Sephardic, whereas in Ashkenazic it has the sound of *s* when it appears without a dot. Two other differences, somewhat less pronounced, are: (1) The vowel "*ö*" in Ashkenazic is pronounced "*aw*" in Sephardic (2) the vowel "*ä*" in Ashkenazic is pronounced "*ě*" in Sephardic.

The difference in Hebrew pronunciation has no bearing upon the differences in prayer liturgies that are also divided along Ashkenazic-Sephardic lines. One may follow the Ashkenazic liturgy, but use the Sephardic pronunciation, as is done in Israeli congregations and in some American synagogues. On the other hand, Hasidic Jews use a liturgical form described as Sephardic, but retain the Ashkenazic pronunciation used by their forebears.

There is no longer any question. Conversational Hebrew is taught today in the Sephardic pronunciation. But since Jewry outside of Israel learned their Hebrew prayers in the Ashkenazic dialect, most synagogues continue to use that dialect for prayer services. Many Jews resist change, some simply because it would be very difficult for them to master and adjust to the new pronunciation; others for halakhic reasons.

The issue in Jewish education is which pronunciation to use when teaching children to *daven*, read their prayers. It is not an issue that affects Jewish values or lifelong Jewish commitments, but it occasionally generates arguments. The issue can be argued pragmatically and halakhically. On the afternoon school level where the major goal is not to make the child proficient in Hebrew but to prepare him for participation in the synagogue, the question here is a practical one. Until such time when the adult congregation decides to shift to the Sephardic, shall the children in that congregation be taught a pronunciation that will make it difficult for them to follow the services later? After all, it is really not necessary that Jewry in the diaspora give up its dialect just because Israelis use another. As the language of prayer, the two can continue to exist side by side as was the case throughout the centuries. If, however, the Sephardic pronunciation is the long-range goal, then a long-range view might be in place. By teaching the new pronunciation to the children, that will then become the dominant pronunciation of the congregation over a period of many years.

The other level is on the day school level where mastery of Hebrew is one of the major educational aims. The issue is there seen in halakhic terms. Some religious authorities are of the opinion that the Hebrew prayers must be recited in the same pronunciation used by their forbears. Others point to the fact that no similar ruling was ever set for the variations of pronunciation within the Ashkenazic form itself. The Polish, Hungarian, and Lithuanian pronunciation of Hebrew differ markedly one from the other, although the Lithuanian version eventually became the dominant and "correct" form.

In any event, the desire on the part of some educators and rabbinic authorities to retain Ashkenazic Hebrew for the purpose of prayer, and the impossibility of teaching children to read and speak in different pronunciations simultaneously, has led to some interesting variations in the practice of day schools under Orthodox auspices. Some teach only the Ashkenazic pronunciation, both for prayer as well as for conversation. Others use the Ashkenazic pronunciation for the first four or six grades, until such time as the children have mastered the prayers, and then shift to the use of the Sephardic pronunciation for Hebrew conversation in the upper grades. Still others have responded to the Israeli influence and teach the Sephardic pronunciation from the very first grade for both prayer and conversation.

In concluding this chapter about the different issues in Jewish education, I wish to note that the last few issues may seem peripheral to the central task of raising Jewish children. After all, does it matter what Hebrew accent is used? The wise and thoughtful parent will, however, consider the ideological issues discussed in this chapter very carefully. The school's position on these questions will greatly affect the quality, the direction, and the effectiveness of the child's formal Jewish education.

CHAPTER

9

*Schools to Choose Among:
Their Strengths
and Weaknesses*

I F we have gained some insight into the ideological and pedagogical questions that may divide schools from one another, it is
now possible to consider the strengths and weakness of the several
types of Jewish schools in America. They are: the day school, the
afternoon school, and the Sunday school. Each school sees itself as
providing Jewish children with "a Jewish education." In their respective promotional material, the sponsors of all three types stress
the need for "a sound Jewish education" and urge you to send your
children to their institution. Yet all three differ considerably in their
educational goals, in their basic structure, and in their course of
study offered. The criteria for what constitutes "a sound Jewish
education" obviously differ widely.

Parents are the ones who make the choice as to the type of Jewish
education to give their children if they live in areas where such
alternatives are available. If they wish to give careful consideration

to all the educational options open to them, they should have a clear idea of what can be expected from each of the three types. Parents should have some awareness of their respective strengths and weaknesses.

In making this evaluation, I ignore the ideological and pedagogical differences already discussed. While these differences have profound educational implications and ultimately influence the preferred type of schooling, I restrict myself in this chapter to evaluating each type of school irrespective of its ideology or its sponsoring group.

While the Sunday school has always been the chief instrument of the Reform movement's educational program, and the afternoon school has been that of the Conservative movement, and the day school that of the Orthodox groups, none of the three "denominations" sponsors only that type of school with which they have been most identified. Orthodox groups have always sponsored and continue to sponsor afternoon schools, and even a Sunday or other one-day-a-week program. The Conservative movement has widely sponsored Sunday schools, and, in recent years, has begun stressing the importance of day schools and actively promoting their development. Reform congregations now also widely conduct midweek afternoon schools, and several day schools under Reform auspices have seen the light of day.

To remove all ambiguity arising from differences in terminology, I take note of the parallel names by which these types are known. Sunday schools frequently designate themselves as religious schools. The afternoon school is popularly referred to as either Hebrew school, Talmud Torah, or synagogue school. Many day schools, particularly those under Orthodox auspices, are also called *yeshivah* (plural, *yeshivot*). Outside of the United States, the term *yeshivah* is reserved for schools on a secondary or higher level of Jewish study which devote themselves wholly to the study of Torah.

The Best: The Day School

Let me start with the best. The day school is really the oldest type of Jewish school in America since it was in existence during the Colonial period and for the better part of the nineteenth century before the free nonsectarian public school system came into existence. However, the Jewish studies portion of these schools gradually eroded to just several hours per week, their religious spirit became diluted, and, by 1870, these day schools eventually disappeared from the scene.

The contemporary day school is a development of the seeds sown at the end of the nineteenth century and during the first decades of the twentieth century. Over 90 percent of all Jewish day schools now in existence were founded since 1940. Their rapid growth during this period is indicative of the growing appreciation of the day school as an instrument for the total education of the Jewish child.*

While day schools differ considerably in their ideology and in their educational methods, the general aims of all of them are directed toward preparing the child for Jewish living, for participating in American life, and for developing personality.

Unlike the other two types of Jewish schools, the Jewish day school is the *primary* framework for the child's *total* schooling. It is not merely a supplementary program of studies. It meets during regular school hours and, within that time framework, offers a combined program of both Jewish and general studies. The general studies curriculum is usually patterned after that of the local public school system if that system is operating on an acceptably high level. The same textbooks are used in most instances. The teachers who teach the general subjects are state- or city-licensed personnel who have taught or are still teaching in the public school system. They need not be Jewish. The Jewish studies program of the day school consists of a minimum of fifteen hours per week of classroom instruction.

The term "parochial school" is sometimes used to describe the day school. If what is meant by that term is a school of a religious character attended in lieu of the public school, then it is, of course, descriptive of the day school. If, however, what is meant by "parochial" is a school narrow in its educational outlook, then the term is most inaccurate inasmuch as day schools provide an extra, broader, albeit Jewish dimension to that offered in the public schools. If

---

* From less than 30 Jewish day schools concentrated in the New York area, with an enrollment of less than 10,000 students in 1940, there were in 1975 over 500 day schools scattered throughout the United States and Canada with an enrollment of over 80,000 students.

what is meant by "parochial" is the Jewish equivalent of a parish school operated and controlled by the church, then the term is also very misleading as most *yeshivot* or day schools are not associated with any synagogue. The manner in which they are founded, supported, and controlled, is closer in concept to the private school or to the Jewish communal school. The day schools probably reflect parental control to a far greater degree than do the other types of Jewish schools.

A typical day school is a community of Jewish children where Hebrew study sessions begin at about 8:30 in the morning and last until about noon; the general subjects are studied from approximately 12:30 P.M. until about 3:30 or 4:00 P.M. In some day schools, half the school may be on the opposite schedule to enable the school to provide full-day employment for both Hebrew and English teachers. In still other schools, Jewish and general study classes are interspersed all through the day.

In the lower grades of the day school, we find the same range of Jewish subjects studied as in the afternoon school, except that progress is much swifter and the results more gratifying. For example, fluency of Hebrew reading and conversational ability in simple Hebrew is often attained by the end of the second grade. By that time too, a day school child will be quite familiar with the traditional synagogue service. Hebrew grammar and composition, Jewish history, and the laws and customs of Jewish life are studied in the lower grades and continue to be studied at every grade level.

The study of the Hebrew Bible is begun by the third grade. The goal is to complete major portions, if not the entire text, of the five Books of Moses and the Early Prophets before the end of the eighth grade. In the fourth or fifth grade, the child will be taught to read the special Hebrew script in which many of the biblical commentaries are printed and the child will be introduced to the study of the famous biblical commentary known as Rashi. Time will be allotted to a summary or review of the weekly Torah portion read in the synagogue and the major lessons derived from it. In the fifth or sixth grade, the study of Mishnah will be introduced. It is through the Mishnah that the student is introduced to Talmud.

The very few pages of Talmud studied by the end of the eighth grade are mostly intended as an introduction to its thought processes and to acquaint the student with the basic method of studying Talmud. In those day schools where there is greater emphasis on Talmud, several chapters of Talmud are studied together with one or more of the commentaries.

In some schools Hebrew literature is part of the elementary curriculum which may consist of the stories and poems of Hebrew writers of the past century or of the *Aggadic* portions of Talmud. Jewish home economics is a popular subject for girls at many day schools. Special school assemblies held throughout the year relate to both the Jewish and the American holidays.

Dr. Alvin I. Schiff in his comprehensive study, *The Jewish Day School in America*, states:

> In comparison to those attending the other types of Jewish schools, there is marked superiority among day school students in Hebrew Language, Jewish History, Holidays and Observances. In addition, the day school student enters into the study of areas totally untouched by the others such as the original unabridged classics of the Jewish faith: The Pentateuch, the Prophets and the Writings; the Talmud, the Code books, the traditional commentaries such as *Rashi*, and other Rabbinic writings.[1]

The fifteen or more hours a week devoted to Jewish studies provide a realistic basis for a child to learn to understand and speak Hebrew fairly well; to acquire a basic knowledge of Bible, Jewish law, and Jewish history; and to develop insights into Jewish values. It provides the elementary groundwork for more advanced Jewish studies.

Since Jewish values are not actually taught as a subject, but are drawn out of the classical sacred literature of the Jewish people, the day school student who studies the sacred literature is also more apt to be influenced by the Jewish value system.

An equally important reason for the greater impact a day school makes upon a child is also because it provides many Jewish experiences during the routine life of a school day. The lunch hour, for example, provides an opportunity to master blessings recited before and after eating; school vacations are not keyed to Christmas and Easter, but to the Jewish holidays highlighting the Jewish festivals to a far greater degree than when holidays are limited to school assemblies; daily worship quickly prepares the child to participate in synagogue services; extracurricular activities are often related to contemporary Jewish affairs and concerns; and school bulletin boards provide constant visual reminders that make Hebrew and Jewish life a continuing experience throughout the day. Even as the child studies the general subjects—mathematics, science, social studies—the child does so in a religious, Jewish atmosphere and not in a secular, non-Jewish one.

It is not necessary that the day school child split himself into two distinct personalities: one secular and one Jewish. Even as one imbibes Western culture and learns to express oneself in the music and the arts, the child can give honest expression to his inner Jewish self.

It is also within this total Jewish environment that the child learns the values he shares with all other Americans—the lessons in American history, geography, civics, and local community. America's national holidays, as distinct from the Christian ones, are celebrated in the day school as they are in any public school. Thanksgiving Day, Washington's and Lincoln's Birthday, Veteran's Day, Memorial Day, and Independence Day all serve to emphasize the child's American heritage and good citizenship. The child's American identity does not suffer because his Jewish identity is strengthened.

The total Jewish environment of the day school is not looked upon favorably by everyone. Some regard it as "narrow," as denying a child the opportunity to get to know the children of other faiths and races, thus not preparing him for the "real" world. To such people, the day school smacks of too much separatism. Yet parents prepared to compromise with their children's Jewish education to avoid the alleged "narrowness" of the day school, are very often the same ones who move into predominantly Jewish neighborhoods where the local public schools are populated almost entirely with Jewish children, where even the teachers are likely to be mostly Jewish, and where there is little real opportunity for interfaith and interracial contacts. If day schools provide a narrow ethnic experience, so do the public schools located in densely populated Jewish communities.

I once received a phone call from a public schoolteacher from a small Michigan town about an hour's drive from our suburban Detroit community. She had heard that our synagogue had a school and requested permission to bring her class to visit it. She told me that she was arranging visits to several *Jewish* schools in the area in an effort to broaden the awareness of her class about children of other faiths. When I pointed out to her that our school was only an afternoon Hebrew school and not a day school, she said that it did not matter.

During the visit, I asked her what other schools they were visiting. When she first called, I had forgotten to ask her this question. I thought that she had arranged to see one or more of the three day schools in the area. Her answer surprised me. They were on their way to the Roosevelt School, which was none other than a local public school with a practically 100 percent Jewish student body. In her mind, this, too, was a *Jewish* school.

Yet, this "Jewish" school was lacking in all Jewishness. Its school calendar revolved around the Christian holidays, not the Jewish ones; the values inculcated were either secular or Christian, rather than being authentically Jewish. If it didn't have any negative effects, it certainly didn't contribute anything that was Jewishly positive.

Parents who want their children to come in closer contact with non-Jewish children, even during early childhood, could achieve these aims far better by living in religiously, ethnically, and racially mixed neighborhoods. In this way, children who attend the day school have the opportunity to make friends with non-Jewish neighbors and associate with them during after school hours, weekends, and the considerable vacation periods. There are, after all, only 180 school days in a 365-day year. Neighborly relations and common play activities can contribute far more to interfaith and interracial goodwill than sitting together in the same classroom.

The truth is that the charge of narrowness is quite spurious. The "narrow" ethnic experience of the day schools only partially balances the influences of the general non-Jewish environment to which the child is inevitably exposed. By now, there is considerable evidence to show that those educated in day schools have had no problem in learning to relate to non-Jews and in taking their place on the American scene. Researchers have found that "there is no difference in intergroup attitudes between day school and other Jewish children of similar background." The success of day school graduates in every walk of life should also lay to rest any fears about its "narrowness."

The day schools not only make a Jewish contribution to the cultural pluralism that enriches American society, but they provide a psychological basis for the child's own personality development. The famed psychologist, Dr. Bruno Bettelheim, emphasized that a child's awareness of his own ethnic group can be critical in his development in terms of his personality, his feeling of self-worth and identity. A child deprived of the opportunity to grow up in his own specific ethnic atmosphere with its special customs and culture, harboring feelings that he never "belonged," is in danger of spending his adult years self-consciously seeking an identity.

The ability of the day school to provide a full general studies program equivalent to that of the public school within a half-day schedule is also a matter of record. Day schools are required to conform to the educational requirements set by the state, and they do. Many exceed those requirements. While it is true that not as much time is devoted to some of the minor subjects and free study periods are eliminated, this has had no adverse effect on the academic achievement of day school students. On the contrary, national achievement tests in reading and other subjects consistently place day school students above the national average. Day school students continue to win more than their share of university scholarships and national academic awards. In view of the facts, the question should not be how the day schools manage to cover the same ground in less time, but what the public schools are doing with the extra time at their disposal.

Although the day school offers a double program of studies, it is not intended solely for the superior child. There are some Jewish day schools who try to enhance their elitist role by limiting admission to those of superior intelligence and ability. I am personally opposed to that practice. I believe that day schools should be open to children of all ability levels. Except for the very slow learner who finds great difficulty in coping with a minimum study program, every child can benefit from the intellectual stimulation that results from the double program. Studies have shown that the learning of a second language is best begun in the early school years between the ages of five and seven. Far from being "too hard," the double program stimulates even an average child to higher achievement in both areas and trains children to cope with greater academic loads and more intensive learning situations. While a sixteen-hour credit load may be all an average public high school graduate can cope with in college, the average graduate from a day high school finds the sixteen-hour academic load almost a relief, and the intensive demands made by some outstanding universities as not excessive.

Inasmuch as it is not the main purpose of the day school to serve as a private school for general studies, but to provide an intensive Jewish education, it is important to note that the day school escapes some of the built-in problems that beset the supplementary Jewish schools.

The day school child goes to school when all other children go. By the late afternoon, when the child is tired and other children are at leisure, the day school child, too, is free. In the lower grades, the child is also likely to be free on Sunday mornings. The child does not have to attend yet another school with additional hours of study with whatever restlessness or resentment it may arouse.

Hebrew and Bible, generally regarded as more difficult for the young child than the general subjects, are studied during the morning or early afternoon hours when the child is still most alert, when the child's concentration is at its peak, and when the child can make the most progress. In marked contrast to children who attend the afternoon schools, children in the day schools also tend to *enjoy* their Jewish studies more; a greater percentage is inclined to continue on to Jewish day high schools.

One school, one administration, one report card for all subjects influence the child to relate with equal seriousness to both Jewish and general studies. Favorite subjects are just as likely to be Torah or Hebrew language as arithmetic or science. Jewish history is not treated as any less important than world history or American history. Teachers of general subjects do not become the "real" teachers, while the teachers of the Jewish studies are seen in a secondary role. Unless parents themselves influence the child's attitude by assigning more weight to one area over the other, no artificial barriers are created between general and Jewish learning. The child's own interests and abilities are given a broader scope within which to function and be expressed.

Since the day school is widely regarded as having a more effective religious influence on the child, parents who are themselves not observant or only moderately traditional express fears about an inevitable clash of values within the home. The fact that a large percentage of children now attending the day schools come from nonobservant homes should perhaps reassure such parents that the problem is not all that serious. If it were, the general enthusiasm such parents continue to show for the day school could not be sustained, and these children would not for very long have remained enrolled.

But it is a problem, and it merits discussion. The problem actually exists on several levels: that of the parents, that of the child, and that of the school itself.

There are several types of nonobservant parents who choose the day school. There are those who themselves feel a yearning for Jewish life and are happy to encourage their children to adopt the Jewish religious practices taught at the school. Such parents often make a sincere effort to draw the family closer to Jewish living and to adopt more of the traditional observances.

Other parents want their children to acquire the higher level of Jewish knowledge the day school provides and are pleased with the cultural aspects of Judaism the child acquires, but resist adopting some of the traditional ritual observances of Judaism. They insist on maintaining a dichotomy between home and school. Where such a dichotomy exists, experience has shown that it is the family's values that will have the greatest impact upon the child. In those instances where the school does make the greater impact, it is more likely that the child will create a religious island for himself at home where he will do what he believes he is required to do rather than create conflict.

The problem of possible conflict between a nonreligious home and the Jewish school should not be seen only in relation to the day school. It exists also with the other types of Jewish schools, wherever Jewish laws and customs are taught, and wherever the school aims to instill faith and conviction. A particularly effective teacher in an afternoon Hebrew school or even a Sunday school can cause the same clash of values to erupt. Where it erupts in an afternoon school, the demands made by the child on the home are likely to be even more intense and persistent, precisely because he has so few other avenues where he can express his religious yearnings and commitments. Where he spends the major part of his day in the

173

intensely Jewish environment of the day school, and where other extracurricular weekend activities are available, *there may be less need for him to pressure parents to adjust their lives to his convictions.*

One views with some bemusement that the same problem of value conflict can exist also with the Reform Sunday school. The chairman of the religious school committee of a large Reform congregation once wrote:

> The children . . . suffer from a kind of mild schizophrenia. *Here* are the rabbi, director, cantor and teachers; *there* are the parents. . . . *Here* is supernaturalism, prayer, the Ten Commandments, Jewish customs and ceremonies. *There* is science, atomic facts, sex and Mickey Spillane, American ways and values. . . . So it comes about that the attempt to make children more secure as members of the Jewish community has in many cases the opposite result. . . . Uncertainty and insecurity are increased and the children's suspicion of adult hypocrisy is strengthened because the *traditions, customs and beliefs of the religious school are at complete variance* with home life.[2]

The problem, however, also exists from the child's point of view. For the child who comes from a nonobservant home, the problem is one of confusion and perhaps also of guilt. On the one hand, he is taught that God requires of Jews that they abide by a whole range of commandments and observances. On the other hand, he realizes that his own parents whom he admires and loves fall far short of the standards. The child may resolve this home-school conflict by simply detaching himself emotionally from the religious values taught by the school, doing in school what is expected of him there, but reverting to parental standards when at home. Or he may search for support from teachers and friends and seek to observe at home as best he can the Jewish tradition he has been taught.

How well this confusion and/or guilt is resolved depends to a large degree on how intelligently and sympathetically the school and the religious teachers meet the challenge of the problem. Here it becomes the school's problem. The wise teacher will first instill in the children the traditional lessons about respect and reverence for parents. These commandments are part of the same Torah that calls for the observance of the Sabbath. The teacher may then explain parental nonobservance as due to a lack of training over which they had no control, but as a result of which they never learned to fully implement the Jewish way of life, and that once launched in one direction it is difficult to change habits. Examples of simple habits difficult to change can be given from the child's own experience. The teacher may emphasize the point that the child's very presence at the Jewish school is an indication of parents' positive attitudes and their interest in his religious growth.

To the child who cannot implement all the religious teachings in the immediate present, they can be presented to him as the goal to strive for when he is on his own and assumes responsibility for himself. Meanwhile, the school serves as a source for Jewish experiences from which the child will be able to draw upon as he grows older.

While the problem is not limited to the day school, it emerges as more of a real problem in the context of the day school only because the day school is taken more seriously by both children and their parents and makes a greater impact on their lives. Still, there is no reason to fear serious conflict that cannot be satisfactorily resolved with goodwill and understanding.

From time to time, one comes across instances where children are sent to a day school although parents have little interest in an intensive program of Jewish education for their children. Decades ago, nonreligious working mothers found the nine-to-five schedule of the day schools a very convenient way to have their children cared for until they returned from work and, because of it, many children were saved for Judaism and grew up to contribute much to Jewish life. More recently, the deterioration of local public schools in some changing neighborhoods provided the incentive. In some instances, the private nature of the Jewish day school or the excellence of its general studies program was the spur. Although the right reason for attending a day school is preferred, I do not disparage the attendance of those who turn to the day school for the wrong reasons. In this matter, the Talmud provides a guideline: "A good deed done out of improper motives will eventually be done for the proper motives." [3] One does not make the purity of a man's motives a condition for accepting a charitable contribution from him; neither should one's motives be a deterrent when he seeks to have his children admitted to a school that offers intensive Jewish training. Our primary concern must be with the Jewish development of the child. Such a parent must only be given to understand the nature of the program, the aims of the school, and what will be expected of the child and the family.

When evaluating the day schools, it is important to note that those who are themselves alumni of day schools are its most ardent fans. Studies show that the great majority of day school alumni, while they vary widely in occupation, prefer the day school for the education of their own children even in the face of the considerable costs involved. Can one ask for a better testimonial of its worth?

Second Best: The Afternoon School

The afternoon school is the type chosen by parents who want their children to attend the local public school and, yet, want them to have a better Jewish education than the Sunday school can provide. It is a system in which many parents place great hope; a hope that is shared by some Jewish educators.

Most afternoon schools in America are conducted by synagogues representing every one of the "denominations." In some cities, these schools are conducted by a central educational agency under community auspices.

The standard program consists of about five to six hours of instruction per week. The hours are usually divided into three, two-hour sessions meeting for two afternoons during the week and on Sunday morning. The United Synagogue Commission on Jewish Education recommends for sound pedagogic reasons that these hours be apportioned into four, one-and-a-half-hour periods so as to increase the frequency of the learning situation.

The afternoon school is generally programmed as a five-year course that begins when the child enters the third grade of public school at about the age of eight. Most afternoon schools also sponsor primary departments where the child may attend kindergarten, and first and second grades on a one-day-a-week basis. Some have high school departments in addition to the elementary five-year course.

A typical afternoon school program devotes the better part of the first year to teaching the child to read Hebrew and to introduce the child to the prayer book. The child is also taught to write the Hebrew alphabet and to understand and speak simple Hebrew words and sentences. The rest of the time is devoted to each of the holidays with its special customs, ceremonies, and historical background; and to teaching the early biblical period of Jewish history.

During subsequent years, the first ten or fifteen minutes of each session is usually spent in prayer. The major events and periods of Jewish history are studied as are the important historic figures in what amounts to an elementary survey of Jewish history. A great percentage of the time continues to be spent on developing reading fluency, increasing basic vocabulary, and furthering the child's understanding of simple Hebrew stories. Some attempt is made to encourage Hebrew conversational skills. The holidays continue to be reviewed each year, and selected Jewish laws and customs are studied.

Beginning with either the third or fourth year, the study of Bible is introduced. This usually takes the form of studying selected passages from the five Books of Moses, sometimes from the actual biblical text, but more often from textbooks containing the biblical stories in condensed form. Almost all schools allocate some time to a discussion of Jewish current events. Children's current event magazines may be used.

The *minimum* aims of this educational program are to enable the child to proficiently participate in synagogue services, to give him a basic Hebrew vocabulary that allows him to understand and speak simple Hebrew, to acquaint him with the details of all the festivals and the basic Jewish laws and customs, and to familiarize him with some major events in Jewish history.

Over the past several decades, professional Jewish educators have continuously been seeking ways to improve the quality and the effectiveness of the afternoon school program. They are constantly devising new textbooks; developing audiovisual material; and experimenting with new teaching methods in Hebrew language, Bible, and other subjects. The standard five-year course most schools now offer is already an expansion of the four- and even three-year courses that had prevailed for many years. There is also great emphasis on requiring teachers to be licensed in both Jewish subjects and pedagogy.

Yet, the educational results of the afternoon schools have been disappointing. The percentage of pupils who actually achieve the level of learning and Jewish commitment that the afternoon schools aim for is low. Jewish educators have been known to bemoan the shallowness of this educational endeavor, terming it "a mile wide and an inch deep." Although an inspiring and effective teacher is probably the key to achieving better results from the afternoon school, there are some built-in difficulties that are imbedded within the very structure of the afternoon school and that adversely affect the effectiveness of the best of teachers and of the best administered schools. It is important that parents understand what these problems are.

From a purely pedagogical view, classes are held at just about the worst time of the day. After a six- or seven-hour day in public school, the child is mentally and often physically fatigued. It is asking a great deal to expect a child to maintain at that hour a high level of interest and concentration, the two necessary ingredients of learning.

Any Hebrew schoolteacher will tell you that class behavior and learning progress is far better when the class meets on a Sunday morning than when it meets on a Tuesday or Thursday afternoon. Of course! It is surprising that the children behave as well as they do, that class discipline is as good as it is, and that some learning actually does take place. Great energy and skill is exerted by Jewish educators to overcome this barrier to learning. But the barrier exists in the very set up of the afternoon school.

While the afternoon Hebrew school is an unquestionable improvement over the Sunday school in terms of hours of instruction, it is still too abbreviated a period in which to successfully cover the entire gamut of Jewish studies to which it is dedicated. For this reason, the National Commission on Torah Education recommends increasing the weekly instructional period to seven and a half hours. But the typical school retains the five to six hours per week schedule.

This may seem adequate, but one should bear in mind that this time period is not devoted to just one course. The curriculum attempts to cover an entire Jewish "liberal arts" program: Hebrew language, Jewish history, Jewish life and religious practices, Bible, and Jewish music and art. The hours of study are divided among many subjects so that the time spent on each subject is measured in terms of minutes instead of hours.

For example, the following is a typical schedule for time allotment in the third grade of a Hebrew school (attended by ten year olds): prayer, 20 minutes, 3 times per week; Torah (Bible), 40 minutes, 3 times per week; Hebrew language, 30 minutes, 3 times per week; Jewish laws—life, 20 minutes, 2 times per week; and Jewish history, 25 minutes, 1 time per week.

Schools may vary by ten or fifteen minutes one way or the other from this schedule, but the variations are not educationally significant.

Bear in mind that an elementary public school devotes five hours a week to the study of every major subject, that the learning situation takes place five consecutive days each week, that it lasts for a period of eight years, and that, then, the child has only attained an elementary knowledge of the subjects. Contrast the afternoon Hebrew school schedule to this, and one should begin to appreciate the difficulty in trying to penetrate the surface of Jewish knowledge and understanding in that setting.

Hours per week are not the only problem. I believe we wait too long before enrolling the children in the afternoon school program, usually at the age of eight, and then we lose them too soon after Bar-Mitzvah.

A current five-year program is now offered not because Jewish educators think it ideal, but because many parents resist starting the child in Hebrew school simultaneously with entering public school at the age of six. They even regard the age of seven as a trifle too soon. It was not too long ago when the accepted norm for starting Hebrew school was at the age of nine, and it was only after much effort that educators succeeded in lowering the age. It needs to be lowered even further if better results from afternoon Hebrew schools are to be forthcoming.

The very fact that afternoon Hebrew schools are treated as a *supplementary* program of education, and not as an extension of one's *primary* schooling has, in itself, some adverse effects. While parents certainly want their children to go to Hebrew afternoon schools, or else they wouldn't be sending them, and most children who go accept the fact that they are required to do so, most Hebrew school students and their parents simply don't relate to the studies in the Hebrew school with the same seriousness that they do to those in the public school. They don't see it as possessing the same "compulsory" quality.

Children have been known to refer to their public schoolteacher, in contrast to their Hebrew schoolteacher, as "my *real* teacher." The subtle implication is that the Hebrew schoolteacher is not being seen by the child on the same level of authority or importance as the public schoolteacher.

Parents' less serious attitude toward this "supplementary" program of studies is reflected in still other ways: by showing less concern about a child's grades or homework assignments from Hebrew school than those from public school; by thinking nothing of making doctor and dentist appointments, or scheduling shopping trips during Hebrew school hours, which these parents would rarely do during public school hours; and by requesting Hebrew school principals to excuse their children from classes to participate in such activities as Little League baseball when, again, the same parents would never think of asking that their children be excused from public school classes for anything but the most dire emergency or illness.

If many parents were able to change these attitudes in themselves, there is no doubt that the afternoon schools could be more successful overall than they are now.

Again, and it cannot be said often enough, the home plays *the* vital role. If the home influence serves to complement that of the Hebrew school, then the chances for the latter to make a meaningful impact is greatly improved. If, however, the home influence serves to complement only that of the secular public school, the odds are overwhelmingly against the afternoon Hebrew school.

I do believe that the afternoon Hebrew school can become a more effective instrument of Jewish education than it is if:

- parents provide a meaningful and intensive Jewish life at home;
- children begin attending at the first grade and stay through the twelfth grade;
- the schedule is extended to at least seven and a half hours over a four-day week;
- and full advantage is taken of the summer months to attend Jewish educational day or overnight camps.

Better Than Nothing (But Not By Much):
The Sunday School

Initially introduced into America in the middle of the nineteenth century by the Reform movement, the one-day-a-week school continues to draw a great number of children. The Sunday school program was also later adopted by Conservative and even Orthodox congregations, although in neither group did it represent the educational aspirations of its rabbinate or of its educational spokesmen. They sponsored it to attract children whose parents were not willing to "burden" them with any Jewish program that required a greater investment of their time. While the Sunday school provided an acceptable level of Jewish learning for the Reform movement, Conservative and Orthodox leaders continued to stress the educational insufficiency of the one-day-a-week program and constantly tried to prevail upon parents to transfer their children to the other types of schools.

The basic curriculum of all Sunday schools is essentially the same. Risking the charge of oversimplification, the lower elementary grades generally concentrate on holiday and Bible stories; the intermediate grades emphasize Jewish history as the core of the program; and in the upper grades of the Sunday school (the ninth through the twelfth grades), one studies about the Bible, Jewish principles of faith, and Jewish life in America. Since time is set aside for music and current events, and for reviewing and celebrating each of the Jewish holidays, the two-hour-a-week program is more than filled.

The two-hour-a-week schedule simply leaves no time for the study of Hebrew; or of the text of the Hebrew Bible; or of the Mishnah; or even for a thorough review of ancient, medieval, and contemporary Jewish history. The question is not only whether the subjects covered in the Sunday schools constitute an adequate minimum Jewish education, but whether, considering the time limitations, it is possible to do justice even to the subjects that are studied.

I recall one attempt to teach Hebrew reading within the framework of a traditional Sunday school. By the end of the first year only about half of the reading primer was completed and, even when the entire primer was completed at the end of the second year, the level of reading was uniformly poor. The explanation is simple. The time lapse of one week between sessions, and of a long summer vacation between the two halves, dimmed the recall needed for reinforcement. Progress was slow and laborious. When the same Hebrew primer was studied at least three times a week on alternate days, the primer was completed with far more successful results in less than four months.

"I went for ten years and didn't learn anything" is invariably the feeling of most young people whose Jewish education was limited to the Sunday school. It should not have come as a surprise. If one stops for a moment to add up the total number of hours that goes into ten years of Sunday school, it comes to approximately two-thirds of the time spent in any *one year* of a regular school program! Moreover, these approximately 700 hours are not concentrated into a short period of time, but are stretched over a decade that ranges from early childhood to the threshold of adulthood. It must also be remembered that a good part of those hours are devoted to recurring holidays, to school assemblies, and to arts and crafts.

It is surely an unrealistic expectation to be able to master an entire heritage, a whole culture, and a complex faith in this limited number of hours. The sense of disappointment comes with the awareness that after devoting ten years to Jewish schooling, one's level of knowledge is still quite elementary.

No responsible Jewish educator from any of the religious segments will today make any claims for the adequacy of the Sunday school as an acceptable minimal program of study. Even the Reform movement's Commission on Jewish Education has expressed its "firm opinion that, beginning with the intermediate grades, more than one session a week is required if the religious school is to accomplish its goals." Yet, the one-day-a-week program continues to serve as the required basis for their confirmation, while the supplementary midweek curriculum is offered on a voluntary basis.

The educational goals set forth for the Sunday school are usually couched in glowing terms. A statement issued by one prominent Reform temple reads as follows:

> Our primary goal is to educate our youth so that upon high school graduation and entrance to college, they have a strong identification with their religious faith. Our young people should possess a knowledge of Judaism that stands them in good stead when they are away

from the security of home and the warmth of Temple life. We must nourish the roots of Judaism so that they can grow and flourish in early adulthood. Adequate Hebrew instruction, for those who do not attend weekday Hebrew classes, should enable them to participate in and fully enjoy a worship service.[4]

In "An Outline of the Curriculum for the Jewish Religious School," the Reform movement's Commission on Jewish Education is even more ambitious. It lists specific objectives that include knowledge of Bible, Jewish history, Jewish ceremonies, Hebrew, worship, post-biblical Jewish literature, and Jewish ethics and theology. Also emphasized is the importance of developing proper attitudes toward all these areas in addition to an appreciation of Jewish art, music, and dancing. The development of habits that positively reflect all the aforementioned study is also stressed. There is little in the listed objectives to which educators from the Conservative and Orthodox camps could object. One only wonders whether such ambitious goals can be attained even in a six-hour-a-week program, much less in a two-hour-a-week program.

Some Jewish educators object to sponsoring any one-day-a-week program on the grounds that they become a party to deceiving parents. The very noteworthy goals enunciated in promoting the Sunday school program, backed by respect for the sponsoring institution and its religious leadership, will lead the average unsophisticated parent to assume that one's child will receive what "the experts" feel is an adequate minimum Jewish education. This is simply not the case.

Jewish parents who choose the Sunday school route should be under no illusions about the results they can anticipate. They should be aware of the candid reservations expressed even by those who sponsor the Sunday school. The Sunday school is only "a taste" of the real nourishment; it cannot satisfy a child's spiritual hunger.

Secondary Schools

Each type of school discussed in this chapter operates not only on the elementary level, but also on the secondary level. The secondary program may be an extension of a school's elementary program;

it may be offered by a school operating only on the secondary level, or as a preparatory division to a college of Jewish learning.

Some parents may be satisfied with the Jewish knowledge accumulated on the elementary level, regarding it as sufficient for their children, and so exert no pressure for their children to continue. The decision to confine Jewish education to the elementary level is actually made by parents, though they often hide the fact by insisting that it is the child who does not wish to continue and that they, the parents, cannot fight with the child. If the youngster was to indicate a disinterest in continuing public high school beyond the legal requirements, one can imagine the furor these same parents would raise and how quickly they would fight with their children and lay the law down on the issue.

The disinclination of children to continue their Jewish schooling is most often a direct result of parents' indifference, or at best lukewarm support, on the question of continuing through the high school years, plus the lack of friends who are continuing. Parents are entitled to feel the way they do. But they should not deceive themselves about the educational ramifications of their decision.

Learning that is not reinforced is soon enough forgotten, especially if the knowledge has not been too deeply digested in the first place. This accounts for the fact that by the time the average Jewish youngster is admitted to a college at about the age of eighteen, he will have forgotten almost everything he learned on the elementary level, particularly if it was of the Sunday or afternoon school type. Very often, he will barely be able to even read the Hebrew letters, much less recall the broader aspects of the Jewish heritage. There is retrogression to the first grade level.

Assuming that other factors, such as regular synagogue attendance or participation in religious youth activities keeps him in contact with what he had learned, or that the child's own superior qualities enable him to retain much that he had learned until the eighth grade, one must appreciate the fact that he learned it all on an elementary level. As he continues to mature mentally and emotionally, as his knowledge of the world and of other subject areas continues to expand, his understanding of Judaism does not correspondingly grow or mature. It should not come as a surprise then if an attitude of disdain develops toward Jewish studies or that

Jewish education comes to be regarded as worthy "for children only." It is as though a doctoral university student in science related to American history only on the level of George Washington chopping down the cherry tree. In this respect, the Jew who has had no Jewish elementary schooling at all is probably under less illusions and develops less of a negative attitude toward Jewish study than one who studied just a bit. The latter, believing that he had received a Jewish education, never learns to relate to Jewish studies with the intellectual seriousness they merit.

The most important reason for not cutting off a Jewish education at the elementary level is that the teenage years are the most crucial in fashioning the child's lifelong values and commitment. It is precisely during these years that the child should have daily contact with teachers who can answer the questions that the child raises about Judaism, about the Jewish people, and about one's own Jewish identity. The child should be in contact with an environment that will seek to instill Jewish loyalties and feelings. For such purposes, the adolescent years from the ages of thirteen to eighteen are more crucial than the growing years from the ages of six to thirteen. Elementary schooling teaches basic skills and conveys basic information, but it cannot and does not address itself to those ultimate questions that only begin to interest and trouble children as they grow older. The questions that interest a sixteen and seventeen year old are worlds apart from the ones that interest a thirteen year old. The difference in their levels of comprehension is also vast. Even where the same question is asked, a good teacher does not give the answer in the same way.

Elementary education must be seen as a stepping-stone to further study. No elementary Jewish program of schooling, even the more intensive program offered by the day school, can do more than offer a foundation on which to build. Parents must appreciate the fact that Jewish secondary schooling, particularly under contemporary conditions, is a necessary prerequisite to the raising of a Jewishly committed and knowledgeable generation.

EPILOGUE

Where Do We Go from Here?

WHILE a gloomy future for American Jewry can be easily forecast, I believe that a significant percentage of young Jewish parents will in the years ahead take their Jewish responsibilities more seriously and actively guide their children ever closer to Judaism. While assimilation may continue to erode Jewish life and lead to a reduction in the quantitative size of the identifiable Jewish community, I believe that the spiritual quality of the surviving community will be vastly superior to our own. In any given family, however, the prospect that children and grandchildren will be counted among that Jewish community depends very much on the young mothers and fathers in this generation.

I dream of a Jewish community where despite differences in practice, the Jewish community will consist of people where the vast majority are highly knowledgeable of their Jewish heritage, where a distinctive Jewish way of life will become commonplace, and where the basic Jewish values will dominate the life of the community and leave a worthwhile impact on non-Jewish friends and associates. I like to think that parents will create a true partnership with their rabbis and the Jewish community's lay leadership for the purpose of reaching their common goals.

The lay leadership of the Jewish community could, of course, help simplify the parents' task. They could provide the incentive, or at least remove some of the barriers. For example, it is not beyond the resources of the Jewish community to see to it that the Jewish day school provides a free education to every Jewish child wishing to attend it. If only the will to do so were there! It is certainly in the Jewish community's interest that it be done. How it should be done is not a question to be dealt with here. But finances should not be a consideration in the minds of parents when they weigh the relative advantages of the different types of schooling available to their children. The costly tuition requirements of the day school are a definite barrier for many parents, limiting such schooling only to the most dedicated and self-sacrificing or to the affluent.

A wise Jewish leadership, concerned with Jewish survival and unencumbered by ideological hang-ups about loyalty to the public school system, would see to it that intensive Jewish education had some chance to compete for the Jewish child. Free day school tuition might well encourage some parents to shift their children from Sunday schools or the afternoon Hebrew schools. Jewish leaders who mean what they say about Jewish education ought to welcome that prospect and not be frightened by it. The nonpublic schools have an honorable place in the history of American education, and there need be no qualms about all out support for free Jewish day schools. Jewish leaders who see the growth of the Jewish day school as dangerous to the survival of the American public school system are guilty of grossly exaggerating the impact that might be made by a partial shift of students from a minority group who in their entirety number less than three percent of the American population.

I would like to see mass scholarship incentives for Jewish children to attend the educational summer camps and the various Shabbaton programs. I would like to see Jewish organizations underwrite scholarships to high school and college youth for one-year study programs at schools in Israel.

The Jewish community has shown a readiness to spend vast amounts of money to finance research on how to improve Jewish education, and for the administrative machinery to support those studies. The time is now ripe for it to turn to encouraging the more than one million Jewish youngsters of school age to take advantage of the educational services which are already available to them.

I would like to see a basic Jewish library established wherever there is a Jewish presence. It should consist of at least three to four thousand volumes covering every area of Jewish knowledge and catering to all age levels. Such libraries should be housed in places where they would be easily accessible to the Jewish population. These could include mobile library units, or special sections of local public or college libraries. These libraries could be housed in neighborhood synagogues or Jewish centers, even in business or commercial centers.

It should be made as easy as possible for parents and children to come into contact with all kinds of Jewish books, to browse through them, in order to make them familiar with the great range of Jewish knowledge. There is no telling what interests might be aroused, how much learning would result. A by-product of such a program would be to encourage scholars to devote even greater attention to areas of Jewish content and to engage in creative writing for the Jewish market. A ready market of several thousand small libraries all over the country would also encourage publishers to publish many important works that they might otherwise not publish due to the limited sales potential.

I would like to see the Jewish community grant its honors not only to those who make magnanimous financial contributions to the welfare of the Jewish people, but also to scholars, teachers, artists, and religious leaders who contribute to the spiritual or cultural life of the Jewish community. The positive impact this can make on the Jewish upbringing of our youth is enormous. If children were to see Jewish learning as something valued by the community, it would encourage them to take their own Jewish studies more seriously. It would make the task of conscientious Jewish parents that much easier.

I firmly believe that the implementation of these and other similar proposals can make a profound impact on the direction in which American Jewry is headed. It can help create the much-needed partnership among parents, rabbis, and community leaders in their common goal of assuring the creative survival of the Jewish community and of simultaneously enriching the lives of Jewish children with the meaningful and eternal values of the Jewish heritage.

No family can afford to wait until community policies change and optimum conditions are reached. Such changes are at best a slow and laborious process, and in the interim another generation that we cannot afford to lose is growing up. Your child is part of that generation, and regardless of whether community policies are good, bad, or indifferent, the policies adopted by each individual parent must represent one's best effort in each of the areas that affect the upbringing of one's children. The informal education provided at home, the nature of the personal relationship between parents and children, the influence exerted by the different environments with which the child comes in contact, and, finally, the nature of the formal education that the child receives are the most important aspects in the raising of a Jewish child. Each parent is personally responsible for providing for the Jewish future and spiritual well-being of one's own child. It is my prayer that every parent will rise to this challenge, and thereby bring fulfillment both to oneself and to one's children.

Notes

Chapter 1

1. William Barrett, *Irrational Man* (London: Heinemann, 1961), p. 31.
2. Ibid., p. 69.
3. Eugene Borowitz, "The Problems Facing Jewish Educational Philosophy in the Sixties," 1961 *American Jewish Yearbook* (Philadelphia: Jewish Publication Society, 1961), p. 150.
4. Shabbat 119b.
5. Ibid.

Chapter 2

1. Avot 1:17.
2. Pesikhta Aikha Rabati 2; Hagigah (Yesushalmi) 1:7.
3. Berakhot 54a.
4. Avot 3:21.
5. Abraham Isaac Kook, *Mussar Avikha Umidot Ha'reiyah* (Jerusalem: Mossad Harav Kook, 1973), pp. 125–126.

Notes

6. Berakhot 28b.
7. Kook, *Mussar Avikha Umidot Ha'reiyah*, pp. 125–126.
8. Nedarim (Yerushalmi) 89:4.
9. Shabbat 30b.
10. Avot 1:12.
11. Kook, *Mussar Avikha Umidot Ha'reiyah*, p. 94.
12. Avot d'Rabbi Nathan 16:5.
13. Yoma 9b.
14. Tana d'bai Eliyahu Rabbah: 11.
15. Leviticus Rabbah 30:9–12.
16. Avot 4:1.
17. Avot 4:15.
18. Avot 2:15.
19. Baba Metzia 58b; see also Berakhot 43b.
20. Avot 3:14.
21. Mishna Sanhedrin 4:5.
22. Ibid.
23. Samuel Belkin, *The Philosophy of Purpose* (New York: Yeshiva University, 1958), pp. 31–32.
24. Viktor E. Frankl, *Man's Search for Meaning* (New York: Washington Square Press, 1963), p. 154.
25. Belkin, *The Philosophy of Purpose*, pp. 10–11.
26. Avot 5:25.
27. Shulhan Arukh, Yoreh Deah 246:1.
28. Eruvin 54b.
29. Nachmanides (Ramban) on Numbers 33:53; Ketubot 110b; see also Maimonides, *Mishneh Torah*, Hil. M'lakhim 5:9.
30. Sifri, Deuteronomy 12:29.
31. Shabbat 133b.
32. Chafetz Chaim, *Ahavath Chesed*, trans. by Leonard Oschry (Jerusalem and New York: Feldheim Publishers, 1967), p. 15.
33. Yevamot 79a.
34. Maimonides, *Mishneh Torah*, Hil. Isurai Biah 19:17.
35. Avot 2:4.
36. Berakhot 21b.

Chapter 3

1. Avot 1:13.
2. Ibid., 2:5.
3. Abraham Isaac Kook, *Igrot Ha'reiyah*, Vol. 1 (Jerusalem: Mossad Harav Kook, 1961).
4. Avot 2:6.
5. Nedarim 41a.

6. Tana d'bai Eliuahu Rabbah 11.
7. Kiddushin 40b.
8. Erkhin 16b.
9. Samson Raphael Hirsch, *Horeb: A Philosophy of Jewish Laws and Observances*, Vol. 2 (London: Soncino Press, 1962), #551, p. 408.
10. Louis Ginzberg, *Students, Scholars, Saints* (New York, Meridian Books, Inc., and Philadelphia, Jewish Publication Society, 1958), p. 177.
11. Avot 2:14.
12. Samson Raphael Hirsch, *Judaism Eternal*, Vol. 1, trans. by Isidor Grunfeld (London: Soncino Press, 1956), pp. 171–173.
13. Ibid., p. 170.
14. Kiddushin 30b.
15. Abraham Isaac Kook, *Orot Hakodesh*, Vol. 1 (Jerusalem: Mossad Harav Kook, 1963), p. 65.
16. Kiddushin 29a.
17. Avot 2:2.
18. Shabbat 150a.
19. Kurt Lewin, *Resolving Social Conflicts* (London: Souvenir Press, 1973), p. 183. Also published in New York, by Harper and Row, 1948.

Chapter 4

1. Sifri, Deuteronomy 21.
2. Sukkah 46b.
3. William E. Homan, *Child Sense* (New York: Basic Books, 1969), p. 69.
4. Arthur T. Jersild, "Emotional Development," in *Manual of Child Psychology*, ed. by Leonard Carmichael (New York: John Wiley and Sons, 1954), p. 895.
5. Sotah 47a.
6. William E. Homan, *Child Sense*, p. 16.
7. Baba Batra 21a.
8. Shmot Rabbah 1:1.
9. Avot 4:12.
10. Baba Metzia 58b.
11. Avot 2:16.

Chapter 5

1. Avot 2:19.
2. Ibid., 1:6.

Chapter 6

1. William E. Homan, *Child Sense*, pp. 66–67.

Chapter 7

1. Sotah 20a.
2. Shmot Rabbah 1:16.
3. For further discussion see Hayim Halevy Donin, *To Be A Jew* (Basic Books, 1972), p. 103.
4. Pesikhta Aikha Rabati 2; Hagigah (Yerushalmi) 1:7.
5. For a detailed explanation of this procedure see Donin, *To Be A Jew*, pp. 280–284.
6. Ibid.

Chapter 8

1. John L. Childs, *Education and Morals* (New York: Appleton-Century, Crofts, Inc., 1950), p. 7.
2. Uriah Z. Engelman and Alexander M. Dushkin, *Jewish Education in the United States*, vol. 1 (New York: American Association for Jewish Education, 1959), p. 32.
2a. Theodore I. Lenn, *Rabbi and Synagogue in Reform Judaism* (New York: Central Conference of American Rabbis, 1972), pp. 98–100.
3. Jacob J. Petuchowski, "The Limits of Liberal Judaism," *Judaism*, vol. 14, no. 2 (Spring 1965), p. 154.
4. For extensive discussion of Halakha see Donin, *To Be A Jew*, pp. 28–32.
5. Eruvin 13b.
6. Menahot 64b; Sotah 49a.
7. Ibid., 99b; Peah (Yerushalmi) 1:1.
8. Ibid.; Shulhan Arukh, Yoreh Deah 246:1.
9. Ibid., 246:6.
10. Chafetz Chaim, *Mikhtavei Chafetz Chaim*, letter no. 70, ed. by Aryeh Leib Hacohen (New York: 1953), p. 181.
11. Maimonides, *Mishneh Torah*, Hil. Sanhedrin 2:1; Kiddush Hahodesh 17:24.
12. Isidor Grunfeld, Introduction to Hirsch, *Judaism Eternal*, p. xxi.
13. Ibid., pp. xxi–xxii.
14. Midrash Aikha Rabati 2:17.
15. Shulhan Arukh, Yoreh Deah 245:4.

Chapter 9

1. Alvin I. Schiff, *The Jewish Day School in America* (New York: Jewish Education Committee Press, 1966), p. 144.

2. Ibid., p. 195.

3. Erkhin 16b.

4. *Temple Israel Messenger*, vol. 8, no. 13 (November 26, 1965), Temple Israel, Detroit, Michigan.

Since the untimely passing of our beloved father, z'l, in 1982, there has been a veritable explosion of resources available to Jewish parents—in terms of books, recordings, videos, computer software, as well as in the development of resources for the disabled. How exciting it would have been for an educator like him, and how much he missed! Working on the new edition of *To Raise a Jewish Child* was truly a labor of love, and it is our hope that our father would have been as proud of us as we were of him.

Out of the wealth of Judaica that has been published, the books and educational materials recommended here include many important works but the list is far from exhaustive. We are certain that they will provide hours of enjoyment to both children and adults from all backgrounds. We encourage all, however, to visit their local Hebrew bookstores and libraries, where possible, and to utilize the catalogues of the various publishing and mail-order houses and the bibliographies referenced for a more comprehensive listing.

We wish to acknowledge and thank Dr. Israel Lerner and Ida Bobrowsky of the Board of Jewish Education; Susan Young, librarian for Bais Yaakov of Queens and Temple Beth Shalom; and the numerous others who so willingly gave of their time to assist us in compiling the updated resource material.

Haviva Donin Peters   *Rena Donin Schlussel*

March 1991

APPENDIX A

~~~~~~

Resources for the Jewish Education of Children

Books

Books to Read to the Preschool Child

A Child's Picture Hebrew Dictionary. Ita Meshi Adama, 1985.
And Shira Imagined. Giora Carmi. Jewish Publication Society, 1988.
Bible Heroes I Can Be. Ann Eisenberg. Kar-Ben Copies, 1990.
Cakes and Miracles—A Purim Tale. Barbara Diamond Goldin. Viking, 1991.
Donny and Deeny K'teeny Help the King. Ella Adler. Mesorah Publications, 1990.
I Can Celebrate. Ann Eisenberg. Kar-Ben Copies, 1988. (Board Book.)
I Have Four Questions. Madeline Winkler and Judy Groner. Kar-Ben Copies, 1988.
  (Board Book.)
Mendel the Mouse. Ruth Finkelstein. Torah Umesorah, 1974.
Mother Goose Rhymes for Jewish Children. Sarah G. Levy. Bloch Publishing, 1945.
My Body is Something Special. Howard Bogot and Daniel B. Syme. Union of American
  Hebrew Congregations, 1981.
The Beginning of the World. Neva Goldstein-Alpern. Judaica Press, 1987. (Board
  Book.)

The House on the Roof—A Sukkot Story. David A. Adler. Kar-Ben Copies, 1976.
The Mouse in the Matzoh Factory. Francine Mendoff. Kar-Ben Copies, 1983.
The Purim Parade. Madeline Winkler and Judy Groner. Kar-Ben Copies, 1986. (Board Book.)
The Ten Plagues of Egypt. Shoshana Lepon. Judaica Press, 1988.
The Very Best Place for a Penny. Dina Herman Rosenfeld. Merkos L'inyonei Chinuch, 1984.

Books for the Young Child, Ages 5–8

NOTE: Some of the titles in the listing for preschool children may also be suitable for the younger children in this age group.
A Picture Book of Jewish Holidays. David A. Adler. Holiday House, 1981.
Brothers. Florence B. Friedman. Harper & Row, 1985.
Could Anything Be Worse? Marilyn Hirsh. Holiday House, 1974.
From Head to Toe, A Book About You. Yaffa Ganz. Feldheim Publishers, 1988.
Honi and His Magic Circle. Phillis Gershator. Jewish Publication Society, 1979.
Jewish Days and Holidays. Greer Fay Cashman. SBS Publishing, 1976.
Joseph Who Loved the Sabbath. Marilyn Hirsh. Viking, 1976.
Just Enough Is Plenty. Barbara Diamond Goldin. Viking, 1988.
My Little Siddur. Adama, 1986. (Also *My Little Machzor* and *Ma Nishtana.*)
The Aleph-Bet Story Book. Deborah Pessin. Jewish Publication Society, 1946.
The Best of K'tonton. Sadie R. Weilerstein. Jewish Publication Society, 1980.
The Carp in the Bathtub. Barbara Cohen. Kar-Ben Copies, 1987.
The Magician. I. L. Peretz and Uri Shulevitz. Macmillan, 1985.
The Number on My Grandfather's Arm. David A. Adler. Union of American Hebrew Congregations, 1987.
The Old Synagogue. Richard Rosenblum. Jewish Publication Society, 1989.
The Story of Mimmy and Simmy. Yaffa Ganz. Feldheim Publishers, 1985.
The Tattooed Torah. Marvell Ginzburg. Union of American Hebrew Congregations, 1983.
What the Moon Brought. Sadie R. Weilerstein. Jewish Publication Society, 1942.

Books for the Growing Child, Ages 9–12

A Child's Book of Midrash. Barbara Diamond Goldin. Jason Aronson, 1990.
All-of-a-Kind Family. Sydney Taylor. Follett/Dell, 1951. Other books in this series include: *All-of-a-Kind Family Downtown, All-of-a-Kind Family Uptown, More All-of-a-Kind Family,* and *Ella of All-of-a-Kind Family.*
Becoming Gershona. Nava Semel. Viking, 1990.
Hanukkah: Eight Nights, Eight Lights. Malka Drucker. Holiday House, 1980. Also: *Shabbat: A Peaceful Island* and *Sukkot: A Time to Rejoice.*
Haym Solomon—Liberty's Son. Shirley Milgrim. Jewish Publication Society, 1979.
Henrietta Szold: Israel's Helping Hand. Shulamit Kustanowitz. Viking, 1990.
Number the Stars. Lois Lowry. Houghton Mifflin, 1989.
Our Golda: The Story of Golda Meir. David A. Adler. Viking, 1984.
Reb Aryeh. Tzira Kallenastein. Feldheim Publishers, 1989.

Savta Simcha and the Incredible Shabbos Bag. Yaffa Ganz. Feldheim, 1980. Other books in this series include: *Savta Simcha and the Cinnamon Tree* and *Savta Simcha and the Seven Splendid Gifts.*

The Jewish Kids' Catalogue. Chaya M. Burstein. Jewish Publication Society, 1983. Also: *A Kid's Catalogue of Israel,* 1988.

The Mystery of the Coins. Chaya M. Burstein. Union of American Hebrew Congregations, 1988.

The Seven Good Years and Other Stories. I. L. Peretz. Jewish Publication Society, 1984.

The Story of the Jewish Way of Life. Meyer Levin and Toby K. Kurzband. Berhman House, 1959.

The Wise Men of Helm. Solomon Simon. Berhman House, 1945. Also: *More Wise Men of Helm.*

We Remember the Holocaust. David A. Adler. Henry Holt, 1989.

Yossi Asks the Angels for Help. Miriam Chaikin. Harper & Row, 1985. Other books in this series include: *Yossi Tries to Help God* and *Feathers in the Wind.*

Zlateh the Goat and Other Stories. Isaac Bashevis Singer. Harper & Row, 1966.

Books for Teenagers 12 and Up

NOTE: Many of the titles on pages 213–16 are also suitable for the mature young teenager.

A Tzaddik in Our Time. Simcha Raz. Feldheim Publishers, 1976.

As a Driven Leaf. Milton Steinberg. Jason Aronson, 1987.

Dawn. Elie Wiesel. Avon Books, 1969.

Forever My Jerusalem. Puah Shteiner. Feldheim Publishers, 1987.

Jewish Stories One Generation Tells Another. Peninah Schram. Jason Aronson, 1987.

Night. Elie Wiesel. Avon Books, 1970.

The Adventure of Gluckel of Hameln. Paul Sharon. United Synagogue Commission on Jewish Education, 1967.

The Diary of a Young Girl. Anne Frank. Doubleday, 1967.

The Gideonites: The Story of the Nili Spies in the Middle East. Deborah Omer. Hebrew Publishing, 1968.

The Passover Anthology. Philip Goodman, ed. Jewish Publication Society, 1961.

The Purim Anthology. Philip Goodman, ed. Jewish Publication Society, 1952.

The Rosh Hashana Anthology. Philip Goodman, ed. Jewish Publication Society, 1970.

The Scent of Snowflowers. R. L. Klein. Feldheim Publishers, 1989.

The Shavuot Anthology. Philip Goodman, ed. Jewish Publication Society, 1974.

The Story of Israel in Stamps. Gabriel and Maxim Shamir. Wilshire, 1970.

The Sukkot and Simhat Torah Anthology. Philip Goodman, ed. Jewish Publication Society, 1973.

The Yom Kippur Anthology. Philip Goodman, ed. Jewish Publication Society, 1971.

The Young Reader's Encyclopedia of Jewish History. Ilana Shamir and Shlomo Shavit. Viking, 1987.

Bibliographies of Books for Children

A Comprehensive Guide to Children's Literature with Jewish Themes. Enid Davis. Schocken Books, 1981.

The Selected Children's Judaica Collection. Once Upon a Time Bookstore, Inc., and JCC Jewish Book Council, 1990. Available through the JCC at 15 E. 26th St., New York, NY 10001, or from the bookstore at 77 Quaker Ridge Road, New Rochelle, NY 10804. (Mail order available.)

Books of Jewish Interest for Children. Published by Eeyore's Books for Children, 2212 Broadway, New York, NY 10024. (Mail order available.)

Magazines and Newspapers

Jewish Current Events. Published by J. B. Harris, P.O. Box 15780, San Diego, CA 92175. Ages 10+ (newspaper/semimonthly).

Noah's Ark. 8323 Southwestern Freeway, Suite 250, Houston, TX 77074. Ages 6+ (newspaper/monthly).

NOW—News of the World. Published by Schaffzin & Schaffzin, 37 Overbrook Parkway, Wynnewood, PA 19096. Ages 10+ (newspaper/monthly).

Olomeinu—Our World. Published by Torah Umesorah—National Society for Hebrew Day Schools. 6101 16th Avenue, Brooklyn, NY 11204. Ages 10+ (magazine/monthly).

Shofar Magazine. Published by Senior Publications, 43 Northcote Drive, Melville, NY 11747. Ages 10+ (magazine/monthly).

Music

Books

Come Sing with Me—Hebrew Songs for the Young. Velvel Pasternak. Tara Publications, 1984.

Eretz Eretz—60 Favorite Israel Songs. Kinneret Publishing House, 1986.

Hebrew Songs for All Seasons. Susan Claire Searles. Tara Publications, 1987.

Holiday in Song. Velvel Pasternak. Tara Publications, 1985.

Israel in Song. Velvel Pasternak. Jewish Education Press, 1974.

Sing Along with Effi Netzer (2 vols.). General Federation of Labour Histradrut Culture and Education Enterprises.

The Songs We Sing. Harry Coopersmith. United Synagogue Commission on Jewish Education, 1951. Also: *More of the Songs We Sing,* 1971.

Recordings

FOR YOUNGER CHILDREN

Apples on Holidays and Other Days. Leah Abrams.
Because We Love the Shabbat. Leah Abrams.
Latkes and Hamantashen (Hanukah and Purim); *Mostly Matzoh* (Passover); *The Seventh Day* (Shabbat). A set of 3 tapes. Fran Avni and Jackie Cystrobaum. Tara Publications.
Uncle Moishe and His Mitzvah Men. A set of 7 tapes. Suki and Ding.
51 Songs for Eyal—The Best of the Best Israeli Children's Songs (cassette and book with English translation and transliteration of songs). Isradisc, Tel Aviv, Israel. Also: *51 Songs for Limor and 51 Holiday Songs for Limor.*

FOR ALL AGES

Fifty Songs—Forty Years. The Givatron (3 cassettes).
Naomi Shemer Sings Her Songs.
Yehoram Gaon—Greatest Hits and *Greatest Hits II.*

You may want to write or call for a catalogue of music publications. Two such catalogues are:
Tara Publications, 29 Derby Avenue, Cedarhurst, NY 11516. (516-295-2290)
Nefesh Ami—Soul of My People. P.O. Box 651, Hicksville, NY 11801. (516-933-2660)

Videos

Shalom Sesame. Children's Television Workshop. A series of videotapes with the Sesame Street characters in Israel, combining Hebrew and English conversation.
Shirim K'tanim. Hebrew songs for children. Scopus Films (Contains English translation and subtitles.)
The Shabbat. Ergo Media, Inc. Four short animated segments relating to the Sabbath. Ages 6–9.

Videos are available at Hebrew bookstores, Jewish libraries, and specialty catalogues. Two such catalogues are:
Ergo Home Videos. Ergo Media, Inc. P.O. Box 2037, Teaneck, NJ 07666.
Jewish Video Library, 300 Raritan Avenue, Highland Park, NJ 08904

Arts and Crafts

A Jewish Arts and Crafts Book—An Artist You Don't Have to Be. Joann Mangus with Howard I. Bogat. Union of American Hebrew Congregations, 1990.

Arts and Crafts Around the Jewish Calendar (2 vols.). Shoshana Mermelstein and Chava Shapiro. Torah Umesorah, 1988.

Creative Puppetry for Jewish Kids. Gail Warshwasky. Alternatives in Religious Education, 1985.

Let's Celebrate. Ruth Esrig Brinn. Kar-Ben Copies, 1977. Also: *More Let's Celebrate.*

The Sabbath. Herbert and Barbara Greenberg. United Synagogue Commission on Jewish Education. A kit of visual and tactile materials for preadolescent and adolescent children with learning and perceptual disabilities.

Together, A Child-Parent Kit. Melton Research Center of the Jewish Theological Seminary of America, 1985. Ages 8–9. In the same series: *Windows: Together 2.* Ages 11–13.

Games

Alef Bet School Blocks. Aviv Judaica Imports. Ages 18 months–5 years.

Brochos Lotto. Aviv Judaica Imports.

Color Shapes—A Jewish Puzzle Game. Jewish Educational Toys.

Draw and Guess—The Jewish Game of Guess the Picture. Beit Yesharim. Ages 6 and up.

Jerusalem Bus Stop. Beit Yesharim. Ages 8–adult.

Kosherland. Jewish Educational Toys. Ages 3–8.

Mitzvah Monopol. Beit Yesharim.

Noah's Ark. Beit Yesharim. Ages 4–7.

Religious Objects Dominoes. Ktav Holiday Products.

Torah Slides and Ladders. Torah Educational Toys. Ages 4–12.

You may want to write to the following companies for their catalogues:
Aviv Judaica Imports Ltd., 4415 First Avenue, Brooklyn, NY 11232.
Jewish Educational Toys, P.O. Box 250469, Brooklyn, NY 11225.

Computer Software

Two companies that produce Judaic and Hebrew software for personal computers are:
Davka, 7074 N. Western, Chicago, IL 60645
Kabbalah Software, 8 Price Drive, Edison, NJ 08817. (908–572–0891)

Jewish Bookstores

Books about the Jewish people and Jewish faith are sold in bookstores or book departments throughout the country. However, their selection is, of necessity, very limited. The Jewish bookstore, specializing as it does in Jewish books of all kinds is therefore a splendid place for browsing. You will find new titles, old favorites, and very useful but little-known textbooks. If you do not find what you are looking for, ask for it. The book dealer may be able to get it for you.

The Jewish bookstore is also the place where you can purchase such religious articles as *Tallit, Tefillin, Mezuzah,* and Sabbath candlesticks. They will carry Hanukkah candles before Hanukkah, Lulav and Etrog before Sukkot, Passover plates and Haggadahs before Passover, and Hebrew New Year cards before Rosh Hashanah.

You are also likely to find a rich selection of music, ranging from modern Hebrew songs to cantorial liturgical music and popular Hasidic melodies. Jewish games and videos will also be found in any well-stocked Jewish bookstore.

You might think of the Jewish bookstore as a general store for Jewish supplies. If you live near one, make a point of visiting it. If there is no such store near you, there are a number of mail-order catalogues, a few of which are listed below. If there is a specific item you would like to order, you might write or call one of the Jewish bookstores listed below. They will be happy to ship it to you.

Here is a partial list of such stores around the country and catalogues to write for.

California

Atara's Bookstore	450 North Fairfax
	Los Angeles, CA 90036
	(213) 655–3050
Jerusalem West	6512 El Cajon Blvd.
	San Diego, CA 92115
	(619) 582–2013
Joseph Herskovitz Hebrew Bookstore	442 ½ N. Fairfax
	Los Angeles, CA 90036
	(213) 852–9310

J. Roth Bookstore

9020 W. Olympic Blvd.
Beverly Hills, CA 91211
(213) 276-9414

Solomon's Hebrew and English
  Bookstore

447 N. Fairfax
Los Angeles, CA 90036
(213) 653-9045

The Jewish Quarter

365 N. Beverly Dr.
Beverly Hills, CA 90210
(213) 288-0364

Connecticut

Jewish Book Shop

570 Whalley Ave.
New Haven, CT 06511
(203) 387-1818

The Judaica Store

262 S. Whitney St.
Hartford, CT 06105
(203) 236-9956

Florida

Judaica Enterprises, Inc.

1074 N.E. 163rd St.
North Miami Beach, FL 33162
(305) 945-5091

National Hebrew Israeli Gift Center

736 41st St.
Miami Beach, FL 33140
(305) 532-2210

Torah Treasures

1309 Washington Ave.
Miami Beach, FL 33139
(305) 673-6095

Illinois

Hamakor Gallery

4150 Dempster
Skokie, IL 60076
(708) 677-4150

Rosenblum's World of Judaica

2906 Devon Ave.
Chicago, IL 60659
(312) 262-1700

The Museum Store

Spertus College of Judaica
618 S. Michigan Ave.
Chicago, IL 60605
(312) 922-9012

Maryland

Abe's Jewish Bookstore

11250 Georgia Ave.
Wheaton, MD 20902
(301) 942-2237

Central Hebrew Bookstore

228 Reisterstown Rd.
Baltimore, MD   21208
(301) 653–0550

Lisbon's Hebrew Books and Gifts

2305 University Blvd. W.
Wheaton, MD   20902
(301) 933–1800

Massachusetts

Davidson's Hebrew Bookstore

1106 N. Main St.
Randolph, MA   02368
(617) 961–4989

Israel Book Shop, Inc.

410 Harvard St.
Brookline, MA   02146
(617) 566–7113/4

Michigan

Borenstein's Book and Music Store

25242 Greenfield Rd.
Oak Park, MI   48237
(313) 967–3920

Spitzer's Hebrew Books and Gift Center

21770 W. Eleven Mile Rd.
Southfield, MI   48076
(312) 356–6080

Minnesota

Brochin's Book and Gift Shop

4813 Minnetonka Blvd.
Minneapolis, MN   55416
(612) 926–2011

Missouri

Midwest Jewish Books and Gift Center

8318 Olive Street Rd.
St. Louis, MO   63132
(314) 993–6300

New Jersey

Highland Park Judaica

227 Raritan Ave.
Highland Park, NJ 08904
(201) 246–1690

Sky Hebrew Bookstore

1923 Springfield Ave.
Maplewood, NJ   07040
(201) 763–4244

The Judaica House, Ltd.

19 Grand Ave.
Englewood, NJ   07631
(201) 567–1199

Resources for the Jewish Education of Children

New York

Eichler's Religious Articles and Gifts

5004 13th Ave.
Brooklyn, NY 11219
(718) 633–1505
1429 Coney Island Ave.
Brooklyn, NY 11230
(718) 258–7643

Hebrew Books and Gift World

72-20 Main St.
Kew Garden Hills, NY 11367
(718) 261–0233

Jewish Museum Bookshop

1109 Fifth Ave.
New York, NY 10028
(212) 399–3344

J. Levine Company

5 West 30th St.
New York, NY 10001
(212) 695–6888

Lazar's Sefer Israel, Inc.

150 West 26th St.
New York, NY 10001
(212) 929–6411

Louis Stavsky Co.

147 Essex St.
New York, NY 10002
(212) 647–1289

Theodore C. Cinnamon, Ltd.

420 Jerusalem Ave.
Hicksville, NY 11801
(516) 935–7480

West Side Judaica

2404 Broadway
New York, NY 10024
(212) 362–7846

Ziontalis Book Division

48 Eldridge St.
New York, NY 10002
(212) 925–8558

Ohio

Frank's Hebrew Bookstore

1647 Lee Rd.
Cleveland Heights, OH 44118
(216) 321–6850

Hebrew Union College Bookstore

3101 Clifton Ave.
Cincinnati, OH 45220
(513) 221–1875

Jacob's Judaica

13962 Cedar Rd.
Cleveland, OH 44118
(216) 321–7200

Pennsylvania

Bala Judaica Center

222 Bala Ave.
Bala Cynwynd, PA   19004
(215) 664-1303

Pinsker's Hebrew Books

2028 Murray Ave.
Pittsburgh, PA   15217
(412) 421-3033

Rosenberg's Hebrew Bookstore

409 Old York Rd.
Jenkintown, PA   19046
(215) 884-1728
6408 Castor Avenue
Philadelphia, PA   19149
(215) 744-5205

Rhode Island

Melzer's Hebrew Bookstore

97 Overhill Rd.
Providence, RI   02906
(401) 831-1710

Canada

Rodal's Hebrew Bookstore

4689 Van Horne Ave.
Montreal, P.Q. H3W 1G8
(514) 733-1876

Alef Bet Judaica

3453 Bathurst St.
Toronto   M6A 2C5
(416) 781-2133

Israel's—The Judaica Centre

897 Eglinton Ave. West
Toronto   M6C 2C1
(416) 256-1010

Negev Book and Gift Store

3509 Bathurst St.
Toronto   M6A 2C5
(416) 781-9356

Mail-Order Catalogues

Shop-at-Home Judaica from Ziontalis

48 Eldridge St.
New York, NY   10002
(212) 925-8558

Hamakor Judaica

6153 Mulford
Unit D
Niles, IL   60648
800–426–2567

Jewish Book Publishers

There are a number of Jewish educational agencies that specialize in the publication of books for children. There are also a number of publishing houses that specialize in the publication of Jewish books, many of them suitable for children of different ages. You may want to write for their catalogues or list of books and recordings they have for children.

Educational Agencies

Board of Jewish Education, 426 W. 58th St., New York, NY   10019.
Merkos L'inyonei Chinuch, 770 Eastern Parkway, Brooklyn, NY   11213.
Torah Umesorah Publication Department, 6101 16th Ave., Brooklyn, NY   11204.
Union of American Hebrew Congregations—Book Division, 838 Fifth Ave., New York, NY   10021
United Synagogue Commission on Jewish Education, 155 Fifth Ave., New York, NY   10010

Commercial Houses

Alternatives in Religious Education, 3945 S. Oneida St., Denver, CO   80237.
Berhman House, 235 Watchung Ave., West Orange, NJ   07052.
Bloch Publishing, 37 W. 26th St., New York, NY   10010.
Feldheim Publishers, 200 Airport Executive Park, Spring Valley, NY   10977.
Hachai Publishing, 705 Foster Ave., Brooklyn, NY   11230.
Jason Aronson, Inc., 230 Livingston St., Northvale, NJ   07647.
Jewish Publication Society, 1930 Chestnut St., Philadelphia, PA   19103.
Judaica Press, Inc., 123 Ditmas Ave., Brooklyn, NY   11218.
Kar-Ben Copies, Inc., 6800 Tildenwood Lane, Rockville, MD   20852.
Ktav Publishing House, Inc., 900 Jefferson St., Hoboken, NJ   07030.
Mesorah Publications, 4401 Second Ave., Brooklyn, NY   11232.
Schocken Books, 201 E. 50th St., New York, NY   10022.

Schools

Day Schools in the United States and Canada

A state-by-state listing of elementary and secondary day schools in the United States and Canada will be found in the day school directories published by Torah Umesorah—The National Society for Hebrew Day Schools, 160 Broadway, New York, NY 10038, and the Solomon Schechter Day School Association, 155 Fifth Ave., New York, NY 10010.

Both of these groups publish a Day School Directory listing the schools affiliated with or serviced by them. The Torah Umesorah directory lists over 500 schools; the Solomon Schechter directory lists over 60 schools.

The directories indicate the name, address, and phone number of the school, the number of grades it teaches, the language of instruction, and the name of the principal.

Comprehensive List of Jewish Schools and Educational Agencies

A comprehensive list of all types of Jewish schools and educational bureaus throughout the United States and Canada is available through A. B. Data Information and Marketing Service, 8050 North Port Washington Rd., Milwaukee, WI 53127 (800–558–6908). The directory lists about 3,000 congregational and communal schools from nursery through high school level. A directory of Central Agencies for Jewish Education is available through the Jewish Education Service of North America, Inc., 730 Broadway, 2nd fl., New York, NY 10036.

Information about day schools and afternoon schools, and help in formulating their curriculum, is also available through the National Commission on Torah Education, 500 W. 185th St., New York, NY 10033. This agency functions under the aegis of Yeshiva University.

Summer Camps

A directory of Jewish camps under the auspices of Jewish communal organizations is available from the JCC Association, 15 E. 26th St., New York, NY 10016. The Association of Jewish Sponsored Camps also has a directory of Jewish camps in the Northeast region. A copy is available by writing to the association at 130 E. 59th St., New York, NY 10022.

The directories provide information on whether the Sabbath and kashrut are observed at the camp, the camp's requirements for general counselors, and its special programs. However, not all the camps in the directories meet the criteria for Jewish and religious observance noted on pages 101–102. It would be wise to consult the rabbi in your community when selecting a camp for your child. He may know of some good ones not listed in the directories, or may have more intimate knowledge of the camps that are listed. If not, he may be in a position to obtain such information for you.

National Youth Organizations

Synagogue-Affiliated

National Conference of Synagogue Youth (NCSY) is affiliated with the Union of Orthodox Jewish Congregations of America, 70 W. 36th St., New York, NY 10018.
National Federation of Temple Youth (NFTY) is affiliated with the Union of American Hebrew Congregations (Reform), 838 Fifth Ave., New York, NY 10021.
United Synagogue Youth (USY) is affiliated with the United Synagogue of America (Conservative), 155 Fifth Ave., New York, NY 10010.
Young Israel Youth is affiliated with the National Council of Young Israel, 3 W. 16th St., New York, NY 10011.

Zionist-Affiliated

Betar Youth Organization is affiliated with the Herut, one of the right-wing parties of Israel, 218 E. 79th St., New York, NY 10021.
B'nai Akiva of North America is affiliated with the Religious Zionists of America, 25 West 26th St., New York, NY 10010.
Hashachar is a union of Young Judea and Junior Hadassah, which is affiliated with the Zionist Organization of America, 50 West 58th St., New York, NY 10019.
Hashomer Hatzair is affiliated with the left wing of Israel's kibbutz movement, 27 West 20th St., New York, NY 10011.

Other

B'nai Brith Youth Organization (BBYO) is affiliated with the B'nai Brith of America, 1640 Rhode Island Ave., Washington, D.C. 20036.
Zeire Agudath Israel (boys) and Bnos Agudath Israel (girls) are affiliated with the Agudath Israel of America, 84 Williams St., New York, NY 10038.

On the College Campus

The B'nai Brith Hillel Foundation publishes "The Hillel Guide to Jewish Life on Campus—A Directory of Resources for Jewish College Students," which provides information about Jewish life on campus, activities of the Hillel Foundation, availability of kosher dining facilities, religious services, Jewish studies, Jewish residential housing options, and other general information about Jewish life on campus. The directory may be purchased at your local Jewish bookstore, or write to B'nai Brith Hillel Foundations, 1640 Rhode Island Ave. N.W., Washington, D.C. 20036. Another well-researched guide on the subject is "The Jewish Student's Guide to American Colleges," by Dr. Lee and Lana Goldberg (published by Shapolsky Publishers, 136 W. 22nd St., New York, NY 10011).

A current listing of Young Israel Kosher Dining Programs is available from National Council of Young Israel, 3 West 16th St., New York, NY 10011 (212-929-1525).

Programs in Israel

"A Guide to 3-Month to 1-Year Programs in Israel," published by the Department of Aliya and Absorption of the Jewish Agency, covers the many academic and work/study programs available in Israel, including high school, kibbutz/ulpan, university, work/study, professional work, leadership training, and Judaic Studies/Yeshivot. There are programs geared for every level of study. A copy of this booklet, as well as general information and advice regarding the programs, can be obtained from your local Jewish Community Center, Israel Aliya Center, or Jewish Federation office, or by writing to American Zionist Youth Foundation—Israel Programs, 110 E. 59th St., New York, NY 10022 (212-339-6002).

The AZYF also annually updates its "Complete Guide to Israel Programs Under the Auspices of the American Zionist Youth Foundation," which includes summer, winter, and long-term programs run by many of the Zionist and synagogue youth organizations listed on page 210. Information about programs run by the World Zionist Organization and the Zionist Organization of America can be obtained by contacting them directly: 110 E. 59th St., New York, NY 10022 (WZO); 4 E. 34th St., New York, NY 10016 (ZOA).

Children with Special Needs: Resources for the Disabled

Raising a disabled or handicapped child can be a fulfilling yet overwhelming experience. Such children are often forced to neglect the Jewish side of their education because of the extra pressures on them and the difficulty in finding materials and activities for them. If your child has special needs, we urge you to contact and utilize the many Jewish organizations that have programs and material available to you. Start with the partial listing below. These organizations will gladly assist you in any way possible and will offer you guidance on other organizations to contact.

Information on programs in North America for the learning-disabled is available through:
JCC Association, 15 East 26th St., New York, NY 10010 (212–532–4949) (for a listing of camps serving children and youth with special needs).
Jewish Education Service of North America, Inc., 730 Broadway, 2nd fl., New York, NY 10003 (212–529–3000).
Special Education Center, Board of Jewish Education, 426 W. 58th St., New York, NY 10019 (212–245–8200).
Special Education Committee of the United Synagogue Commission on Jewish Education, 155 Fifth Ave., New York, NY 10019 (212–533–7800).

Visual Disabilities

The Jewish Braille Institute of America, Inc., provides services such as braille books, audio book cassettes, and large-print books to the visually impaired and reading-disabled. They can be contacted at 110 E. 30th St., New York, NY 10016 (800–433–1531). All services are free of charge.

APPENDIX B

~~~~~~

Resources for the Jewish Education of Parents

Books

Primary and Classical Works

Chumash with Rashi. A. Silbermann and M. Rosenbaum. Feldheim Publishers.
Judaica Books of the Prophets—Mikraot Gedolot: Joshua, Judges, Samuel I & II, Kings I & II, Isaiah I & II, Jeremiah I & II, The Twelve Prophets I & II. English translation of the text, Rashi and Commentary Digest. Judaica Press.
Sefer Hahinnuch (vols. 1–5). Translated by Charles Wingrov. Feldheim Publishers.
Talmud El-Am, Modern English Edition. Selected tractates in paperback edition. El-Am Publishing.
The Authorized Daily Prayer Book. Commentary by Joseph H. Hertz. Bloch Publishing, 1948.
The Complete Artscroll Siddur. Translation and commentary by Rabbi N. Scherman. Mesorah, 1984.
The Jerusalem Bible. Hebrew, with English text revised and edited by Harold Fisch. Koren Publishers, 1986.
The Pentateuch and Haftorahs. Commentary by Joseph H. Hertz. Soncino Press, 1966.

Resources for the Jewish Education of Parents

The Soncino Books of the Bible. Complete set: 14 vols. Soncino Press.
The Soncino Talmud. 18 vols., English edition. Soncino Press.

Reference Works

Encyclopaedia Judaica. 16 vols. Keter Publishing, 1972.
The Complete English-Hebrew Dictionary. Reuben Alcalay. Massadah, 1965.
The Complete Hebrew-English Dictionary. Reuben Alcalay. Massadah, 1965.
The Talmud, The Steinsaltz Edition: A Reference Guide. Adin Steinsaltz. Random House, 1989.

Jewish Law and Observances

A Maimonides Reader. Isadore Twersky, ed. Berhman House, 1972.
Horeb: A Philosophy of Jewish Laws and Observances. 2 vols. Samson Raphael Hirsch. Soncino Press, 1962.
The Book of Our Heritage. Eliyahu Kitov. Feldheim Publishers, 1978.
The Jewish Way in Death and Mourning. Maurice Lamm. Jonathan David Publishers, 1969.
The Jewish Way in Love and Marriage. Maurice Lamm. Harper & Row, 1982.
To Be a Jew: A Guide to Jewish Observance in Contemporary Life. Hayim Halevy Donin. Basic Books, 1972.
To Pray as a Jew: A Guide to the Prayerbook and the Synagogue Service. Hayim Halevy Donin. Basic Books, 1980.

Jewish Philosophy

A Philosophy of Mitzvot. Gershon Appel. Ktav, 1975.
Challenge: Torah Views on Science and Its Problems. Aryeh Carmell and Cyril Domb, eds. Feldheim Publishers, 1976.
Encounter: Essays on Torah and Modern Life. H. C. Schimmel and Aryeh Domb, eds. Feldheim Publishers, 1989.
Faith and Doubt: Studies in Traditional Jewish Thought. Norman Lamm. Ktav, 1986.
God in Search of Man: A Philosophy of Judaism. Abraham J. Heschel. Jewish Publication Society, 1955.
Halakhic Man. Joseph B. Soloveitchik. Jewish Publication Society, 1983.
Man of Faith in the Modern World: Adapted from the Lectures of Rabbi Joseph B. Soloveitchik. Abraham Besdin. Ktav, 1989.
Man Is Not Alone: A Philosophy of Religion. Abraham J. Heschel. Farrar, Straus, Giroux, 1951.
Rav A. Y. Kook—Selected Letters. Translated and annotated by Tzvi Feldman. Maaliyot Publications, 1986.
The Essence of Judaism. Leo Baeck. Schocken Books, 1987 (rev. ed.).
The Faith of Judaism. Isadore Epstein. Soncino Press, 1954.
The Kuzari. Judah Halevi. Schocken Books.
The Nineteen Letters. Samson Raphael Hirsch. Feldheim Publishers, 1960.

Jewish History

A History of the Jewish People. Max Margolis and Alexander Marx. Atheneum, 1969.
A History of the Jews: From Earliest Times Through the Six-Day War. Cecil Roth. Schocken Books, 1970.
A Vanished World. Roman Vishniac. Farrar, Straus, Giroux, 1983.
From Time Immemorial: The Origins of the Arab-Israeli Conflict over Palestine. Joan Peters. Harper & Row, 1984.
Fulfillment: The Epic Story of Zionism. Rufus Learsi. Herzl Press, 1972.
History of the Jews. Vols. 1–6. Heinrich Graetz. Jewish Publication Society, 1891.
Jewish Life in the Middle Ages. Therese and Mendel Metzger. Chartwell Books, 1982.
My People: The Story of the Jews. Abba Eban. Random House, 1968.
Pillar of Fire: The Rebirth of Israel. Yigal Lossin. Shikmona Publishing, 1983.
The Sequence of Events in the Old Testament. Eliezer Schulman. Investment Company of Bank Hapoalim and Ministry of Defense Publishing, 1987
The Siege: The Saga of Israel and Zionism. Conor Cruise O'Brien. Simon & Schuster, 1986.
The Temple Scroll: The Hidden Law of the Dead Sea Sect. Yigael Yadin. Weidenfeld & Nicolson, 1985.
The Western Wall. Meir Ben Dov, Mordechai Naor, Zeev Aner. Ministry of Defense Publishing House, 1983.

Holocaust Studies

A Holocaust Reader. Lucy S. Dawidowicz. Behrman House, 1976.
Blessed Is the Match: The Story of Jewish Resistance. Marie Syrkin. Jewish Publication Society, 1947
Dawn. Elie Wiesel. Avon Books, 1969.
Justice in Jerusalem. Gideon S. Hausner. Schocken Books, 1968.
Night. Elie Wiesel. Avon Books, 1970.
Quiet Neighbors: Prosecuting Nazi War Criminals in America. Allan A. Ryan, Jr. Harcourt Brace Jovanovich, 1984.
The Abandonment of the Jews. David S. Wyman. Pantheon Books, 1984.
The Belarus Secret. John Loftus. Knopf, 1982.
The Destruction of the European Jews. Raul Hilberg. Quadrangle Books, 1961.
The Holocaust. Martin Gilbert. Holt, Rinehart & Winston, 1985.
The Holocaust in History. Michael R. Marrus. University Press of New England, 1987.
The War Against the Jews. Lucy S. Dawidowicz. Bantam Books, 1975.

General

A Treasury of Tradition. Norman Lamm and Walter S. Wurzburger, eds. Hebrew Publishing, 1967.
Ethics from Sinai. Irving M. Bunim. Feldheim Publishers, 1966.
Nine Questions People Ask About Judaism. Dennis Prager and Joseph Telushkin. Simon & Schuster, 1981.
Great Jewish Personalities in Ancient and Medieval Times. Simon Noveck, ed. B'nai Brith, 1959.

Great Jewish Personalities in Modern Times. Simon Noveck, ed. B'nai Brith, 1960.
Great Jewish Thinkers of the Twentieth Century. Simon Noveck, ed. B'nai Brith, 1963.
How the Hebrew Language Grew. Edward Horowitz. Ktav, 1967. (rev. ed.)
Jewish Worship. Abraham Millgram. Jewish Publication Society, 1971.
Popular Judaica Library. Leon Amiel Publishers, 1974. *Passover,* Mordell Klein; *Shavuot,* Asher Margaliot; *Sukkot,* Hayim Halevy Donin; *The High Holy Days,* Naphtali Winter; *Minor and Modern Festivals,* Priscilla Fishman; *Marriage,* Hayyim Schneid; *Family,* Hayyim Schneid; *The Synagogue,* Uri Kaploun; *Hasidism,* Aryeh Rubinstein; and *The Return to Zion,* Aryeh Rubinstein.
The Essential Talmud. Adin Steinsaltz. Basic Books, 1976.
The Holiday Anthologies. Philip Goodman. Jewish Publication Society. *The Passover Anthology; The Purim Anthology; The Rosh Hashanah Anthology; The Shavuot Anthology; The Sukkot and Simhat Torah Anthology; The Yom Kippur Anthology.*
The Sabbath. Dayan I. Gruenfeld. Feldheim Publishers, 1959.
This Is My God. Herman Wouk. Doubleday, 1959.

Jewish Book Clubs

You may want to join a Jewish book club. Two such clubs are the Jewish Book Club, P.O. Box 941, Northvale, NJ 07647–0941, and the Jewish Publication Society, 1930 Chestnut St., Philadelphia, PA 19103 (the latter sells only those titles that it publishes itself). Write to them for details of membership. They offer fine selections at very good prices.

Note: Judaica Book News, published semiannually by Bookazine, 303 West 10th St., New York, NY 10014, reports on all the latest books of Jewish interest that are published by the general publishing houses as well as by those specializing in Judaica. It is a good way to keep yourself informed.

Magazines for Parents

Compass, New Directions in Jewish Education. Published by Union of American Hebrew Congregations, 838 Fifth Ave., New York, NY 10021.
Your Child, a newsletter for parents of young Jewish children. Published by the United Synagogue Commission on Jewish Education, 155 Fifth Ave., New York, NY 10010.

Periodicals

The American Jewish community is blessed with a great many periodicals that will keep you abreast of issues, ideas, and trends affecting Jewish life and the Jewish people. Their contents reflect all the views current in the Jewish community, ranging from the very popular to the most sophisticated. Become acquainted with them before subscribing by spending a little time in the periodicals section of your library. Read as many of them as you can and subscribe to the ones that appeal to you most. Here is just a partial listing of what is available.

Weekly and Biweekly

Near East Report. A weekly Washington letter on American policy in the Near East. 440 First St. N.W., Washington, D.C. 20001 (202-638-1225).

Jerusalem Post. The international edition of Israel's English newspaper. P.O. Box 282, Brewster, NY 10509 (914-878-9522).

Sh'ma. A biweekly journal debating the problems that beset the Jewish community. P.O. Box 567, Port Washington, NY 11050 (516-944-9791).

Monthlies and Bimonthlies

B'nai Brith International Jewish Monthly. Published by B'nai Brith, 1640 Rhode Island Ave. N.W., Washington, D.C. 20036 (202-857-6645).

Commentary Magazine. Published by the American Jewish Committee, 165 East 56th St., New York, NY 10022 (212-751-4000).

Congress Monthly. Published by the American Jewish Congress, 15 East 84th St., New York, NY 10028 (212-879-4500).

Hadassah Magazine. Published by Hadassah, The Women's Zionist Organization of America, 50 West 58th St., New York, NY 10019 (212-355-7900).

Jewish Frontier. Published by Labor Zionist Letters, Inc., 275 Seventh Ave., New York, NY 10001 (212-645-8121).

Jewish Observer. Published by Agudath Israel of America, 84 Williams St., New York, NY 10038 (212-797-9000).

Midstream. Published by the Theodore Herzl Foundation, Inc., 515 Park Ave., New York, NY 10022 (212-752-0600).

Moment. Published by Jewish Educational Ventures, Inc., 3000 Connecticut Ave. N.W., Washington, D.C., 20008 (202-387-8888).

Reconstructionist. Published by the Federation of Reconstructionist Congregations and Havurot, Church Rd. and Greenwood Ave., Wyncote, PA 19095 (215-887-1988).

Tikkun. Published by the Institute for Labor and Mental Health, 5100 Leona St., Oakland, CA 94619 (415-482-0805).

Quarterlies

Conservative Judaism. Published by the Rabbinical Assembly, 3080 Broadway, New York, NY 10027 (212-678-8049).

Jewish Spectator. Independent, P.O. Box 2016, Santa Monica, CA 90406 (213–393–9063).

Journal of Reform Judaism. Published by the Central Conference of Reform Rabbis, 192 Lexington Ave., New York, NY 10021 (212–684–4990).

Judaism. Published by the American Jewish Congress, 15 East 84th St., New York, NY 10028 (212–879–4500).

Present Tense: The Magazine of World Jewish Affairs. Published by the American Jewish Committee, 165 East 56th St., New York, NY 10022 (212–751–4000).

Response: A Contemporary Jewish Review. Published by Jewish Education Ventures, Inc., 27 W. 20th St., New York, NY 10011 (212–675–1168).

Tradition: A Journal of Orthodox Jewish Thought. Published by the Rabbinical Council of America, 275 Seventh Ave., New York, NY 10001 (212–807–7888).

The English-Jewish Press

In every major American city, and some smaller ones too, there is at least one English-Jewish newspaper devoted to news about the local Jewish community in addition to news about Israel and Jewish communities elsewhere. Most appear on a weekly basis.

The English-Jewish press varies in quality from excellent to mediocre. The extent of coverage differs greatly, and on many important issues there is a wide variety of editorial opinion. Yet if one wishes to become familiar with what is going on within the Jewish community and to remain alert to new developments, a subscription to an English-Jewish newspaper is important. The daily American press simply does not and cannot provide adequate or balanced coverage to the Jewish community.

The English-Jewish press keeps you in contact with fellow Jews and apprises you of opportunities available to you and your children for Jewish study and participation in community life. If you are not acquainted with the Jewish newspaper(s) in your area, inquire about them at your synagogue.

APPENDIX C

Wisdom from the Sages
on the Education
of Children

It seems fitting that in closing a book on Jewish child-raising and education, we allow the classical sources to speak for themselves. While many biblical and Talmudic passages have been liberally interspersed throughout this book, I hope that an additional selection arranged by topics, would be welcomed by some readers and might serve as an inspirational resource.

Most of the passages which follow are from the Talmud. The parenthetical citation which follows each selection signifies the name of the volume and page number.

Torah Study as a Religious Duty

"All who are obligated to observe [the Torah] are obligated to study it" (Yevamot 109b).

"A scholar may not dwell in a city that does not have the following ten services . . . a [religious] teacher for the children" (Sanhedrin 17b).

"Seven are excommunicated in the sight of God . . . he who has children and does not raise them to the study of Torah" (Pesahim 113b).

"Jerusalem was destroyed [70 C.E.] only because the schools for the children were closed down" (Shabbat 119b).

On the Importance of Torah Study

"He who teaches Torah to the child of his friend is regarded as though he gave birth to him" (Sanhedrin 19b).

"A man who has many good deeds to his credit and also studies much Torah can be compared to a man who sets his bricks on a foundation of stone" (Avot d'Rabbi Nathan 24).

"Just as a man is not embarrassed to say to a friend, 'Give me some water,' so should he not be embarrassed to say to one younger than he, 'Teach me Torah.' " (Tanhuma, Leviticus, Vayakhel 8).

On Students

"Four are the characteristics found among students: quick to learn and quick to forget, his gain is cancelled by his loss. Slow to learn and slow to forget, his loss is cancelled by his gain. Quick to learn and slow to forget, his is a happy lot. Slow to learn and quick to forget, his is an unhappy lot" (Avot 5:15).

"Four characteristics are found among those who attend the house of study: he who attends but does not practice has the reward of going. He who practices but does not attend has the reward of his practicing. He who both attends and practices is of saintly character. He who neither attends nor practices is wicked" (Avot 5:17).

"As one piece of iron sharpens another so do two students sharpen each other [when they study together]" (Taanit 7a).

"Much have I learned from my teachers; even more so from my colleagues; but more than from all of them did I learn from my students" (Taanit 7a).

On Educational Methods

Rabbah would first put his students into a joyous, cheerful mood before starting on the lesson (Pesahim 117a).

"Said Rabbah: 'One should always study that part of the Torah that his heart desires [to which his interest draws him]' " (Avodah Zarah 19a).

"If one is inattentive, put him next to a diligent pupil" (Baba Batra 21a).

"Even if a child does not know how to read, he is not to be expelled from the class but is to sit with the others in the hope that he will eventually understand" (Shulhan Arukh, Yoreh Deah 245:9).

"A teacher must not become angry with his pupils if they do not understand him, but must repeat his explanation as many times as necessary until they understand . . . nor shall the pupil say 'I understand' when he really does not but should question over and over again until he does understand" (Shulhan Arukh, Yoreh Deah 246:10).

"Teach each one according to his strength [ability]" (Shmot Rabbah 5).

"If you see a pupil for whom learning is as difficult as iron, it is because he has failed to systematize his studies [he has not been given a proper foundation] . . . it is because the teacher is not pleasant to him" (Taanit 7b-8a).

"The fool says: 'there is so much Torah, when can I learn it?' and so he turns away [and studies nothing]. The wise one says, 'I will study one chapter every day' and does so until he completes the entire Torah" (Leviticus Rabbah 19, Devarim Rabbah 8).

"The number of pupils assigned to a teacher is twenty five" (Baba Batra 21a).

"The honor of your pupil should be as dear to you as your own" (Avot 4:12).

On Discipline

"Be it ever your way to thrust off with the left hand and draw to you with the right hand" (Sotah 47a).
"If you punish a pupil, hit him only with a shoe string" (Baba Batra 21a).

On Equal Opportunity

"I teach the children of the poor as well as those of the rich; I take no fees from any who cannot afford to pay" (Taanit 24a).

"Be careful regarding the children of the poor, for it is from them that Torah does come forth" (Nedarim 81a).

"The School of Shammai said: One should not teach [Torah] to another unless he be wise, modest, wealthy and from a distinguished family. The School of Hillel said: One should teach [Torah] to every person, for many transgressors who were drawn to the study of the Torah became righteous, pious and worthy people" (Avot d'Rabbi Nathan 3).

On Teachers

"No teacher should be appointed for the young unless he is a God-fearing person and possesses the qualifications to teach accurately" (Shulhan Arukh, Yoreh Deah 245:17).

"The easily angered person cannot teach" (Avot 2:5).

A teacher's background must be unsullied, free of suspicion of improper behavior: "If a teacher resembles a messenger of the Lord, seek instruction from him; otherwise do not" (Moed Katan 17a).

The effective teacher has few equals on the scale of merit: " 'They that turn many to righteousness like the stars for ever and ever' " (Daniel 12:3) applies to teachers of young children" (Baba Batra 8b).

A teacher must be patient, capable of explaining a point many times over: "A person must go on teaching his pupil until he has mastered the subject" (Eruvin 54b).

A teacher must be conscientious in his work: "A teacher who leaves his students and goes out of the room or engages in other work while in their presence or shows carelessness in teaching them comes under the ban of Jeremiah (48:10). 'Cursed be he who does the work of the Lord deceitfully' " (Maimonides, Mishneh Torah, Hil. Talmud Torah 2:3).

"The Ark was overlaid with gold from within and from without, so the teacher's inner and outer self should be consistent" (Yoma 72b).

Those who neglect their outward appearances bring contempt upon the Torah: "Any scholar upon whose garment a stain is found is worthy of death" (Shabbat 114a).

"A teacher of young children . . . is liable to be dismissed immediately [if inefficient]. The general principle is that anyone whose mistakes cannot be rectified is liable to be dismissed immediately [if he makes one]" (Baba Batra 21b).

"A teacher cannot prevent another teacher [from establishing a school in the same street] for the reason that 'the jealousy of scribes increases wisdom' " (Baba Batra 21b–22a).

On Guidance

"He who guides his sons and daughters in the right way . . . to him does the verse apply: 'And you shall know that there is peace in your tent' " (Yevamot 62b).

Index

A

Abraham, xvii, 36, 40, 84, 90, 105
Absalom, 69
Adolescence, 74, 92–95, 116, 126;
  See also Teenagers
Adopted child, 125–127
Afternoon school (synagogue school;
  Talmud Torah), 4, 20, 102, 141,
  170;
  curriculum in, 176–179;
  educational results in, 178, 184,
  effective teachers in, 173, 178;
  free tuition and, 187;
  Hebrew-language vs. religious instruction in, 157–159;
  limitations of, 116–118;
  other names for, 165;
  resistance to attendance, 110;
  sponsorship of, 164–165;
  standard program of, 176–179;
  as "supplementary," 179–180;
  See also Hebrew school
Agudat Israel, 155
Ahavat haShem (Love of God), 24

Ahavat Yisrael (Love for all Jews), 28
Akiva, Rabbi, 27
America, *see* United States
American Jewry, future of, 186–189
Americanization, 3–6
Anti-Semitism, 6, 55
Arithmetic, 51, 172
Art, 45, 48–49, 169, 179
Arts and crafts, 182
Ashkenazic pronunciation of Hebrew
  language, 161–163
Assimilation, xvii, 3–6, 42, 148, 151,
  186
Authority, parent-child relationship
  and, 59–60
Awe toward God, sense of, 25–26

B

Babylonian Talmud, 157
Bar-Mitzvah, 5, 43, 88, 91, 112–115,
  127, 128

223

Index

Hirsch, Samson Raphael, 52, 53, 152
Holidays, *see* Christian holidays; Jewish holidays; National holidays
Holiness, striving for, 31–33
Homan, William, 62, 68, 100
Home environment, 132;
  adolescents and, 92–95;
  conflict between school and, 172–175;
  elementary school children and, 86–91;
  preschool children and, 78–86
Honesty, 50, 61
"Honor thy father and mother," obligation to, 17–18, 60, 129
Human dignity, respect for, 29–30
Hypocrisy, 120–122

I

Identity, Jewish, 4; mental health and, 54–55
Immersion in a mikveh, 126–127
Interdating, 130–131
Intermarriage, 3, 6, 17;
  objections to, 131–133;
  reactions to, 135–136;
  rejection of Halakha and, 148
Isaac, 84, 90, 105
Isaiah, xix, 36
Israel: attitude toward state of, 153–155;
  cherishing land of, as basic value of Judaism, 35–36;
  Hebrew language in, 105, 106, 159, 161–163;
  Independence Day in, 154, 155;
  study programs in, 106–107, 211;
  visits to, 21, 101, 105–106, 160
Isserles, Rabbi Moses, 151, 157

J

Jeremiah, 39
Jewish community: civic responsibility to, 38–39;
  future of, 186–189;
  philanthropy within, 14
Jewish Day School in America, The (Schiff), 168
Jewish day schools, *see* Day schools
Jewish dropout, the, 115–116
Jewish education (Jewish schooling; Jewish studies), 3–4, 20, 91, 112, 159;
  in America, history of, 165–166, 181;
  Bar-Mitzvah as deterrent to, 113–115;
  character training in, 49–51;
  cultural education in, 45–49;
  early start in, 86–87;
  elementary, 116, 184;
  general studies in, 51–52;
  Hebrew language in, *see* Hebrew language;
  occupational training in, 53–54;
  parents' mixed feelings about, 14–18;
  physical education in, 52–53;
  Torah studies and religious training in, 43–45;
  vagueness of goals of, 9–10;
  whole child as concern of, 41–42;
  See also Schools
Jewish history: in afternoon schools, 117, 177, 178;
  books on, 215–216;
  in cultural education, 45–46, 49;
  in day schools, 167, 168;
  in Sunday schools, 117, 183
Jewish holidays, 54, 167, 177;
  staying out of school on, 122–124;
  See also specific holidays
Jewish identity, 4; mental health and, 54–55

227

Index

Mikveh, immersion in a, 126–127
Mishna, 27, 29, 30, 31, 38, 143;
  study of, 33, 44, 45, 152, 157, 167, 181
Mixed marriage, *see* Intermarriage
Moses, 18, 31, 38, 80, 143
Mourning, week of *(shiva)*, 35, 128, 135
Music: in afternoon school curriculum, 179;
  cultural education and, 45, 48–49;
  in day schools, 169;
  See also Jewish records; Songs, Hebrew
Music books, 200–201

N

National Commission on Torah Education, 178
National holidays, 169
National Religious Party, 154
Nature, reverence for God and, 25
Neighborhoods, 170; selecting a, 95–96
Newspapers, English-Jewish, 218
"Nondenominational" schools, 142
Nondirective techniques in child-rearing, 63
Numbers, book of, 45

O

Occupational training, Jewish education and, 53–54
Oral Torah, 44, 45, 143
Orthodox Judaism: Conservatism and, 150;
  day schools and, 142, 153, 156–157, 165;

as "denomination," 10–12;
Halakha in view of, 148–149;
Kashrut and, 103;
religious standards for standards and, 156;
Sunday schools and, 165, 181;
Torah in view of, 145

P

Palestine: ancient, 161
  See also Israel
Parents: obligation to honor, 17–18, 60, 129;
  rebellion against, 60, 69;
  resources for Jewish education of, 213–218;
  single, 128–130;
  as teachers, 77–79;
Passover, 82, 123, 124
Passover seder, 12, 85, 86, 129
Peer groups, influence of, 93, 99–101
Pentateuch (Five Books of Moses), 33, 45, 159–160
Periodicals, 214–215
Petuchowski, Jakob J., 146
Philanthropy, within Jewish community, 14
Philosophy, books on Jewish, 214–215
Physical contact, in communicating love to children, 64–65
Physical education, 52–53
Physical punishment, 68–69
Poor, Talmud on children of the, 221
Prayer Book, High Holyday, 28, 68
Prayers, 33, 45, 174;
  Hebrew language and, 47, 54, 79–81, 163;
  Land of Israel and, 36;
  during preschool years, 79–80;
  public, 38–39;
  during weekend retreat, 107